THE
GOSPEL
ACCORDING TO

SAINTS, SAVIORS &
SINNERS

THE
GOSPEL
ACCORDING TO

SAINTS, SAVIORS &
SINNERS

HYPERION

Edited by Jay Lovinger
Introduction by Hunter S. Thompson

Book Designed by Walter Bernard and Milton Glaser

ART DIRECTOR: Walter Bernard

PHOTO EDITOR: Donna Aceto

ASSOCIATE EDITOR: Craig Winston

ASSISTANT ART DIRECTOR: Julia Zichello

RESEARCH: Jim Jenks (director), Michael Corbo, Heath Henry, Howie Schwab, Matthew Wilansky

EDITORIAL ASSISTANT: Elizabeth Massa

SPECIAL CONTRIBUTORS: Bill Burdick, Michael Cooper, Russ Davis, Wayne Duke, Tim Evans, Raymond Franklin, Sue Friedman, Bill Gallo, Dan Galvin, Allen Guttmann, Jim Hawkins, Carl Kirker-Head, Liam McHugh, Roger Jackson, Wellington Mara, Dave Marsh, Gueorgui Milkov, William Nack, Tip Nunn, Terry Pruyne, Jane Schwartz, Pam Shriver, Eleanor Smeal, John Sparkman, Rusty Staub, D.W. Stump, Grace Thorpe, Darrell Trimble, Patrick Trimble, Garry Trudeau, Jules Tygiel, Justin Yungfleisch

ISBN: 0-7868-6754-X

Hyperion books are available for special promotions and premiums. For details, contact Hyperion Special Markets, 77 W. 66th Street, 11th floor, New York, New York 10023-6298, or call 212-456-0100.

First Edition

10   9   8   7   6   5   4   3   2   1

Opening Illustrations

Title page: "Jupiter and Thetis"
by Jean-Auguste Dominique Ingres

Contents page: "St. Sebastian"
by Pietro Perugino

Introduction: "The Last Judgment"
by Michelangelo

HE SIMILARITIES AND POINTS OF CONFLUENCE BETWEEN SPORTS AND RELIGION range from the mundane to the eerie.

On the simplest level, we have teams named the Saints, the Padres, the Crusaders; players nicknamed Preacher, the Minister of Defense, the Four Horsemen of the Apocalypse; plays immortalized as the Holy Roller, the Hand of God Goal, the Immaculate Reception; and various sports stadia, arenas and Halls of Fame commonly referred to as shrines and meccas.

But deep down, both are all about myth. And whether the myth is about the nature of existence or Babe Ruth's "called shot," the real point is, to quote the great Mets reliever Tug McGraw:

"You gotta believe."

And in what, exactly, are we supposed to believe?

Religion? If you are willing to give yourself to God, and live your life the way you know you should live your life, that life will be fruitful . . . and there will be an afterlife, an eternity of serenity.

Sports? If you play fair and try hard, you will win games, and championships, and you will be worshipped like a god. Your life will be fruitful, and your heaven will be here on earth . . . enormous riches and fame, and records that may never be broken (though, of course, one of the articles of our sports faith is that all records are made to be broken).

What we most deeply believe in, whether we are talking about the sacred or the profane, is the mythmakers—the Gods, the Prophets, the Saints, the Saviors, even the Sinners, who form the core of both faiths.

This book is about those mythmakers from the world of sports, who they are, why we care and need and worship them, why, if they didn't exist, we would have had to invent them.

But lucky us—we didn't have to. All we had to do was kneel down, open our eyes and hearts, and prepare ourselves to receive.

—JAY LOVINGER

073720

■ Contents

Enough to Make a Man Believe

by Hunter S. Thompson

". . . and whosoever was not found written in the book of life was cast into the lake of fire."

—REVELATIONS 20:15

HIS WAS THE THEME OF A SERMON I DELIVERED OFF THE 20TH-FLOOR BALCONY of the Regency Hyatt House in Houston on the morning of Super Bowl VIII—a crazed and futile attempt, as I recall, to explain the nature of my relationship with the National Football League. It was just before dawn when the urge to speak came on me. I had not planned a sermon for that morning—or any other morning, for that matter—but now, looking back on that outburst, I see that I'd been cranking myself up for it, in a slow and violent way, for at least two months and maybe three or four.

It was sometime in late November, I think, when Oakland Raider managing general partner Al Davis decided—for reasons he refused to explain—that my name should be stricken at once from the Raiders' Book of Life and that I should be cast, figuratively or even physically if necessary, into professional football's lake of fire. . . .

Instant excommunication and total banishment from any personal or professional contact with the Oakland Raiders; barred from the press box, locker room, practice field and for all practical purposes—because of the ominous assumptions that would inevitably be made by NFL security watchdogs—from any bar, restaurant, zoo or shotgun store in the Bay Area frequented by any Raider players.

There was nothing accidental about my choice of themes—except maybe for the fact that I happened to find this small, eight-page comic book in a huge pile of discarded newspapers on the floor of a hotel mezzanine bathroom. It had probably been there for several days, a tiny little chunk of low-level Jesus propaganda that only a freak in the grip of some kind of personal desperation would notice and immediately pick up.

I sensed a karmic influence . . . I was, in fact, in a very peculiar state of mind at that point—and when this weird little booklet appeared in front of me on the floor, I knew, at once, that it was definitely meant to be.

I normally pay no attention to Jesus-freak pamphlets, but after 48 hours of stone boredom in Houston, I was ready for anything. So I seized the little bugger off the floor and read it straight through—and it was on the very last page that I suddenly came face-to-face with that line about "the lake of fire."

I am, after all, a certified man of the cloth and a natural-born Sportswriter with four pages to fill in the new issue of the once-proud *Rolling Stone*—so it was only natural that I would be sifting through the rubbish on bathroom floors of the official Super Bowl hotel to seek out whatever sports or religious wisdom I could glean. That is the way we like to work, us preachers who love Sports too much.

Indeed. My credentials are impeccable. I scrimmage with holy men and preach my sermons to thugs. It is the flip side of Tough Love Gone Wrong.

So it would seem. On the evidence of my suave qualifications, I would seem to be exactly the right man to question about the long-standing love affair between big-time sports and *The Church* in America.

The last time I was grilled about it, the conversation went like this:

Q: Is Sports a Religion in America?

A: Yes.

Q: Is it an organized religion?

A: No. It does not *appear* to be Organized—but if it were, we would all be members of a very powerful church. We would be a political majority in the U.S.A.

These are strong words in any language. From "powerful church" to "political majority," they are reminiscent of Adolf Hitler and the Nazi Third Reich. All we need now are some Sporting terms like "stomp them" or "dominate them" or "crush the life out of them"—as in Terminate, Kill or Croak. It is hard to argue that this kind of language does not warn strongly of violence. Trouble is in the air.

Think about this: At 52 million, the Catholic Church is the most dominant religion in this country. But a quick estimate of the number of sports fans would produce at least 100 million fans who think of themselves as "rabid," in that they will gamble at least $20 on one game every two days per year. Yes sir, that is real

money—until you consider that the United States is spending that much every day on our mysterious "War" on Terrorism. Who knows what the real cost might be?

Let's have a fling at the math: Ho ho, that is over $1 billion being spent feverishly *every day* by bull-fruits who love War. Some people would question this, but the math is unassailable. War and Sports are symbiotically linked in America, on the same queer level as Brutality and The Church (of Rome). . . . We are all beasts, in the end.

Right. But let us not be wandering off on tangents, eh? Our subject is Sports and Religion, and whether or not they are more and more becoming one and the same.

The answer to that one is *Yes*, of course; and the only reason that Sports is not yet completely organized, like a feverish fan club of some famous Hollywood whore, is that nobody, except perhaps the IRS, has quite figured out how to collect membership fees from 100 million people. But that is not far off; it will happen before 16 moons have passed.

"Anyone who will tear down sports will tear down America. Sports and religion have made America what it is today." —WOODY HAYES, 1976

ANY QUESTION OF RELIGION AND/OR SPORTS WILL NECESSARILY INVOLVE Muhammad Ali. Ali is the gold standard for magic living in the U.S.A. Even flirting with Ali was like dancing on water. When Muhammad walked into a public room and sized it up for some action, he walked in strong. It was an elegant thing to see. That man could handle any room in the world. The price Ali paid for his courage is deeply troubling to me, on a personal level, but there is no doubt in my mind that he would do it all over again, step by step, if he ever got the chance.

"Would you do it again?" is a deceptively complex question for most people, but an extremely simple query on its face. What it asks is what it says, no hooks and

no tricks. It is an opportunity that some people find awkward—as I have from time to time, and so will you, or Britney Spears or Colin Powell.

Yes sir, good old Colin—he will have some lurid moments with this one. Like many of us, he may not exactly remember all the fear and grief and pain that came with some of our finest hours—but he will, and so will Britney, in time.

I know for a fact that Muhammad Ali will see both sides of the picture, because I have been there in person for some of it. The Champ and I have gone through a whole fistful of "never again" experiences, and I will have to brood for a while before I decide whether to do any of them over again. A few involved real loss or anguish. I remember moments of humiliation and failure that came along with some of my highest memories. . . . Muhammad Ali was like that: Love me up, love me down; buy the ticket, take the ride. That is the bottom line in Sports: Take it or leave it. Mercy is not an option.

Ali took that for granted, in religion as well as sports, and I suspect he would do it again, note for note—including the shocking loss to Leon Spinks and losing three years at the top of his career to jingo bigots for being a Muslim and refusing to be drafted.

One of the many things that sports and religion have in common is that we take both of them far too seriously, when in fact less than half of what we learn in this world about either one is true. Think quickly about the "Black Sox" scandal of 1919, or "the legendary" Knute Rockne, who invented the forward pass—but no. They are both *gossip*, pure balderdash, queer rumors from consistently unreliable sources. They are stories that were born innocent, and not always by knowing liars. This gibberish is passed from skull to innocent skull, sometimes by accident, like some unseen virus from Hong Kong.

The sporting world is full of ugly moments, and that is the way we like it. Moments of shame and failure are elevated to the status of myth and legend by sports fans who wept and cursed and raved at each other when they saw the foul things actually happening. There are people in Boston who still jam burning ciga-rettes into their own flesh at the mention of that horrible error that caused the Red Sox to lose the 1986 World Series, just as thousands of football fans in Dallas still cry out in pain when they see a TV replay of Jackie Smith dropping that touchdown pass in the end zone against Pittsburgh in Super Bowl XIII.

■ AH, BUT WHO CARES, ANYWAY? HITLER STARTED WORLD WAR II, AND LOOK what happened to him. The 1,000-Year Reich lasted 12 years and five months. But Hitler wasn't counting, they say; he was a full-bore Joker with morbid tastes. And he called himself a sports fan—he always loved the speed events.

So did Caligula, of course, and who could blame him for it? I have always enjoyed speed, myself. It will get us where we want to go, but not as fast as a virus, or a strange football story. That will travel at the speed of light, which is pretty damn fast.

Almost as fast as Muhammad Ali in his prime. You bet—that man was fast. He would catch flies in his hand behind his back while he was looking you right in the eye. He was three times as fast as Sugar Ray Robinson. And he ate flies, too, with a whooped-up grin on his face. Nobody has ever been as fast as Cassius Clay. He could hit you 225 times in 60 seconds, if you wouldn't call him by his right name. Yes sir, you could say the Champ was *touch*y about that . . . *real* touchy.

Which reminds me of Mike Tyson, somehow. He was a man of strong convic-tions, back then, and maybe he still is. We will see soon enough. Or maybe not . . . maybe we will never know. Maybe he'll find Jesus. Or maybe he will have his license jerked in all 50 states, if he doesn't go back to prison for rape.

That could happen, but it won't. There is too much money involved. We are not a nation of honest men, despite our love and trust of Sports and all the swill it pumps out. In our hearts we are circus people.

Sportswriting is a primitive trade on most days, but not always. Even a pig will find love in his own barnyard now and then. Life is weird for animals. They will never know the real value of gold, even when they root in a field of it. That kind of truth is not in them, despite their innocent souls. It is one of life's tragedies . . .

Ah, but never mind the animals, my dear, I just want to suck on your back . . . We are talking about top-of-the-line Sportswriting, and I suspect I am letting my odd sense of humor get in our way.

WHICH IS NOT WHAT THIS BOOK IS ABOUT. WHAT WE HAVE HERE IS A MULTITUDE of exceptions to the dismal rule. The best of Sportswriting can be as smart and as elegant as any other kind of journalism; in the hands of a master, it can sing like a beast in heat.

I have said some nasty things about sportswriters, from time to time, some in jest and others deadly serious, and I am certainly not here to take them back or apologize. I could do that, "but it would be wrong," as Richard Nixon liked to say.

Nixon was a monster, but on some days he could be downright charming, and I can tell you for sure that Richard Nixon knew football. Yes sir. He worshipped the Green Bay Packers. Nixon would have understood this book in his bones.

The Boss was in a league of his own when it came to talking football and politics at the same time. When he was running for president in 1968, nobody in the press corps was confident enough to match wits and wisdom with the Boss when he wanted to "cool out and talk football," as he called his downtime sparring—and this included reporters from *The New York Times* and *The Boston Globe* who were serious sports fans.

But Nixon was more than just serious: He was a flat-out fanatic. Not even his trusted speechwriters dared challenge him when the talk turned to football. Nixon was nothing if not competitive, and he showed no mercy to frauds. He was fast track—too fast for even the best and brightest of political writers in need of a private interview for the weekend edition. They were afraid of him.

Nixon getting back into presidential politics was news, but weird news. There was a sizable press corps at the New Hampshire primaries. I was not among the best and brightest in those days, but I did know football, which is why I got along splendidly with the Boss, despite our mutual hatred on political issues. He and I were congregants of the same house of worship. I was also drunk—or at least drinking, as they say in AA wards—but that didn't bother Nixon in the slightest. He was gracious, full of smiles, and happy in a way that I still find amazing. He was always good company.

I arrived in Manchester dressed in Levi's and a ski jacket, and who did I run into but Pat Buchanan? He spotted me while I was demanding a room in the Manchester Holiday Inn. . . . There were about 40 people in the press corps, all of them main political reporters; I wasn't one of them, but I had written *Hell's Angels*, and I was notorious. They had sent Buchanan down to have a word with the weirdo who was insisting on being in Nixon's wing of the hotel. (Nixon had reserved the whole wing of the Holiday Inn for him and his staff.) That was the beginning of our fine friendship.

A few days later, Buchanan was assigned by Nixon to go out and "talk to those bastards in the press and see if you can find any of them who knows anything about football." He had a long ride ahead of him in the back of a yellow Mercury, a big sedan with a cop driving and his speechwriters Buchanan and Ray Price in the front, and he wanted to talk football. It was time to pray, and he was looking for someone to kneel down with him.

Buchanan had tried not to allow me to do this, of course. Anybody but me . . . I was known as an enemy sympathizer. But nobody else in the press corps would claim to know football well enough to talk it with the Boss. And what the hell—football is one of my strong suits. I kept telling Pat, "Yeah, I can talk football, I'm an expert, a sportswriter," and he'd laugh and say: "Shut up, Hunter. Get back on the bus." He tried to get somebody else to do it, anybody. I knew it was a rare chance for an interview with Nixon—personal time, Christ.

Buchanan had no choice; he was finally forced to say, "Ah well, it's you, Hunter. I guess it's you. But if you say a goddamn thing about the tear gas or Vietnam, we'll put you out of the car instantly." It was about 10 below, a horrible, horrible March night in New Hampshire, so I had no trouble at all with Nixon. I got into the backseat with him and took my drink in with me. We didn't talk about anything but football.

I thought I'd show off a little bit, so I brought up a play by an obscure player in the previous season's Super Bowl. It was a second-down play about halfway through the second quarter, an extraordinary down-and-out pass to a No. 4 or 5 receiver— it was spooky to see the guy on the field when they had so many other good receivers. But the guy caught the pass and kept his feet inside the end zone, an amazing catch. Nixon looked into the darkness and ether for a minute, then he slapped me on the thigh and said, "Ah yes, the Miami Boy! The guy's name was Bill Miller from the University of Miami!"

Miami Boy! Even the most obscure sports-desk freak wouldn't know a thing like that. You'd have to be a religious fanatic.

"God almighty!" I exclaimed. "That was good, man—that was very good." I almost slapped him on the knee, but thought better of it. The Boss was grinning at me. It was a moment of strong bonding, and it turned out to be a fateful night in my career as a journalist. From that point on, I was a "political correspondent." It was a personal epiphany, enough to make a man believe in God, or at least some kind of supreme being. I was a proven professional sportswriter, and because I'd just spent a long year with the Hell's Angels, Richard Nixon didn't seem particularly dangerous to me. I was not afraid of anything—I could walk the talk and talk the walk. This political stuff looked like a free lunch.

I was wrong, of course. There is no free lunch, and Nixon turned out to be a monster. But that is another story, and we will leave it for later.

PROPHETS ARE SCARY

IF TAKEN SERIOUSLY, WHICH IS WHY WE MOSTLY TRY TO SHUT THEM UP, IGNORE THEM OR MISINTERPRET THEM. IF THEIR PROPHECIES COME TRUE, THEN NOTHING WILL EVER BE THE SAME; THE WORLD WILL TAKE A TURN AND OUR LIVES WILL CHANGE. AT THE VERY LEAST, IN SPORTS, WE'LL HAVE TO GO OUT AND BUY SOME BRAND-NEW CAPS AND JERSEYS.

THERE WERE THREE GREAT SPORTS PROPHETS OF THE 20TH CENTURY, AND THEIR INFLUENCE IS SHAPING THE 21ST. THEY WERE NOT ONLY PROPHETS OF GAMES; THEIR IMPACT ON CLASS, NATIONALISM, RELIGION, RACE AND GENDER (WHAT ELSE IS THERE?) WAS PROFOUND.

PROPHETS
by Robert Lipsyte

Of the three, Avery Brundage probably had the most impact. In his fierce stewardship of the Olympic Games, he promoted sports as a social force, a moral vehicle and a crucible for character and for nation-building, as well as a mass entertainment that could bind the globe. Brundage, who looked and sounded like a thundering prophet of the Old Testament, begat Muhammad Ali, who carries the Koran, and Billie Jean King, as New Agey a prophet as sports has ever seen.

■ Love and Compassion Most Austere

Prophets tend to be self-anointed and self-righteous, nourished by the "essential task," in the words of Abraham J. Heschel, an expert on such matters, "to disclose the future in order to illumine what is involved in the present." In their times, Muhammad, Moses, Jesus, the Buddha, Joseph Smith and Nostradamus have all been called prophets, although the great thundering Isaiah (who may have been put to death for his insistence on kindness, pity and justice) may come closest to Heschel's pithiest description of our model: "The words of the prophet are stern, sour, stinging. But behind his austerity is love and compassion for mankind."

The followers of Avery Brundage have always more or less said that.

Brundage was the prophet of Olympism, the secular religion that believed in amateurism, sports for the love of it, sports as a preparation for real life. The Olympic Games were the high holy days of Olympism. The cardinals and archbishops (the officials) were more important than the congregation (the fans), or the priests and nuns (the athletes), who were treated like children and given small allowances. Athletes were punished for behaving badly, which usually meant performing below expectation or disregarding the officials' rules. No wonder the authoritarian team became a model for countries, armies and corporations.

Ali was the prophet of free agency, the athlete's challenge to the authority of owners, officials, coaches and the media. The morning after he first won the world heavyweight boxing championship, he announced: "I don't have to be what you want me to be, I'm free to be what I want." This was so shocking we tended not to deal with it. It was 30 years before the message percolated up, until the basketball star Charles Barkley, in a Nike commercial, said, "I am not a role model."

People were outraged; **what right did this overpaid ingrate have to abdicate his responsibility to give our children the example of acceptable behavior we were too busy, selfish or greedy to give them?** But by then, it didn't much matter. Ali had so frightened us about the power of athletes as role models that we no longer allowed them any power greater than selling food, drinks and clothes. (Check out that fading icon, Michael Jordan.) Ali had prophesied that, too.

"When I'm gone, boxing be nothing again," he told us when he was still in his 20s. "The fans with the cigars and the hats turned down'll be there, but no more housewives and little men in the street and foreign

An exultation of minor prophets: (left, from top) Joe Namath, Roone Arledge, Bill Veeck, Howard Cosell and St. Jerome in his study (right, in a painting by Antonello da Messina)

Billie Jean King (top left, holding up the coveted Wimbledon singles trophy in 1968); Muhammad Ali and Avery Brundage (bottom left, as a track star, circa 1914) were all well armed for the job of major prophets. At right, minor prophets Arnold Schwarzenegger (during his Mr. Universe period) and Grantland Rice, the first superstar sportswriter.

presidents. It's goin' to be back to the fighter who comes to town, smells a flower, visits a hospital, blows a horn and says he's in shape. Old hat. I was the onliest boxer in history people asked questions like a senator."

Billie Jean King is the prophet of Fair Shake Feminism, of a total equality of opportunity that includes the right to choose to be a product or an entrepreneur, an entertainer or a moral symbol, or all of the above and more. Billie Jean was the one who should have been the senator.

"Almost every day," she said in the '60s, "someone comes up to me and says, 'Hey, when are you going to have children?'

"I say, 'I'm not ready yet.'

"They say, 'Why aren't you at home?'

"I say, 'Why don't you go ask Rod Laver why he isn't at home?' "

Nowadays, those lines sound like dialogue from a sitcom in the broadcast museum. But then, they were deal-breakers. If you believed her, you could also believe in a feminist fantasy of the level playing field. You could believe that someday your Venus would come. And bring her sister.

A Gaggle of Minor Prophets

There were plenty of minor prophets along the way, promoters such as Bill Veeck, who believed customers should have fun in the temple of baseball; ABC's Roone Arledge, who opened a window on the wide world of sports, and Phil Knight, who just sold it. There were performers like Babe Didrikson, Jesse Owens, Grantland Rice, Howard Cosell, Jim Bouton, Joe Namath, Arnold Schwarzenegger, Magic Johnson and Tiger Woods, all of whom, by words or actions, prophesied future innings.

All were begat by the Olympic dictator Avery Brundage, who bellowed, "The Games must go on!" through every crisis that demanded at least a tap on the pause button. Paradoxically, for all his lip service to an amateur elite, it was his furious devotion to the survival of the Games that eventually led to the ultimate band of touring professionals, the so-called Dream Team at the 1992 Barcelona Olympics.

Brundage was long dead by then, but he had left a prophetic epitaph, not unlike Ali's, which reminds us that all great prophets share one thought: Après moi, the game's over.

Brundage said: "When I'm gone, there's nobody rich enough, thick-skinned enough and smart enough to take my place, and the Games will be in tremendous trouble."

Of course, he was right. Prophets always are, eventually.

We must never forget the Prophets, because they reassembled the mind, body and spirit of every athlete and fan they touched, who in turn touched so many millions more. The Prophets were no ivory tower intellectuals or mountaintop hermits; they breathed the air of contemporary politics, cold cash and communications technology, and some of them smoked the right stuff.

These are prophets, not saints.

THE BOOK OF AVERY

The Prophet of Olympism

VERY BRUNDAGE WAS A RIGID, FASCISTIC, HYPOCRITICAL, SELF-indulgent, self-righteous prig. He was also a strong, pragmatic, passionate, visionary politician. He worshipped at the altar of Olympism, and he would sacrifice anyone—as would most heads of churches—for the good of the institution he claimed was the "one place in this troubled world free from politics, from religion, from racial prejudice."

He is best remembered for controversial, draconian decisions that often seemed idiosyncratic, even outrageous, the prophet shaking his staff from the mountaintop. Yet taken as a pattern—he was more involved in some decisions than others—they show a leader who came to believe that nothing was more important than The Games, and that the goals of Brundage, the Olympics and Civilization were all the same, or should be. Because he competed against—and lost to—Jim Thorpe in the 1912 Stockholm Games, he is often blamed for the Native-American decathlete's later troubles with the Olympic Committee. Thorpe's gold medals for winning the decathlon and pentathlon, as well as several jewel-encrusted trophies awarded to him by kings, were taken back when it was revealed in 1913 that he had played summer baseball for money years earlier. Thorpe's family believes that it was Brundage, still an active athlete then, who dug up the information and fed it to the press. Whether or not that's true—no hard evidence has ever surfaced—there's no question that Brundage agreed with the decision to strip Thorpe of his championships. **The rules of amateurism were stringently maintained to keep out the kind of riffraff then dominating baseball and to keep track and field the province of gentlemen under the control of the rich, pure-hearted guardians of the flame.**

Brundage was surely a rich guardian of the flame, but the purity of his heart has been questioned. He allowed himself the worldly gratifications that some prophets take as entitlements. Long married, he had many mistresses and a secret second family; he treated his illegitimate sons poorly. He pleasured himself with Asian art, possibly looted. He flouted Olympic conflict-of-interest conventions when there was a chance to drum up business for his construction company. Meanwhile, for example, Brundage had no problem with the decision to throw the sexy swimmer Eleanor Holm off the team for drinking and carousing on the voyage to Berlin in 1936.

Before those Olympics began, he conveniently dismissed Nazi Germany's discrimination against its Jewish athletes (a violation of the Olympic charter), and he fought the growing movement in American sports circles to boycott those Games. In Berlin, he did nothing to impede, or at least investigate, the American coaches' last-minute decision to

The 1948 Olympics in St. Moritz, Switzerland (right), was Brundage's first as vice president of the IOC. He looks happy enough, but he was no fan of the Winter Games, which he allowed to become embroiled in controversy, seemingly whenever possible.

remove Marty Glickman and Sam Stoller, both Jews, from a relay team. The prophet of Olympism was there when Tommie Smith and John Carlos were thrown off the team and out of Mexico in 1968 for raising their gloved fists in the black power salute on the victory stand, one of the mildest political gestures of that hard year. Brundage ordered the Games to go on in Munich in 1972 after 11 Israeli athletes were abducted and murdered by Palestinian terrorists.

■ Models of Muscular Christianity

Brundage was an early acolyte of Pierre de Coubertin, the French baron who created the modern Games in 1896 as a patriotic reaction to the Franco-Prussian War of 1870-71, which France had lost so badly. De Coubertin's followers maintained that the baron was trying to bring athletes together as a step toward world peace; his critics thought he was just trying to get French youth in shape for the rematch. The victorious Prussians had discipline, conditioning, will, experience, good leadership. Decadent France was in bad shape, split between right-wing monarchists and left-wing democrats, jingoism versus justice. Politics-as-usual was disguised by the claim—false as it turned out—that one Captain Dreyfus had given military secrets to the Germans. Baron Pierre was anti-Dreyfus. He stocked the leadership of the Games with aristocrats.

       The baron's concept of these Games was half ancient Greece, half *Tom Brown's School Days*. He admired the British and, by extension, the American ways of sport as models of muscular Christianity and of pre-

Thorpe (second from left in photo) and Brundage (center) line up for the start of the 1,500-meter race in the decathlon at the 1912 Olympics in Stockholm, Sweden. At the finish of the 1,500-meter race in the pentathlon, Thorpe was by himself (right). Though he set world records in both the pentathlon and the decathlon, Thorpe was later stripped of both gold medals for having played professional baseball years earlier.

combat training. Wars were won on the playing fields of Eton.

Brundage was no aristocrat. He was born on September 28, 1887, in Detroit. When he was 5, the family moved to Chicago, where he was raised. His father, a drinker, deserted when Avery was 6, never to be seen again. (He would die in a car crash.) His mother became a seamstress. Avery, poor, with bad eyes and no father, became a dedicated athlete and a role model in the Horatio Alger mold. He even had a paper route at 12. By that time, the Games were under way.

Selling the American Way of Life

The American team at the first modern Games in 1896 were mostly Ivy Leaguers in Athens at their own or a patron's expense. They did well in track and field and came home with what many observers feel was a sense of scoreboard nationalism that would eventually overwhelm Coubertin's romantic patriotism. This scoreboard nationalism had a missionary aspect —American victories would be a way of selling our way of life to the world, of showing that democracy was stronger than monarchy and, eventually, communism.

That was the foreign policy aspect of the Olympic movement in America. The domestic policy was powerful, too—this sense of elite amateurism, of sports for the love of it, of the nobility of games played with no reward other than what we now call bragging rights.

It's worth noting that amateurism flourished in America in an historical climate different from that of any other country. Amateurism—a word that now has the negative connotations of being unschooled, second-rate, a bumbler—was a mark of pride. It meant you played sports for love, not money, you were pure, you were upper class, you had the free time for grace and style.

It also would mean, for most of the century, that by using the Olympic template of rules and codes, promoters and officials would be able to manipulate athletes in all amateur sports, including intercollegiate. The stick would be the threat of being banned from competition for violating any one of hundreds of ambiguous and bendable regulations about clothing, employment, drugs. The carrot would be secret under-the-table payments to box-office stars. **Amateurism was a form of control. The Olympics did not invent that control, but they perfected it, and through their patina of purity gave it credibility and power.**

Like Kenesaw Mountain Landis, the judge who was brought in as baseball commissioner after the Chicago White Sox were accused of fixing the 1919 World Series, Brundage was generally perceived as a principled autocrat whose harsh methods were a small price to pay for the integrity of the Games. But since little happened in the Olympics without his approval, or at least his willful blind eye, some of the prices Brundage helped fix may have been higher than fans knew.

In 1968, for example, as part of cleaning up Mexico City for the

THE WHEELS OF JUSTICE GRIND SLOWLY

Grace Thorpe, the fourth of eight children, led the campaign for the return of her father's two gold medals. They were returned in 1982— almost 30 years after his death and 70 years after he won them in Stockholm. Thorpe, an environmental activist, lives in Prague, Oklahoma, on the Sac and Fox Reservation.

■ I remember asking him about mooching the medals and all, and all he said was, "Grace, I never once wrote a letter or asked that I get those medals back." Then he shut up and wouldn't say another word, and went back to reading his newspaper.

Dad was not a talker to start with. I could tell he didn't like talking about the subject. I think he probably resented it. So he personally didn't do anything to get the medals back, but that didn't stop others from doing it, of course.

Though he didn't speak about Brundage, Mother did. She thought Brundage was probably jealous of Dad because he was in the same Olympics in 1912, the same events, and didn't even place.

Brundage was dead when the medals were returned. They say that's one reason they were returned. Probably, if he'd still been alive, they wouldn't have been.

THE GAMES ALWAYS CAME FIRST

Allen Guttmann is president of the North American Society for Sport History and the author of The Olympics: A History of The Modern Games.

■ During the 20 years (1952-1972) of his autocratic reign as president of the International Olympic Committee, Avery Brundage was fanatically committed to the belief that the Olympics were more than a mere sports event. They were part of "a religion with universal appeal which incorporates all the basic values of other religions." Brundage was moved by a utopian vision of the Olympics as a school of virtue (fair play and good sportsmanship) and as an example of international peace and reconciliation.

  Neither Adolf Hitler's treatment of German Jews nor Japan's invasion of China nor the Mexican government's massacre of student demonstrators budged him from his belief that the Olympics scheduled for Berlin (1936), Tokyo (1940), and Mexico City (1968) should not be moved or cancelled. Brundage's response to the massacre of Israeli athletes at the 1972 games was, therefore, perfectly predictable. Like most of the world, he was horrified when a group of Palestinian terrorists infiltrated Munich's Olympic Village, murdered several athletes, and took others hostage. After hours of tense negotiations, after the terrorists were lured to the airport, after a botched assault that left most of the terrorists and all of the hostages dead, Brundage agreed to interrupt the games long enough for a memorial ceremony.

  Many voices called for cancelling the remaining events, but Brundage—with the support of the Israeli government—was adamant. "We have only the strength of a great ideal," he said. "The Games must go on."

  They went on. They still do.

Brundage was determined not to let anything interfere with his beloved Games, including terroristic mass murder (above, a burned-out helicopter in which some of the Israeli athletes died during the Munich massacre at the 1972 Games) and the Nazis' plan for world domination. At the 1936 Games in Berlin (right), Brundage—between two German military officers—leads the American team into the Olympic Village.

Games, student demonstrators were machine-gunned in the streets. Their blood was scrubbed off the cobblestones, the story concealed from the press for many years.

(At those same Games, Brundage's Swiss and Mexican girlfriends had a screaming match in the stands over a piece of jewelry that had been sent to the wrong one, another story concealed from the press for many years.)

By that time, Brundage had earned his media sobriquet as "the most powerful man in sport." He had worked his way up methodically and with some skill—he may have learned a few moves from his uncle, a Chicago politician.

Brundage was graduated from the University of Illinois in 1909 with a degree in engineering and a reputation as one of the Midwest's finest athletes. A runner, competitive walker and handball champion, he preferred individual to team sports; he liked to stand on his own, he said, which nicked with his rise as a self-made millionaire. He looked down on professional athletes as "trained seals" and mercenaries, an interesting position for a construction mogul with thousands of employees.

By 1929, he was president of both the Amateur Athletic Union and the U.S. Olympic Committee, and from that command perch was able to force a peaceful coexistence with the National Collegiate Athletic Association until 1960, when TV upped the ante and the struggle for amateur power resumed.

While accounts of male athletes competing as women, of drug use and of secret payments from national organizations generally blamed individuals, it is hard to believe that senior Olympic officials were not aware of systemic corruption. **"Just don't get caught" seems to have been the Olympic motto; the most important country from a commercial standpoint, the United States, never publicly lost a superstar athlete to an Olympic rule.** In the years when the Olympics were a sporting Cold War, there was never a serious challenge to the state-supported teams of the Soviet bloc.

Enlightened Self-Interest

For the most egregious Olympic violation—the years of payoffs to IOC members by cities applying for the Games—there was no real punishment; a few greedy officials lost their gigs in the Salt Lake City scandal, but Salt Lake didn't lose the Games. Brundage was long gone by this time, but this was the system he had set in motion. His own attempt to make money from his support of the Nazi Olympics makes that clear.

Two immensely powerful turn-of-the-century stewards of the Games, Juan Antonio Samaranch of Spain and Dick Ebersol of NBC, learned their lessons from Brundage and Roone Arledge of ABC (Ebersol's mentor); uncovering wrongdoing in the Olympic movement was not only never a priority, it was to be assiduously avoided, lest it interfere with expansion

and enrichment.

From their re-booting in 1896, the Games never have been quite what they seemed, quite what their PR machines—and the press, the TV, the host countries, the corporations, all those elements with financial interests in the Games' success—would have us believe. **The Games have always seemed determinedly, and appealingly, out of fashion, yet they have been arbiters of international sports style.** The Games have been a kind of secular religion, yet it is very hard to find any consistent moral base beyond the Rules. The Games have rituals and high holy days and infallible leaders, as well as judgments, rewards and punishments for keeping or breaking the faith, and, like all religions, the certainty that nothing is more important than the survival of the institution. Which has made them relentlessly crass.

That the Olympics have been, in their time, racist, sexist, anti-Semitic, commercialized and corrupt might have stirred our blood in a more innocent time, 50 years ago, but why are we still outraged? Is it because the Olympics, like all sports—and the Olympics at its best is sports at its best—is one human activity with the possibility to bring us together in a pure physical, emotional, mental, even spiritual community that rarely exists? Even as our religions pull us apart, our sports have the power to bring us together in a joy that transcends border and birth.

And for some of that we can thank or blame Avery Brundage, who in 1936 was elected a member of the International Olympic Committee, just in time for the Berlin Games, in which the American hero Jesse Owens won four gold medals.

The Nazi Olympics

By the time Owens got to Berlin, four different past, present and future IOC presidents were complicitous in promoting the so-called Nazi Olympics, in defiance of their own organization's spirit and charter. Two of them, Brundage and the Belgian Count Henri de Baillet-Latour, would have profited handsomely from their German friends if World War II had not disrupted many business plans. That was a foreshadow of Salt Lake City.

Information about Brundage and Baillet-Latour moldered in archives for years until it was dug out and spread around by the Los Angeles-based Simon Wiesenthal Center.

THE FIVE-RING CIRCUS

Scandals have always been part of the tradition of the Olympic Games. Usually at the center of the controversy are athletes who seek to win at all costs, or nations that confuse athletic excellence with political power. In the Games, the act of one athlete, judge or administrator can leave a lasting mark.

Summer Games

■ 1904: As American Fred Lorz is to be awarded the gold in the marathon, it is discovered that he had stopped running after 9 miles, ridden 11 in a car, and then resumed running. Officials slap him with a lifetime ban from Olympic competition.

■ 1936: Eleanor Holm had won gold in the backstroke at the '32 Games. But while en route to Berlin aboard a luxury liner, she parties with sportswriters. Avery Brundage kicks her off the team for inappropriate behavior. After the incident, it is written: "Brundage had a discus where his heart belongs."

■ 1972: The USA basketball team enters the gold medal game against the Soviets with a 62-0 all-time record. With three seconds left and the Americans at the free throw line, the Soviets call a time-out that is not acknowledged by the officials. The Americans lead by a point when the clock is reset to three seconds—the time remaining when the Soviet coach originally tried to call time-out. The Soviets score on a layup to win. The U.S. loses its protest before a Jury of Appeal by one vote.

■ 1988: Canadian Ben Johnson sprints to a world-record 9.79 seconds in the 100-meter final, but is disqualified. He becomes the first renowned athlete caught cheating with steroids. He subsequently admits to taking drugs, and is stripped of his gold medal and his world record.

■ 1988: Roy Jones Jr.: The American appears to have convincingly beaten Park Si-hun for the light middleweight gold medal, but three of the five judges give the victory to the Korean. Observers of all nationalities agree the decision was biased—even some Korean fans are embarrassed, and Park apologizes to Jones.

Winter Games

■ 1936: Alpine skiing is included for the first time in the Games, although the IOC overrules the sport's governing body, mandating that ski instructors can't take part in the Olympics because they are professionals. Incensed, the Austrians and the Swiss skiers stage a boycott.

■ 1972: Karl Schranz, the Austrian champion and gold medal favorite, is banned from the Sapporo Games by Brundage because he was paid to test and develop ski products. Schranz, a critic of Brundage, returns to Vienna, where he is greeted by 100,000 fans and a ticker-tape parade.

■ 1994: Tonya Harding conspires with her husband Jeff Gillooly to club Nancy Kerrigan in the knee to stop Kerrigan from competing at the U.S. Nationals and qualifying for the Olympic team. Kerrigan is given the team's second spot, and will win a silver medal in Lillehammer. Harding will later plead guilty to conspiracy and be banned for life by the U.S. Figure Skating Association.

■ 1998: A Utah TV station breaks a story about the SLOC informing the daughter of a Cameroon IOC member that the SLOC would no longer pay her university tuition. It will be revealed later that many IOC members sold votes to cities bidding to host future Games. By March 1999, four IOC members will resign and six will be expelled.

■ 2002: The French judge Marie-Reine Le Gougne is banned for three years by the International Skating Union for misconduct in judging the pairs' free program. She confesses that she was pressured by her own skating federation to vote in favor of the eventual winners, Russians Elena Berezhnaya and Anton Sikharulidze.

While Nazism didn't faze Brundage in the slightest (above left, at the 1936 Olympics), drinking by women and Jews winning gold medals were verboten. He had Eleanor Holm (above, center in photo) booted from the '36 U.S. women's swim team for drinking on the boat that carried the U.S. team to the Berlin Games; and the Jewish Marty Glickman (right) was not allowed to run in the finals of the 4 x 100-meter relay, which was won by the U.S. with two subs.

Brundage's papers at the University of Illinois include a 1938 letter from the president of the German Olympic Committee, assuring him that his Chicago construction company's bid to help build the German embassy in Washington had been accepted.

There also was an April 12, 1933, letter to "My dear Avery," from Sigfrid Edstrom, the Swedish engineer who became IOC president after Baillet-Latour died in 1942. On stationery identifying him as an IOC member, Edstrom wrote: **"It is too bad that the American Jews are so active and cause us so much trouble.** It is impossible for our German friends to carry on the expensive preparations for the Olympic Games if all this unrest prevails."

While the Wiesenthal Center was hardly the first to charge that Brundage and others willfully ignored German sports officials' discrimination against their Jewish athletes, in violation of Olympic regulations, its indictment of Brundage as a potential bribe-taker was new. As evidence, it offered an August 8, 1938, letter from Hans von Tschammer und Osten, the so-called Reichssportfuhrer, President of the German Olympic Committee and a Nazi Party member since 1922.

THE WRITINGS OF CHAIRMAN BRUNDAGE

"Confusion on the subject of amateurism is entirely needless . . . An amateur sportsman is one who participates in sport for the love of it. A professional athlete is one who participates for pay of one kind or another, direct or indirect . . . Professional sport is not a sport at all, but a branch of the entertainment business."

—*"The Ideals of Amateur Sport"* in The Amateur Athlete, *August 1941*

"Every gathering of the nations brings an 'incident.' In the vast scheme of the Olympics these are minor matters, but press hysteria blows them into lurid headlines. Since 1929 I have been on the receiving end of a great many of these brickbats. 'Meanest man in sport,' 'the last living amateur' and 'apostle of hypocrisy' are a few of the things I have been called."

—*"Operation Olympic Games"* in *Bulletin du Comité International Olympique, 1953*

Von Tschammer wrote: "Mr. Von Halt (Karl Ritter von Halt, a German IOC member) forwarded your letter to me at the beginning of July, in which you asked whether your firm could participate in the building of the German embassy in Washington. Having brought your proven record of your friendly attitude toward German sports before the responsible authorities, I can happily tell you that both the German foreign minister, as well as General Building Inspector Speer, have declared to me that you take part."

By November, however, world events trumped Brundage's bid. In a letter to von Halt, Brundage wrote: "Ambassador Diekhoff informed me that the project had been postponed." In the same letter, he discussed the difficulty of staging another track and field meet between Germany and the United States. He wrote that because of "the overwhelming proportion of Jewish advertising, our papers have been filled with anti-Nazi propaganda."

Brundage's most prominent biographer, the Amherst College sports historian Allen Guttmann, did not mention the letters in his 1984 book, *The Games Must Go On.*

When asked about the seeming oversight, Professor Guttmann said, "There were 334 boxes of documents in the archives. I might have overlooked a few. In any case, I'm skeptical of the Center's interpretation of all this. I see no linkage between the present corruption and Brundage. Why

The normally ultra-dignified Brundage has his crash helmet adjusted before a photo-op bobsled run at the St. Moritz Games of 1948.

THEY NEVER PLAYED THE GAMES, BUT THEY RULED THE GAMES

When we think of major sports influences, we usually think first of athletes.
Not necessarily so. As proof, here is a list of the most influential non-athletes in sports history.
And remember, class, those most influential in developing sports need not be as autocratic as Avery Brundage,
but innovation, persistence and daring help when you strive to make an indelible imprint.

Baseball

■ John Montgomery Ward: A 19th-century player and manager, he championed players' rights and helped shape modern baseball. And if that wasn't enough, he also invented the intentional walk.

■ Kenesaw Mountain Landis: Baseball's first commissioner (1920-44) was known for his autocratic style and the banning of eight Chicago Black Sox for life. Avery Brundage was probably a big fan.

■ Rube Foster: In 1920, he founded the first successful pro league for African-American players, the Negro National League.

■ Branch Rickey: He devised the modern farm system in 1919, and integrated the major leagues when he brought up Jackie Robinson to play for the Brooklyn Dodgers in 1947.

Branch Rickey

■ Marvin Miller: As executive director of the Players' Association (1966-82), he challenged the assumption that unions have no place in sports, while increasing average salaries from $19,000 to more than $240,000.

Marvin Miller

Football

■ George Halas: The Chicago Bears' coach/owner (1920-83) was an innovator and the founding father of the NFL. He revolutionized strategy in the late 1930s when he revived the T formation and invented the man in motion.

■ Lamar Hunt: In 1959, he organized and became the first president of the American Football League, which merged its 10 teams with the NFL in 1966.

■ Pete Rozelle: The NFL commissioner (1960-1989) negotiated lucrative TV deals with the networks that made NFL football our national sport, doubled the league's size, and helped create the Super Bowl.

Boxing

■ John Graham Chambers: He wrote the Queensberry code of rules that influenced modern boxing. They were first published in 1867.

■ Don King: The flamboyant and controversial promoter has pretty much controlled the heavyweight division since 1978.

Hockey

■ Lord Stanley of Preston: The Canadian governor-general in 1893 gave hockey the Stanley Cup, the oldest trophy that can be won by pro athletes in North America.

Soccer

■ Jules Rimet: The Frenchman proposed the World Cup and was a major force behind its first staging.

Basketball

■ James Naismith: He was the physical-education director with the ball and peach basket who, in 1891, invented basketball.

■ David Stern: NBA commissioner since 1984, he has presided over expansion in the U.S. (from 23 to 29 teams) and globally, and launched the WNBA in 1997.

Olympics

■ Pierre de Coubertin: This French educator revived the Olympic Games in 1896. He was a founding member of the IOC and its president for 30 years (1896-1925).

Motor Sports

■ Enzo Ferrari: The cars of the Italian manufacturer and designer have often dominated world racing in the second half of the 20th century.

Sports media

■ Grantland Rice: The first celebrated American sportswriter, he chronicled the Golden Age of Sport in the 1920s and greatly influenced the thinking of fans and athletes on a wide variety of issues.

■ Roone Arledge: He ran ABC Sports (1968-86), revolutionized Olympic coverage and made *Monday Night Football* a ritual. He also discovered . . .

■ Howard Cosell: The audacious and rarely silent commentator on *Monday Night Football* (1970-83) was the nation's most loved and most hated broadcaster.

■ William Rasmussen: A sports announcer who founded cable network ESPN in 1978 to broadcast regional sports events; now ESPN and ESPN2 collectively reach 90 million households.

■ Rupert Murdoch: The Australian-born founder of News Corp., a global media company, purchased the LA Dodgers for a record $350 million in 1997. More importantly, as the head of Fox, he has greatly affected rights fees for all the major sports, and has influenced how sports are broadcast all over the world.

James Naismith

Tennis

■ James Dwight: The architect of tennis in America served as president for 21 years of the U.S. National Lawn Tennis Association, which he helped organize in 1881.

Marketing

Phil Knight

■ Phil Knight: He is the founder and chairman of Nike, the multi-billion-dollar shoe and fitness company, which is renowned for using high-profile athletes in its advertising and exercising great influence on high school, college and pro sports programs, especially in basketball.

■ Leigh Steinberg: For 27 years he has epitomized the high-profile sports agent, negotiating more than $2 billion in contracts and orchestrating trades and other kinds of player movements, particularly in pro football.

wouldn't the Germans go to someone with whom they had a relationship to build their embassy? College department chairmen call up their alma maters when they want new faculty.

"Brundage wouldn't need a sweetener. He was pro-German, he was against the boycott of the Berlin Olympics. Believing Brundage would need to be bribed to support the Berlin Games makes as much sense as believing Bill Clinton would need to be bribed to support Hillary for Senator."

◼ Trivial and Tinged with Evil

World War II and the Holocaust made Olympic politics seem both trivial and tinged with evil. The Games were suspended in 1940 and 1944. By the time they resumed, the Soviet Union had replaced Nazi Germany as the Evil Empire.

Cold War sports was a made-for-TV rivalry. Behind the Iron Curtain, Americans were told, were secret athletic camps of "state professionals" brimming with performance-enhancing drugs. Much of that was true, which seemed to justify American drug use and college athletic scholarships. After Eastern Bloc women began winning bushels of gold medals, the treatment of American women athletes improved.

And after the 18-year-old gold-medal winner Cassius Clay stood up for his country when a Russian journalist asked him about civil rights, he became an instant media star.

Eight years later, Muhammad Ali was a central symbol of a proposed Olympic boycott by black athletes.

Dick Gregory, the black comic and civil rights activist, a former college runner, had tried and failed to organize an Olympic boycott in the

During his 20-year run as IOC president—1952-1972— Brundage saw good times (above, awarding a gold medal to American Wilma Rudolph for her victory in the women's 100-meter dash in the 1960 Games) and bad times (right, the famous black-glove protest against racism by Tommie Smith, center, and John Carlos in Mexico City in 1968, about which Brundage said, "Warped mentalities and cracked personalities seem to be everywhere").

early '60s. Harry Edwards, the California sociologist, created an organization that damaged several major pre-Olympic events and helped convince Lew Alcindor to turn down a spot on the Olympic basketball team.

It was a central skirmish of the Athletic Revolution, a fragmented offspring of the anti-war and civil rights movements. Black athletes, in particular, had begun to see themselves as exploited gladiators. But since many of them were depending on athletic fame to get them jobs, demonstrations were risky. Who wants to hire or draft a troublemaker? A plan to have black athletes wear black shoes as a symbolic protest fell through; too many of them were getting secret shoe company payoffs. Such verboten deals were winked at by Olympic officials who had a community of interest with the companies.

■ 20/20 Tunnel Vision

And so, when Tommie Smith (who had earlier said, "I don't want Brundage presenting me any medals") and John Carlos raised their black-gloved fists on the victory stand, not only was it one of the mildest militant gestures of that bloody era, it seemed almost a compromise by sports standards. Perhaps emboldened by the mildness, Olympic officials responded by throwing Smith and Carlos out of Mexico.

Brundage would have been happy if the Winter Olympics had simply disappeared. Luckily, he died before his beloved Games could be despoiled by professionals like Magic Johnson (right, celebrating after the Dream Team captured gold at the 1992 Games in Barcelona).

AVERY'S ISSUES

The highly principled Brundage would have "issues" with many of the changes in the Olympic movement since his death in 1975.

■ Women being allowed to participate in sports previously considered male-only: ice hockey (1998), pole vault and weightlifting (2000) and bobsled (2002).

■ The Games getting boycotted for political reasons: 65 countries, Moscow, 1980, and 14, for Los Angeles, 1984.

■ The advent of corporate sponsorship of athletes and teams.

■ Using the worldwide stage for protests, such as Cathy Freeman displaying the flag of her Aboriginal ancestors at Sydney in 2000.

■ The rampant commercialism, particularly at Montreal (1976), Atlanta (1996) and Salt Lake City (2002).

■ The decision by the IOC to give international governing bodies the authority to allow professionals to compete: tennis (1988), men's basketball and soccer (1992) and ice hockey (1998).

■ The success of the Winter Oympics, which he seemingly allowed to become embroiled in controversy whenever possible.

Brundage's comment, "Warped mentalities and cracked personalities seem to be everywhere and impossible to eliminate," has been unfairly interpreted as racist; his fury was simply at the violation of his bubble.

Brundage came to world attention at the 1972 Munich Games, after the murder of 11 Israeli athletes by Palestinian terrorists. In a famous address from the Olympic Stadium, he declared, "The Games must go on, and we must continue our efforts to keep them clean, pure and honest and try to extend the sportsmanship of the athletic field into other areas."

Some felt he trivialized the murders by linking them to the successful and peaceful protest by black African countries against Rhodesia's appearance at the Games. In his address, he said the Games had been "subject to two savage attacks." The prophet had 20/20 tunnel vision.

Given the Olympics' tacit marketing plan, the murders seemed a rational act; since the Games had become a way for nations to showcase the symbolic superiority of their way of life, why wouldn't a band of terrorists without an official team try to blast their way onto the scoreboard?

The Olympics never seemed to recover the moral high ground after the murders. Brundage lasted only three more years. He died in 1975, at 87, his new 39-year-old wife, a German princess, at his bedside.

Après moi, the game is over. Montreal was nearly bankrupted by the 1976 Games. In 1980 and 1984, the United States and the Soviet Union took turns boycotting the Games, politicizing them in blatant ways that had always been masked. By the time the Berlin Wall came down, and then the Soviet Union collapsed, the East-West competitive rivalry, the Olympics' main marketing tool, was dead.

How would the prophet have felt about the 1992 Dream Team?

The prophet Avery would have made some twisted sense of it all, just so long as his vision of the world's heart kept beating, so long as the Games went on.

THE BOOK OF CASSIUS

Prophet of Free Agency

HENEVER CASSIUS CLAY PASSED A MIRROR THAT FEBRUARY OF 1964 in Miami Beach, he would do a comic double-take, then peer with feigned surprise at the glass and gasp, "So beautiful."

That would invariably set the scribes snarling, "Let's be serious. What if the champ beats you?"

Cassius would laugh. "I won't feel bad. I'll have tricked all the people into coming to the fight to pay $250 for a ticket, when they wouldn't have paid $100 without my talk."

"So this whole act is just a con job, eh?"

The prophet's eyes would sparkle as he proffered wisdom. "People ain't gonna give you nothing no way, you gotta go get it. I'm making money, the popcorn man making money, and the beer man, and you got something to write about."

So many wrote so much that the Book of Cassius swelled into a blimp of words that rose into SportsWorld heaven, where it hovers to this day, threatening to explode and rain upon us a confusion of legend and hard fact, of vilification and beatification. It is hard to remember that the trembling, moon-faced Muhammad Ali who made us weep when he lit the Olympic Flame in 1996 had scared the subpoenas out of the government by refusing to step forward and become Private Cassius Clay. Federal prosecutors earnestly declared that if they lost their case against Ali, the United States might be unable to field enough black soldiers to fight a war. This was in 1967, the middle rounds of Vietnam.

State and municipal boxing commissions, all of whom are stocked with political appointments, responded immediately, refusing to sanction Ali fights. He was effectively blackballed for three years in the prime of his career. Although the United States Supreme Court would eventually overturn his conviction, the lesson of the '60s, supposedly that time of doing your own thing, of standing up for your principles, was very clearly something else for athletes, particularly the black athletes who were emerging as the superstars in the major pro sports, the gladiators of the new mass entertainment.

The lesson was this: Forget about expressing yourself politically or socially; just wear the shoes; take the money and run.

Oh, there were charismatic stars that dominated their games before Ali—John L. Sullivan, Babe Ruth, Arnold Palmer come to mind—but every one of them worked within the system. Ali was the first of that magnitude to challenge it, and he may well be the last for a very long time. Michael Jordan, remember, refused to back political candidates since, as he put it, members of both parties bought shoes. It will be interesting to see if

Ali would grow up to be something of a sporting martyr (right, as a modern St. Sebastian—who was clubbed to death for converting to Christianity—in a classic Esquire *cover photo by Carl Fischer). But his childhood (left, at 12) was no bed of roses either. When he was 13, he saw a photo of Emmett Till, a 14-year-old from Chicago who was brutally murdered in Mississippi for whistling at a white woman. The dead boy's smashed and swollen face haunted him for years.*

Tiger Woods decides to take over golf, and how far he can get.

Cassius Clay started his professional career in a traditional way. Just back from winning the Olympic gold medal, he signed what was considered a fair, even benevolent, contract with the Louisville Sponsoring Group, 11 local white business leaders who had "the complexions and connections to give me good directions."

■ Legend of the Greatest: The First Tale

That was the world Cassius Marcellus Clay Jr. was born into on January 17, 1942. His father was an angry sign painter who felt his artistic talent had gone unrecognized because of racism. His mother, Odessa, was a sweet pillowy housewife whom Cassius and his younger brother, Rudy, called "Bird." There is evidence that Cash, as Senior was called, beat Bird, and perhaps the boys, as well. A loud autodidact, Cash talked about the black nationalist Marcus Garvey and taught his boys that the white man would never let the black man get over. You got to take what you want, he'd say.

Out of that environment, a basically shy, possibly abused, probably learning-disabled youngster could find escape, solace, support in the discipline of boxing and later in the Lost-Found Nation of Islam, the so-called Black Muslim separatist group.

But first, there was the red bicycle. It is the founding tale, the first of seven tales that form the Legend of the Greatest. On a rainy day in October 1954, when Ali was 12, he left his brand-new $60 Schwinn bicycle outside the Columbia Auditorium in Louisville. When he came out,

In an undated photo (above), from left, Cassius, friend Arned Arter, brother Rudy and William Keane—the uncle of Knicks star Allan Houston—enjoy a hot Louisville summer afternoon. He didn't look all that much older when he won gold in 1960 at Rome.

the bike was gone. Furious, Cassius screamed for the cops.

A passerby sent him down to the building's basement, where a white police officer, Joe Martin, ran a boxing gym. Martin was off duty, but sympathetic enough to the ranting, sobbing boy to take a report. But when Cassius described how he was going to "whup" the robber when he found him, Martin gently suggested he first learn how.

The legend, which seems true, comes with commentary. **Joe Frazier, the rival who defined Ali's talent and courage in the ring, would later sneer that an expensive bicycle proved that Ali was a middle-class kid who hadn't come up hard as he did.** That Cassius called for the police indicates that he was no junior gangbanger. He himself admits he was more attracted by the chance to get on Martin's local amateur boxing TV show, *Tomorrow's Champions*, and be a celebrity, than he was by the controlled violence of the sport.

Yet Martin would be the first of his boxing mentors to express wonder and delight at his ability to learn fast, his natural athleticism and, most important, his willingness to work harder than most anyone else around.

There was a hunger in him.

But among the Negro strivers of the late '50s, he was easy to discount. He did poorly in school. He could barely read. He was advanced from grade to grade and finally graduated because he was a cute boy with early celebrity, winning amateur titles as a teenager. No one would be surprised later when a report disclosed he had an IQ of 78.

But he was not isolated from the outside world. His family included teachers, nurses, successful business owners. He was deeply affected by the lynching of Emmett Till, in 1955. A Chicago boy about Cassius' age,

Emmett was murdered for flirting with a white woman while on vacation in Mississippi.

Nevertheless, in 1960, Cassius was able to speak well of his country. After Cassius won the light-heavyweight championship at the Rome Olympics, a Soviet journalist asked him about segregation in America.

Cassius replied, "Tell your readers we got qualified people working on that, and I'm not worried about the outcome. To me, the USA is still the best country in the world, including yours. It may be hard to get something to eat sometimes, but I ain't fighting alligators and living in a mud hut."

Clay became a hero, a symbol of what was right about America—a lineal descendant of Jim Thorpe and Jesse Owens, priests in the Olympic church, pages in the Book of Avery. Here was a young black man, the descendant of slaves, who seemed properly grateful for the advantages of democracy. He wasn't agitating to vote or sitting in at lunch counters. He was knocking down commie boxers, and his only complaint was having to sleep on his back, because when he tried to sleep on his stomach the medal cut into his chest.

The second great tale was the slaying of the monster, which is a standard of heroic epics. He was still Cassius Clay then,

After taking on the thuggish Sonny Liston (above, left) and winning the heavyweight title in Miami Beach in what was considered a monumental upset (right), Ali easily chopped the Beatles down to size (left, during the 1964 tour of America). Before fighting the seemingly unbeatable Liston, Clay—as he was still known—was asked if he was scared. "Black guys scare white guys a lot more than black guys scare black guys," he said.

presented in the media as a self-promoting clown, often dubbed Gaseous Cassius or the Louisville Lip. Depending on the sensibilities of the writer, Cassius was either bringing dishonor to boxing, this Third World outpost of sports, or was being exploited, an innocent lamb being led to slaughter. Clay's doggerel—"This is the story about a man/With iron fists and a beautiful tan" —and his garrulous exuberance infuriated an older generation of white reporters who considered Joe Louis' reticence and repression the gold standard of heavyweight behavior. A younger generation of scribes who wanted a fighter of its own was charmed.

But all were in agreement that cold-eyed thug Sonny Liston was going to hand poor Cassius his head. Going into the fight at Miami Beach on February 25, 1964, the odds were 7-1 that Liston would retain his title.

Clay never should have gotten that title shot after only 19 pro fights. There were heavyweights higher in the rankings. But boxing needed fresh meat for the monster. The big money was now in closed-circuit theaters, and fans were not going to pay for tickets to a one-round knockout, unless the victim was at least interesting. Clay's picture had been on the cover of *Time* magazine, he had performed in Greenwich Village coffeehouses, and he helped promote the fight by stalking Liston's training camp and screaming how he would "whup that big ugly bear." Liston would shake his head

Three of the many faces of Ali: the committed Black Muslim (top left, addressing a Muslim convention in 1968 in Chicago; and clowning with Malcolm X, at left in photo left, after beating Liston in 1964); and the tenderhearted, kid-loving innocent (right, after being "floored" by 9-year-old Keith Green while training for a 1967 title fight with Zora Folley).

at that and say, "I'll get locked up for murder if I fight him."

In the days before the fight, reporters asked Clay, after all his big talk, how he would handle defeat. Clay would laugh and say, "The next day, I'll be on the sidewalk, hollering, 'No man ever beat me twice.' I'll be screaming for a rematch."

Fear of Higher Authority

At the weigh-in the morning of the fight, Clay staged a mad scene that actually left him frothing at the mouth. He ranted and raged, lunging at Liston on the scale. His handlers pretended to be holding him back. Despite the fact that Clay had done this before in an attempt to stimulate ticket sales, the act was taken seriously. One boxing commission doctor said Clay was "scared to death."

If Clay was afraid of anything, it was what prophets are always afraid of—Higher Authority. Rumors had been circulating that Clay, at 17 or 18, had been "fished" off a street corner in Atlanta and brought to a Muslim meeting. The sober and earnest men in the congregation, some former convicts and drug addicts, made an impression on the youngster, as did the preacher's message of black pride, economic independence and contempt for the "blue-eyed devils" who would be swept to death in the coming Armageddon. While the Honorable Elijah Muhammad was the titular leader of the group, it was the fiery Malcolm X who got the headlines;

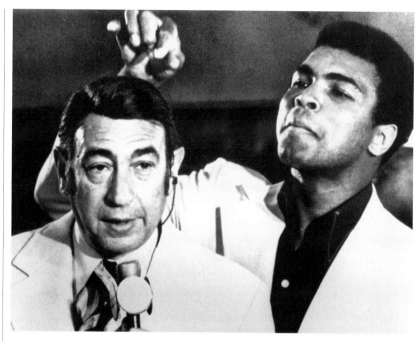

CINEMATIC HEAVYWEIGHTS

Although many boxing movies are flawed, the few good ones keep us coming back. They not only offer finely choreographed fight scenes, but, inevitably, the star's battles with his own demons. These 10 are knockouts.

whites were afraid of Malcolm because they believed, incorrectly, he was a powerful leader who could send rivers of blood down city streets.

Malcolm had been silenced by Elijah for describing the JFK assassination as a matter of violence begetting violence, of "chickens coming home to roost." Elijah didn't want to offend "the white power structure," especially since he had hopes of making alliances with segregationists.

Malcolm X in the Middle

Malcolm, who considered Cassius a kid brother, was the fighter's guest in Miami during the buildup, and he tried to keep a low profile. But when the promoters realized they had scaled the price of tickets too high, they demanded that Clay publicly deny the growing rumors that he was a Black Muslim. It was a ploy to shift blame for a box-office bust from their mistake to the vague excuse that vacationing Jews were boycotting the fight because of the Muslims. Clay refused, the promoters threatened to cancel the fight, he called their bluff, and they backed down.

As far as the promoters were concerned, it was a sharp business tactic that hadn't worked. But to Clay, it was an inkling of what new power he was getting through his Muslim affiliation. He wasn't a boy anymore, he wasn't just a fighter, he was nobody's Olympic nigger. He was a force to be reckoned with.

Certainly in the ring, for starters. When Liston and Clay met in the middle of the ring for the referee's instructions, there was a gasp in the arena; Clay was bigger.

And a better fighter. Liston never came out for the seventh round, claiming he had torn muscles in his left shoulder from swinging and missing. Liston quit his title.

1. *Rocky* (1976): Sly Stallone's famously undervalued script turns into an Oscar-winning best picture. Its success led to boxing's worst movie—*Rocky V*—once again hammering home the old adage: No good deed goes unpunished.

2. *Raging Bull* (1980): Martin Scorsese captures Jake La Motta's violent life beautifully, if gruesomely. Robert De Niro packs on 30 pounds, gets bloodied and wins an Oscar.

3. *Body and Soul* (1947): The gold standard. Hard-luck Charlie Davis (John Garfield) earns a title, then self-destructs. The final fight sequence was cutting-edge for that time.

4. *Champion* (1949): In his breakout role, Kirk Douglas plays an ambitious boxer who rises through the ranks but succumbs to corruption. Nominated for six Oscars.

5. *The Harder They Fall* (1956): In his last film, Bogey is a sportswriter-turned-press agent who exposes a sleazy promoter. Jersey Joe Walcott has a role as a trainer.

6. *Requiem for a Heavyweight* (1962): A washed-up fighter will do anything to make ends meet. The cast includes Anthony Quinn, Jackie Gleason and Mickey Rooney. Cassius Clay and Jack Dempsey have cameos.

7. *The Great White Hope* (1970): James Earl Jones is Jack Jefferson, who endures racism as the first black heavyweight champion. Jane Alexander plays his white love interest. Both are nominated for Oscars.

8. *The Hurricane* (1999): Yes, it lacks authenticity and is poorly told. But Denzel Washington's Oscar-nominated performance transcends the film's limitations.

9. *Somebody Up There Likes Me* (1956): Paul Newman assiduously prepared to depict Rocky Graziano from delinquent to champion. He gets it all right— the boxing, the mannerisms, the speech.

10. *The Boxer* (1997): Daniel Day-Lewis plays Danny Flynn, who, after 14 years in prison, struggles to pick up his career in politically charged Northern Ireland. Underrated.

The new champion looked down at the press corp and shouted, "Eat your words. I am the greatest. I . . . am . . . the . . . greatest."

But at the traditional press conference the morning after the fight, Clay was so subdued that older reporters were convinced that his behavior up until then had been merely a pose to sell tickets. Clay would settle in to become a champion they could live with. Many of the younger reporters, disappointed at Clay's seeming betrayal, tried to provoke him. Was he really "a card-carrying Muslim," a black separatist in this time of civil rights activism?

He snapped back, "In the jungle, lions are with lions and tigers with tigers and redbirds stay with redbirds and bluebirds with bluebirds. That's human nature, too, to be with your own kind. I don't want to go where I'm not wanted."

Reporters argued. Jackie Robinson was invoked; integration was the goal, not further separation. Clay then delivered the mantra of free agency: "I don't have to be what you want me to be, I'm free to be who I want." From a brand-new heavyweight champion, it was a profound and revolutionary mantra, truly the declaration of a prophet.

The third tale in the Legend of the Greatest was his refusal to be drafted, a tale that begins on the mild afternoon of February 17, 1966, in Miami. Ali was in the early stages of training for a fight with Ernie Terrell, and now he was relaxing outside his rented bungalow, ogling schoolgirls on their way home. On television—although not on his television—Senate hearings raged over the war in Vietnam. Sharp political lines were being drawn. A nation was pulling apart. Ali was crooning, "Hey, little girl in the high school sweater, you not gonna pass me by today."

The phone rang inside the house and his cook came out. It was a reporter. When Ali came back, he looked upset. His draft board in Louisville—which had originally classified him unfit for service, perhaps as a gift to the Louisville Sponsoring Group—had just reclassified him 1A, ready for combat.

"Why me?" was his first response. He began to rant. After embarrassing him with a classification that implied he was too dumb or nutty for the Army, how could they reclassify him "without another test to see if I'm any wiser or worser?" Why didn't the draft board call up some poor boys?

Always the consummate performer, Ali makes a grab for Howard Cosell's toupee at the the 1972 Olympic boxing trials (above, far left), a move imitated by Will Smith as Ali and Jon Voight as Cosell in the 2001 movie, Ali *(above, near left). Ali makes his acting debut in the Broadway musical* Buck White, *in 1969 (above, right), well disguised in a wig of his own.*

Think of how many guns and bombs his taxes paid for. It was hardly the response of a principled pacifist.

Television news trucks pulled up, interviewers sensed his anger and provoked him further: "What do you think about the Vietcong?"

Tired, exasperated, Ali blurted out the sound bite that would help define the '60s, a headline sentence that made him simultaneously hated and loved: "I ain't got nothing against them Vietcong."

There was no question that he said it. But the context twists the tale. "I ain't got nothing against them Vietcong" was widely interpreted as either the chant of "unwashed punks" ungrateful to their country, or a humanistic plea to stop killing people of color in an unjust war. But for Ali, at the moment he said it, the phrase really meant, "Why me?"

Nevertheless, the reaction was profound. **He became a hero to war protestors, a traitor to those who felt patriotism meant, "My country right or wrong."**

American boxing commissions found ways to block his title fights, sometimes even by digging up the mob connections of an opponent and then denying him a license. Ali was forced to fight outside the country. It fed his grandiosity.

"All great men have to suffer," he would say. "Jesus was condemned, Moses, Noah, Elijah, Martin Luther King. You can't rank me with no fighter . . . I'm in a class of my own. I'm a jet compared to props."

He fought in Toronto, London twice, Frankfurt, which enhanced his celebrity in America; the fights were replayed on ABC, and the lively chats with Howard Cosell showcased both men at their best. Authorities relented—perhaps they were afraid he was getting too popular abroad or that he wouldn't come back for his draft induction—and he was allowed to fight in America. Always the performer, he invented the Ali Shuffle to enliven a match with Cleveland Williams.

But on a dreary day in Houston, April 28, 1967, when Cassius Clay was called to step forward in a draft ceremony, Muhammad Ali stood firm and his career stopped cold.

The Fourth Tale: Exile

Like Noah and Moses (not to mention Daniel Boone, Davy Crockett and Wyatt Earp, to whom he also compared himself), Ali had his wandering years in exile, the fourth tale of the Legend of the Greatest. While those three and a half years out of the ring were his athletic prime, they were also a time of enormous emotional and intellectual growth. Needing money, he starred in a mediocre Broadway musical (he was mediocre, as well) about a black preacher, he began working on his autobiography, *The Greatest*, a silly and inaccurate book, and he lent his name to Champburgers, a short-lived fast-food chain. He replaced his first wife, a delicious Chicago model who wanted him to resist Muslim influence, with a 17-year-old Muslim bride, and went to work producing four children. He toured college cam-

Ali earned an estimated $60 million in the ring, more than all other heavyweight champs before him . . . combined. In 1987, Ring magazine named him the greatest heavyweight ever. Three reasons why—winning the title from Liston (top right), avoiding Frazier during one of their three classic slugfests (middle right), and mesmerizing Foreman with the Rope-a-Dope during the Rumble in the Jungle. "Man, I hit him with punches that'd bring down the walls of a city," Frazier said. "Lawdy, lawdy, he's a great champion."

Sept. 30, 1975

"A thrilla in Manila"

ALI-FRAZIER

FIGHT OF A LIFETIME

PHILIPPINES

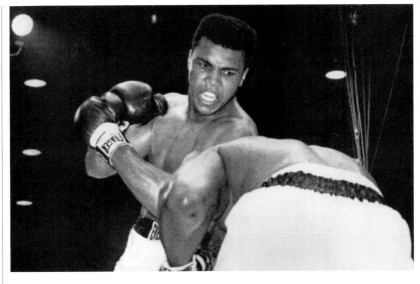

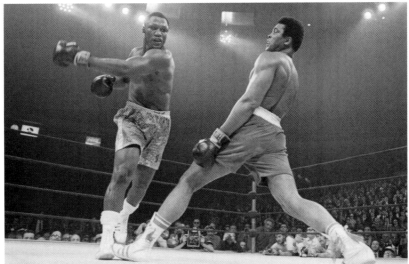

STANDING UP TO ALI

■ It seemed like an odd matchup: follow up the Rumble in the Jungle by taking on the Bayonne Bleeder. Just five months after Muhammad Ali regained the title in 1974 by dismantling George Foreman in Zaire, he squared off against little-known Chuck Wepner, a brute whose nickname was derived by combining his hometown in New Jersey with what he did best in the ring.

Said Wepner, "I got my shot, I fought The Greatest, and it's something I'm proud of, though my life is better today."

The champ's opponent was unexpectedly tough. In the ninth round, the Bleeder became just the fourth man to knock down the Butterfly. (That vicious punch inspired a spectator at the fight named Sylvester Stallone to script a movie called *Rocky*.) Ali put Wepner away in the 15th, the final round, on a TKO with 19 seconds left.

Today, the 63-year-old Wepner is still inspiring: He spends much of his free time giving motivational speeches (he was sentenced to 10 years in 1988 for cocaine possession—he served 3—but has been clean for years). "I enjoy talking about boxing to kids," he said. "I tell them to stay away from drugs, booze and women—all the things I failed to do."

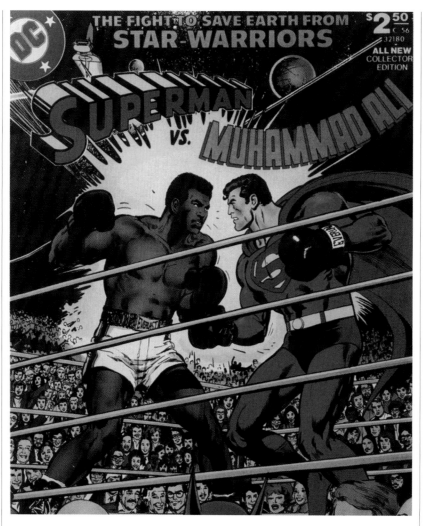

ALI THE MUSE

Muhammad Ali has inspired artists in many mediums since he burst upon the world boxing scene in 1960 at the Olympic Games.

Painting: Widely regarded as the most frequently portrayed athlete on canvas, the Butterfly has been painted by Andy Warhol, whose silk-screened portrait of Ali is among his most recognizable works.

Film/theater: He's been the topic of documentaries, such as the Oscar-winning *When We Were Kings*; feature films, like *Ali*; and even an off-Broadway show— Geoff Ewing's one-man rendition, *Ali*.

Photography: The camera loves Ali, and auction houses like Sotheby's are flooded with his action and portrait photos. Among the most creative pieces of photojournalism involving Ali is Flip Schulke's iconic photos showing the champ training underwater.

Sculpture: Lawrence Holofcener crafted pieces on 20th-century icons like FDR, Gandhi, Kennedy, MLK, Mother Teresa, the Beatles . . . and Ali. And the Charles H. Wright Museum of African American History in Detroit houses the Donald Thibodeaux series that celebrates Ali's life.

Writing: Ali's brashness, poetic speech and turbulent life have attracted many talented writers, including Norman Mailer (*The Fight*), David Remnick (*King of the World: Muhammad Ali and the Rise of an American Hero*) and Thomas Hauser (*Muhammad Ali: His Life and Times*).

puses where he was indeed "the onliest boxer they ever asked questions like a senator."

His legal battles dragged on. He was convicted of draft evasion, and a federal judge made an example of him with a stiff sentence—five years in jail and a $10,000 fine. His lawyers kept him out of jail with appeals and technical speed bumps. As his case became central to both the anti-war movement and the so-called Athletic Revolution, Ali's symbolic importance took on its mythic stature—every athlete who stood up against an oppressive system, or even a bullying coach, invoked his name or drew courage from his strength.

The prophet of free agency's most obvious acolyte was Curt Flood. An All-Star St. Louis Cardinals outfielder, Flood challenged the legality of a team forever owning a player's contract. He refused to be traded, even with a raise in salary. He ultimately lost his case before the Supreme Court, but within a few years free agency changed the game forever.

Politics shaped the fifth tale of the Legend of the Greatest. The growing black power of the New South led to Ali's first fight in three

'The Greatest' Is Gone

and a half years, on October 26, 1970 in Atlanta, against Jerry Quarry, a willing journeyman whose thin white skin predictably and conveniently cut open in the third round. At ringside were Bill Cosby, Sidney Poitier, the Rev. Jesse Jackson, Hank Aaron, Diana Ross and Coretta Scott King, whose foundation awarded Ali the annual Dr. Martin Luther King Jr. medal and called him "a living example of soul power, the March on Washington all in two fists."

Powerful stuff, but not quite enough to beat Joe Frazier in what was justifiably called The Fight.

It was generally conceded that every contender would be a pretender until he fought the true champ—but Frazier was clearly the fighter that Ali had to beat if he would ever reclaim his title. Smokin' Joe was only two years younger than the 29-year-old Ali, and his straight-ahead slugging style, his willingness to absorb two punches to deliver one, was the polar opposite yet complement to the master craftsman's stick-and-dance.

But there was also a rub between the two unbeaten heavyweights. A southern farmboy who won the Olympic heavyweight title in 1964, Frazier felt he exemplified all the hard working, boot strapping American values that seemed to have gone out of fashion in the class strife around the Vietnam War. How could the world prefer this draft-dodger who talked like a pimp?—"I am the prettiest, Frazier too ugly to be champ, he looks like a gorilla," Ali would say, words that sting Frazier to this day. Even if Ali was merely trying to "steam up" the box office by using Frazier as a foil, how could he spew such racial slurs?

Blood Purge

For Ali, that fight, on March 8, 1971, was a blood purge, the second stage in his redemptive return to America's good graces. He had convinced people of his sincerity by standing up for principle, and losing millions. Against Frazier, he convinced people he could stand up and take punishment; his speed and talent had never been questioned, but his "heart" had always been suspect. Frazier tested him to the limits, and Ali passed the test. At terrible physical cost. As expected, Frazier planted his feet and pounded away, offering up his own bumpy face as a lure. But Ali, expected to jab and run, stood and slugged back to prove his manhood.

In what would be a little noticed foreshadowing of the famous Rope-a-Dope against George Foreman, Ali leaned against the ropes and let Frazier bang away. But it backfired. Not only did Frazier fail to punch himself out over the 15 grueling rounds, he deadened the muscles in Ali's arms. Ali had underestimated Frazier's strength and conditioning and overestimated his own. Ali had been away too long. He was knocked down in the 15th. He got up, but Frazier had clinched a unanimous decision.

Frazier's face was raw hamburger, and he was later hospitalized for internal injuries. For the first time, Ali looked like he had been in a prize-fight. The next morning, his face blotched and lumpy, his body marked and

In comic books, Ali was a match for Superman. But in real life (above), Larry Holmes made him look like he'd stayed too long at the ball. "The most virulent infection in the human race is the standing ovation," said boxing analyst Ferdie Pacheco. "Once you've seen that, you can't get off the stage."

sore, Ali again surprised the media. He was relaxed and light hearted. "Just lost a fight, that's all," he said, from his hotel suite. "More important things to worry about in life. Probably be a better man for it."

Three months later, there was official confirmation of Ali's return. On June 28, 1971, Ali pulled up in front of a fresh juice stand on the south side of Chicago, and a man started shouting that he had just heard on the radio that the Supreme Court had reversed his conviction. It was a unanimous decision on a narrow technicality, but it was as good as a knockout. He was free. But, at 29, he was also an old man.

The Sixth Tale: Rumble in the Jungle

The Rumble in the Jungle on October 30, 1974, in Kinshasa, Zaire, the former blood-drenched Belgian Congo, was the central event of the sixth tale of the Legend of the Greatest. The dictator Mobutu Sese Seko sponsored the event as affirmation of his rule. The promoter was an upcoming dictator named Don King.

Ali bathed in the love of the African crowds. He seemed reborn, joyous, a wiser Cassius Clay. Foreman, surly and isolated, was a perfect foil. Decades away from becoming the jolly preacher and grillmeister, he was best remembered for having paraded around the ring with a small American flag after winning the 1968 Olympic heavyweight gold medal in Mexico City. A trainer had stuck the flag in his glove. In Zaire, Foreman showed up with his German shepherd, the breed the Belgian colonials had used to police the Congolese. No wonder the natives chanted, "Ali, *bomaye,*" Ali, kill him.

And so, in the still darkness of the hour before dawn (to accommodate American TV), under a waning moon, Ali and Foreman met in the middle of the ring. Foreman stared balefully as Ali whispered, "You have heard of me since you were young. You've been following me since you were a little boy. Now you must meet me, your master."

Ali struck first, a hard right to Foreman's head. The champ, angry, lunged at Ali, and Ali grabbed him around the neck and forced his head down. The crowd roared. No one had ever tested Foreman so early before, or grappled with him. A moment later, the crowd groaned. Ali was against the ropes and Foreman was pounding on his arms and shoulders. This was the Rope-a-Dope, the tactic that had failed against Frazier. And Foreman had beaten Frazier.

But by the fifth, it was Foreman who was failing, his face lumpy, his arms and legs slowing. Desperately, he threw everything he had at Ali, his chest heaving with the effort of crunching rights and killer left hooks at Ali's face and body. Ali took it.

In the eighth it was Ali's turn, three good rights and a left that left Foreman wobbling. Then the bomb, perhaps the best punch he had ever thrown, a straight right hand. Foreman leaned forward from the waist, then pitched to the canvas.

INVESTING IN ALI

With the exception of Babe Ruth, there is no better investment in sports memorabilia than Muhammad Ali. Although the market is flooded with all sorts of Ali paraphernalia, almost anything that ever touched the boxer—even an X-ray of his broken jaw from his first fight against Ken Norton in 1973 (and signed by both fighters)—is selling for extravagant amounts. The following are some of the Ali collectibles that were auctioned or sold in recent years:

■ $140,000 for an African-patterned robe worn when he beat George Foreman in the 1974 "Rumble in the Jungle" title fight, a record amount for boxing memorabilia; shoes from the fight went for $52,000, trunks for $50,000.

■ $55,000 for a six-page letter sent to the Selective Service in 1966 asking for a draft exemption as a minister of religion.

■ $35,000 for four Andy Warhol screen prints, all signed.

■ $25,000 each for his 1960 Golden Gloves Trophy and the trunks worn in the 1975 Chuck Wepner fight.

■ $20,000 for the robe Cassius Clay wore before his 1964 fight with Sonny Liston, with the words "The Lip" stitched on the back in red letters.

■ $18,000 for the boxing applications filed by Clay and Liston for their first fight.

■ $17,250 for a fingerprint card —part of his application for a New York State boxing license to fight Lucien Banks in 1962— which is signed "Cassius Marcellus Clay."

■ $15,000 for the gloves worn for speedbag workouts that are signed "From Cassius Clay next heavyweight champion, 1962."

■ $8,700 for Cornerman "Bundini" Brown's signed terry cloth robe with "Float like a butterfly, sting like a bee, Ali" on the back.

■ $7,600 for a card that reads "In case of a riot, the bearer of this card will serve as an Honorary Negro (This card must be signed by an original Negro)" with Ali's signature. (The card was handed out in the late 1960s to white members of Ali's entourage.)

■ $1,900 for a cigarette pulled from the mouth of boxing historian Hank Kaplan in 1961 by Clay and signed by him.

Ali was champion again.

He should have quit then. The seventh and final tale of the Legend of the Greatest is about steep decline and gentle rise.

Who can ever tell a prophet when to hang it up? Through the '70s and into the '80s, with children, girlfriends and ex-wives to support, Ali fought all comers, losing the title and reclaiming it for a third time. His second and third fights against Frazier were damaging battles. As he grew older, his zealous religiosity and his grandiosity slipped away. But his capacity for simple kindness never did. Once, in the mid-'70s, running through a small Florida airport late for a flight, he stopped to let a little old white lady take his picture. After the flash popped, a traveling companion tugged at his arm—the puddle-jumper was about to close its door—but Ali had noticed that the woman's lens cap was on. He didn't want her to miss that moment. He reached out, carefully removed it, told her to shoot again.

The "cuddly and kindly" boy his high school classmates remember running alongside the bus has reappeared in the glowing silences of his late middle age. The world trembled with him as he lighted the Olympic torch in 1996. He had become the planet's most famous patient; his courage and unself-consciousness dealing with Parkinson's match anything we have ever seen in any ring. A prophet with yet another vision.

"When you look at Muhammad Ali," George Foreman recently said, "you think about veterans of World War II, really a great war, fought for something special. And when you're sitting in an office with them, and they happen to take off a leg and say, 'Look what happened to me,' or take out an eye and say, 'Look what happened to me in that war,' it's a thing of pride. Muhammad felt like he did something more than box. He made a lot of people feel good about themselves."

HIS LIGHT STILL BURNS

Janet Evans, a five-time Olympic medalist in swimming, was shut out in medal competition during the '96 Olympics in Atlanta. But, as a torchbearer, she was center stage for one of the Games' most suspenseful Opening Ceremonies.

■ I was told three hours before the Opening Ceremony that I would be passing the torch to Ali. The organizers wanted to keep it a secret from me, but they also wanted me to know the alternative plans to light the torch in case Ali had some trouble. I must say that I was pretty nervous about running the torch, much less passing it to Muhammad Ali!

I was born in 1971. I didn't know that much about Ali. But what I saw when I passed him the torch was an incredibly strong man who personified a true champion. Here he was—the greatest and most recognizable athlete in the world—standing in front of 3.5 billion people and lighting the Olympic Flame, even though he was sick. He showed the world that even though he wasn't physically the same person, he was still a courageous man. As an Olympian, I think that there was no one better to light the flame.

We didn't get to talk while he was lighting the flame—the chants of "Ali" made it impossible to hear. I wondered how he felt about that moment. At a luncheon in LA about six months afterward, I walked into a room to find him surrounded by people. Before I knew it, he had stood up, ignored everyone else in the room, and ambled over to give me a big hug. The hug spoke volumes, and it was then that I realized that the moment in Atlanta had been as special to him as it was to the rest of the world.

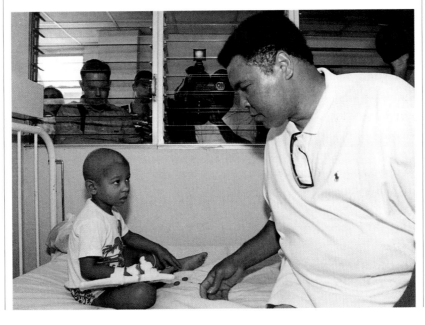

The Louisville Lip is a lot less vocal these days, ravaged by Parkinson's Disease. But he is more beloved than ever (above right, with Janet Evans), and still crazy about kids (right, with 2-year-old cancer patient Fernando Castro in a Havana hospital in 1998). As he says, "Silence is golden when you can't think of a good answer."

THE BOOK OF SISSIE

Prophet of Fair Shake Feminism

I

F CASSIUS HAD HIS LITTLE RED BICYCLE, SISSIE MOFFITT HAD her little white tennis shorts. She was a big, strong tomboy who learned tennis on public courts in Long Beach, California, after she figured out she was not going to make it to the major leagues as a shortstop, much less to the NFL as a quarterback.

Like Cassius, Billie Jean King got early attention because she was such good copy. Until Cassius and Billie Jean arrived, black boxing and white tennis had been beige territories for lively quotes. Sportswriters might label her "kooky"—or at least "outspoken"—to cover themselves with the stiff-necked tennis officials, but they appreciated her honesty, especially when it came to her class consciousness, a forbidden subject in a country-club sport.

"For my first tournament, I was 11 or 12," she has often recalled, "and my mother made me a pair of white shorts. We couldn't go out and afford to buy shorts then. It was a southern California junior tournament, and Perry T. Jones pushed me out of the group picture. He said I should be wearing a tennis dress. I felt bad for my mother."

Sissie's mom was an Avon Lady, and her dad was a fireman. The whole town knew that her kid brother, Randy, was headed for The Show. That all-American start was her strength and her burden, why she drove herself to the top, carrying the closet on her back. Knowing that, it is amazing how much she did, and how she held on to her exuberant passion for performance and competition.

She was a star at 10, the youngest player and shortstop of a softball team that won a Long Beach public parks championship. **At 50, she was still talking about the play in which she caught a sinking line drive at her shoe tops, spun and, without straightening up, threw out a runner at third to end the game.** She never forgot the applause and hugs from teammates.

In describing the joy of shot-making in her 1974 autobiography with Kim Chapin, she said: "My heart pounds, my eyes get damp, and my ears feel like they're wiggling, but it's also just totally peaceful. It's almost like having an orgasm—it's exactly like that."

Making social-psychosexual interpretations is hard to resist, given the carnality of our prophets. In Billie Jean's seeming openness about that early class rejection by lawn tennis society and about her orgasms on and off the court, there is an especial poignancy; her only role model had left a mixed message.

Babe Didrikson was already dying of cancer about the time Sissie Moffitt was rushing to the net and blasting little girls in dresses off the courts. The Babe was Sissie's spiritual mother and critical to understand-

Billie Jean King's family "was considered wrong-side-of-the-tracks. I was a typical lower-middle-class, tract-home kid (who) went to school with rich kids" (left). By the time she played Bobby Riggs in the Battle of the Sexes in 1973 (right, being carried on court by four men), she was rich herself.

ing her. Even prophets need role models, although many girls growing up in the '50s heard, "Don't you be like Babe Dike-rikson," when they tried too hard to win.

Babe

Like Sissie, Mildred Ella Didriksen (the spelling of the last name was Americanized along the way) was born to working-class westerners, on June 26, 1911. Her father, a Norwegian immigrant, was a master carpenter who built a backyard gym for his seven children. Mildred, called Baby until the seventh child arrived, was re-nicknamed Babe in adolescence because she could hit a baseball farther than anyone her age of either gender in Beaumont, Texas. During the 1932 Los Angeles Olympics, she told sportswriters that she wasn't nervous, because "all I'm doing is running against girls." She won gold medals in the javelin throw and the hurdles.

After breaking the world record in the high jump, she was disqualified because her "western roll" technique had yet to be officially recognized. Sportswriters loved her big mouth and wrote what she told them, after cleaning it up, including her age. That made her, at 18, a teen sensation. She was really 21. She routinely claimed to have been born in 1914.

In 1930, she led her high school basketball team to an undefeated season and the state championship in Houston, where she was spotted by the coach of an insurance company team. In those days, industrial league sports were a major promotional tool in the South and Midwest. Babe quit school and moved to Dallas, where she led the Golden Cyclones to a basketball title, then a track and field championship in which she competed in all eight events, winning six and setting four world records. She also won a place on the Olympic team.

She did not necessarily win hearts along the way. **Teammates often resented a personal style that has been characterized as crude, obnoxious, boastful, blunt, flamboyant and immodest.**

Sportswriters loved her act, if they did not all love her, frequently making comments about her flat chest or Adam's apple. After she beat Paul Gallico in a footrace, that influential New York sportswriter rarely wrote about her without some variation on his grand insight that she had become the greatest woman athlete of all time as "an escape, a compensation," because "she would not or could not compete with women at their own best game—man snatching."

The Babe's marriage to the 250-pound wrestler George

Babe Didrikson was a hurdling superstar (left, in 1932) and a role model for King. But first Billie Jean served as a 12-year-old ballgirl (third from right, top row, photo at right), the only time in her life she submitted to such a subordinate role.

Zaharias, whose name she took despite the fact that hers was far more famous (she was known to call him "Za-hairy-ass"), has been interpreted as a ploy for credibility; she needed a man's affirmation to be taken seriously as the founding mother of the Ladies Professional Golf Association, a germinal organization in the creation of professional sports careers for women. Suddenly, the same sportswriters who had found her thin-lipped and "button-breasted" noticed her makeup, lacy clothes and "Valkyrian" bosom.

Her profile was in courage, however; in 1954, two years before she died of cancer, she won the Open wearing a colostomy bag. And she talked about it so other women would not feel ashamed or avoid treatment.

Didrikson's suspected lesbianism has never been completely substantiated. She had long-term relationships with other women, but such friendships are not always sexual. The deep closets of that time have been opened by contemporary lesbian historians who want to claim Didrikson; she is the most compelling of those foremothers who kept women competitive at a time when men found female muscle and sweat threatening. There is no question that lesbian energy and determination is the foundation of current women's sports, but the issue is more complicated. Many men who consider lesbians less than "real women" cling to the idea that female jocks are dykes; how else explain that these women are better athletes than they are?

Many women, some of them lesbian, want to downplay the lesbian component in sports, because it is so often used as a way to devalue their games. It also scares off some sponsors.

But all Sissie Moffitt knew as a kid was that her family encouraged her to take tennis lessons on the local public courts because the sport was the most "lady-like." She quickly channeled her athleticism. An old champion, Alice Marble, became a mentor. In 1961, while still in high school, almost on a lark, Billie Jean and Karen Hantze won the Wimbledon doubles title. In college, she began dating Larry King, a mediocre varsity tennis player on athletic scholarship.

There was no scholarship for her, even though she was high in the

world rankings. She has always given Larry, whom she married when she was 21 (they have since divorced), credit for awaking her feminism.

Like Babe, Billie Jean broke no new ground merely by being female. There had been great women athletes before, among others the swimmers Gertrude Ederle and Eleanor Holm, the tennis players Helen Wills Moody and Althea Gibson, who was black. But they were all amateurs. It was Billie Jean's style of female-ness that was so empowering, unashamedly competitive and commercial, just like the men. And entrepreneurial. While in college, Larry and Billie Jean came up with the idea of World TeamTennis, a combination pro tennis tour and amateur tennis league that still seems like one of the best concepts in all of sports.

Lawn tennis officials were uneasy with Billie Jean. She wouldn't stop asking the killer question: Why should players be amateurs and promoters be professionals? "They especially don't like me," she said, "because I talk about money all the time. I'm a mercenary. A rebel."

The rebellion was successful. In 1971, President Nixon called her up to congratulate her on being the first woman athlete to make $100,000 in one year. (Rod Laver made $293,000 that year on the men's tour.)

■ Much More Than a Tennis Player

In 1966, she was ranked No. 1 in the world, and won the first of three straight Wimbledon singles titles. She would win six altogether. In 1967, she won the U.S. title, the first of four. In 1968, she won the Australian. That was the year tennis went "open," meaning that pros could play for money alongside amateurs playing for silverware.

King began accumulating almost $2 million in career prize money, an astonishing amount, considering the late start and the tiny purses of that time.

And she never stopped talking. "I'd like to get away from this sissified image of tennis," she would say, "I mean, after all, they stop the action, because a player's got a blister. The fans have to laugh; they've seen hockey players get their teeth knocked out and keep playing."

More importantly, she never stopped agitating against the inequity of prize money. Typically, in a 1970 tournament promoted by Jack Kramer, men's first-place money was $12,500, women's $1,500. Atypically, King led a boycott and with eight other women signed $1 contracts with Gladys Heldman, publisher of *World Tennis* magazine.

It caused a sensation; establishment tennis sued and the media treated the women as "radicals" rather than professionals desperate to make a living at their chosen trade.

King whips Evonne Goolagong in the 1973 Wimbledon semis (left), and is congratulated by husband Larry after reaching the 1968 U.S. Open semis (above). When asked what she remembered most from that period, King said, "I was tired. Always tired. I averaged four hours of sleep for years."

TESTAMENT

During the '80s, Pam Shriver was among the world's top 10 players and, with Martina Navratilova, won a record 109 consecutive doubles matches. Now, she's on the WTA's board, works as a tennis TV analyst and is a minority owner of the Baltimore Orioles.

■ You know that term: a life force? Someone with an extra bit of drive, energy, vision and challenge who can articulate. It's a package that doesn't come around very often. The athletes that have leadership charisma as well as that No. 1 swagger are really rare. I think Billie Jean stands alone among female athletes in their impact upon society and on their sport.

An example of her drive is World TeamTennis—Billie Jean's best vision for tennis, a coed team game. She's had to deal with the establishment's mindset as to what tennis should look like: 128-draw, 32 seeds, single elimination . . . your star loses in the opening round, bad luck, you don't get to see him or her again. Whereas Billie Jean's version is more fun.

And she's kept that dream alive. TeamTennis has become a cornerstone of the grassroots effort; people who play tennis for the fun of it and the exercise really love this format. That is the best example of her competitiveness. She's stubborn, she stuck with it, she was true to her heart, and she will keep plugging away. I think it will be one of her main legacies.

In retrospect, the establishment and the press were right to feel threatened. The prophet of Fair Shake Feminism was leading her people to the promised land, a tour of their own.

Women's tennis would not have succeeded then if cigarette advertising had not just been banned from television. Big tobacco looked to sports and music for exposure to a young audience just lighting up and developing brand loyalty. Philip Morris was marketing a new cigarette for women with a slogan that evoked a tough feminism: "You've come a long way, baby." The Virginia Slims tour was born.

That same year, King discovered she was pregnant. There was no time for that baby, she has said. She thought the cost of an abortion, $580, was "ridiculous," and that it was "wrong" that Larry had to sign permission papers. Otherwise, the operation was less painful and traumatic than her knee or gum surgeries, she said.

Her supporters have winced at her handling of the cigarette and abortion stories. She responds to criticism of Philip Morris' sponsorship by writing letters to the editor defending the company that allowed the women's tour to breathe, assuring that no tennis player ever advocated smoking or even smoked in public. After her name appeared in Ms. magazine on a list of women who had had abortions, she waffled at reporters' questions. Apparently, she had signed a pro-choice petition without realizing she was admitting to having had an abortion.

Whatever her seeming contradictions, however, which included her denial of being "a card-carrying women's libber," there was no question that she was the world's most visible liberated woman. Even her marriage, clearly one of convenience and business—they were too busy to get divorced, she said—underlined the obvious; she was living a man's life.

And then she went out and beat a man.

Battle of the Sexes

In any sane sporting society, the match against Bobby Riggs would have as much political resonance as a pro wrestling smackdown. Here was the top woman tennis player in the world at the top of her game, 29 years old, against a 55-year-old junk-shot hustler whose best days were long gone. He was in it for the big score. She was forced into it as a part of the second wave of feminism sweeping the country. As she tells it, she was in Japan on Mother's Day 1973, when she heard that Riggs had routed the Australian star Margaret Court. King said she had "lockjaw," she was so angry. Riggs had pursued King for years with his wheedling plea for a joint payday, but she kept brushing him off. Too busy. She had a movement to spearhead. Now she knew she had to play him.

"I thought it would set us back 50 years if I didn't win that match," she said 20 years later. "You know, I still wake up some mornings thinking I haven't played the match yet."

The buildup was intense, more like a heavyweight title fight than an

Ready to serve a new dish for female ego . . . : one roasted pig (chauvinistic style)!

BILLIE JEAN KING: MYTH DESTROYER

Eleanor Smeal is president of the Feminist Majority Foundation and is a former president of the National Organization for Women. One of FMF's goals is to empower women and girls in sports.

■ Billie Jean King changed everything for women's tennis and in women's sports. She's the reason women tennis players are among the highest-paid. When she started her career, that wasn't the case—she organized them, and they walked off. And it worked.

The King-Riggs match was one of a series of things she did to break the game wide open for women. Everyone watched it. I don't know how many kids know about it, but it doesn't really matter. It was one of the principal ways in which she destroyed the myth that the best woman is not as good as the worst man. This demolished that argument, and you almost never heard it again. It's these mythologies that have helped keep women down. The whole tennis thing was just such a crock. In the early days, at the turn of the century, they said the reason girls could not play tennis was, because of the curves of their bodies, they would always hit the ball crookedly. In the early '70s, the mythology that girls were hopeless in sports was destroyed by Billie Jean, a major myth that was keeping equitable funding away from girls.

Is the fight over? No, we still have the same damn fight. For that matter, Title IX is never secure—there is always a crowd of people trying to destroy it.

To destroy the mythology is very important. I wish there were other matchups between males and females. Frankly, I think the reason there aren't is because this one was so decisive.

Riggs jumps the net to congratulate King for kicking his sexist butt. "They didn't have security," King recalls. "After the match, George Foreman ran out of the stands to escort me off the court."

Annie Oakley

Althea Gibson

Katherine Switzer

FIRST LADIES

Women athletes were never in the game—and not even in the stands—during the ancient Olympics. Through the centuries, women trailblazers have endured sexism and ridicule in order to participate and assume leadership positions in sports. These dared to be first:

■ 396 B.C.—Kyniska, a Spartan princess, wins an Olympic chariot race, but is barred from collecting her prize in person.

■ 1885—Annie Oakley, the sharpshooting star of the Buffalo Bill Wild West Show, shows she can handle a gun better than the best man.

■ 1926—Violet Piercy of Great Britain becomes the first woman to participate in an officially timed marathon. Gertrude Ederle beats the best time to date (man or woman) by two hours for swimming the English Channel.

■ 1932—Babe Didrikson wins three Olympic track and field medals. She also won 10 golf majors and helped establish the LPGA in 1949.

■ 1950—Kathryn Johnston, a 12-year-old, calls herself "Tubby" Johnston in order to play as a boy in Little League.

■ 1957—Althea Gibson, an African American, earns Wimbledon and U.S. Open titles.

■ 1965—Shirley Muldowney becomes the first woman to participate in National Hot Rod Association drag races.

■ 1967—Katherine Switzer becomes the first woman to run in the Boston Marathon, but officials try to tear her number from her back during the race.

■ 1970—Pat Palinkas is the first woman to play for a men's semi-pro football team as a holder for place-kickers.

■ 1973—Billie Jean King co-founds the Women's Tennis Association and serves as its first president.

■ 1975—Marion Bermudez of the U.S.A. boxes in a Golden Gloves tournament—the first woman to do so—in Mexico City.

■ 1977—Janet Guthrie is the first woman to race in the Indianapolis 500.

■ 1979—Ann Meyers signs as a free-agent with the NBA's Indiana Pacers.

■ 1980—Julie Krone wins her first race and goes on to become the first woman to compete on even terms with top men jockeys.

■ 1986—Nancy Lieberman plays in the USBL pro basketball league, becoming the first woman to compete professionally against men.

■ 1986-88—Susan Butcher wins her third consecutive Iditarod Sled Dog Race

■ 1992—Manon Rheaume suits up for the Tampa Bay Lightning against the St. Louis Blues in an exhibition game, becoming the first woman to compete in the NHL.

■ 1994—Martina Navratilova retires as the career leader among men and women in singles titles (167); she becomes one of the first star athletes to acknowledge that she is a lesbian.

■ 1996—Spain's Christina Sanchez achieves the rank of matador in Europe.

■ 1997—Anita DeFrantz is elected vice president of the International Olympic Committee.

■ 1997—Liz Heaston of Willamette University (Salem, Oregon) plays in a men's college football game, kicking two extra points.

■ 2002—In the inaugural women's Olympic bobsled competition, Americans Jill Bakken and Vonetta Flowers take the gold.

Janet Guthrie

Christina Sanchez

Jill Bakken and Vonetta Flowers

HIS GIFT IS HIS SONG, AND THIS ONE'S FOR YOU, BILLIE JEAN

■ *Saturday Night Fever.* Donna Summer. The Village People. The 1970s was a decidedly awkward time for any performer, even Elton John, to interpret Billie Jean King's on-court temperament into a hot single.

In 1974, King was co-founder, a coach and a player in fledgling World Team Tennis; John was a fan. "Philadelphia Freedom," John's 1975 tribute to King and her team, debuted in the top 40 in March. On April 12, the 45 topped the charts and went platinum.

"He told me that the beat came from his perception of how I stomped around the court," said King in her 1982 autobiography, *Billie Jean.*

These days, the WTT (now officially Tyco WTT) continues play with its unique format: teams of two men, two women and a coach, playing in different combinations in each of a match's five sets. Long time friends King and John host an annual charity tennis event, appropriately named All Star Smash Hits.

unsanctioned tennis match, but far more political than any fight since Louis-Schmeling. It became the Super Bowl of the battle of the sexes, stoking family feuds, boiling office water-coolers.

Riggs, playing up his chauvinist pigginess, squealed that he would help drive women back to the kitchen and bedroom where they belonged. King stoutly maintained that she was about "Women's lob, not women's lib." But she was every bit as tough as the old guy. When ABC hired Jack Kramer, that nemesis of women's tennis, to help Howard Cosell broadcast the match, King threatened to pull out. Once Roone Arledge realized King was serious, Kramer was replaced.

The night of the extravaganza, Billie Jean was carried out in a gold litter by four muscular college athletes. Riggs was wheeled in on a rickshaw pulled by six bosomy models. He gave her a huge Sugar Daddy candy bar. She gave him a brown baby pig. The match, before a crowd of 30,492, the largest ever to see a tennis match, was not quite up to its buildup.

Neil Amdur of *The New York Times* wrote: "Mrs. King squashed Riggs with tools synonymous with men's tennis, the serve and volley. She beat Bobby to the ball, dominated the net, and ran him around the baseline to the point of near exhaustion in the third set, when he suffered leg cramps and trailed, 2-4.

"Most important perhaps for women everywhere, she convinced skeptics that a female athlete can survive pressure-filled situations and that men are as susceptible to nerves as women."

Not everyone was quite getting it, however. Up in the broadcast booth, Cosell was committing some amazing commentary, even for those pre-politically correct days. He described King as "a very attractive young lady, and sometimes you get the feeling that if she ever let her hair down to her shoulders, took her glasses off, you'd have someone vying for a Hollywood screen test." This from the father of two grown daughters, TV's champion of fair play who had supported Ali on constitutional grounds?

And then he said, "There's the velocity that Billie Jean can put on the ball, and walking back she's walking more like a male than a female." The final score was 6-4, 6-3, 6-3, and King also had the last word, another independent athlete's declaration of independence. "This is the culmination of 19 years of work. Since the time they wouldn't let me be in a picture, because I didn't have on a tennis skirt, I've wanted to change the game around. Now it's here. But why should I want a rematch? Why any more sex tennis? Women have enough problems getting to compete against each other at the high school and college levels. Their programs are terribly weak. Why do we have to worry about men?"

■ An Ill-Timed Palimony Suit

King became an effective spokeswoman for Title IX, the new educational legislation mandating equity between men's and women's sports in any institution that receives federal funds. The law would eventually change the geography of sports. Enforcement would be resisted, but Title IX made it possible for the next pool of talent to be female, following the African American and Hispanic migrations to sports.

This did not add to King's popularity in tennis. Her characterization in *People* as the "fiery feminist dynamo" explained why tennis was so happy to have her replaced by the "placid All-American teenager" Chris Evert, labels both women disliked. By 1981, King was winding down her playing career. A monster deal for a line of clothing was about to be announced, and Larry was getting World TeamTennis off the ground.

And then Marilyn Barnett served papers. There had always been rumors on the tour that King's attractive blonde secretary/hairdresser/traveling companion was also her lover. But Billie Jean was popular, important to tennis, and Larry King was still her husband, although there were rumors that he played in other beds. Barnett, who was being evicted from a Malibu house King owned, sued for half of Billie Jean's income during the seven years they were allegedly lovers. The damage control was clumsy, first a denial, then a Barbara Walters interview in which Larry claimed his

With sometime doubles partner Martina Navratilova (right). "People sometimes say, 'You should have come out like Martina.' They forget Martina was going to be outed by a newspaper. I wasn't sorry for being outed; I was sorry because I was married, and I believe in monogamy."

BEING KING IS A FULL-TIME JOB

■ When Billie Jean King's name comes up, the words "first" and "founder" are invariably in the sentence.

But today she works mostly behind-the-scenes as a social compass, constantly trying to reposition the debate on issues dear to her heart, such as gender equity in sports. "I'm still very much an activist and trying to help make the world a better place on a tiny scale of what Bono is trying to do, but he's just so much more high profile, he can get a lot more done."

She isn't under the same glaring spotlight as Bud, David or Paul, perhaps because her to-do list includes consciousness-raising of the kind that doesn't make headlines but quietly moves mountains. Her schedule, however, is no less crammed than any sports exec's.

A short list includes World Team Tennis, board meetings, Fed Cup (as team captain), TV announcing, charity work and fund-raising, and helping with gay and lesbian issues.

King, named one of the "100 Most Important Americans of the 20th Century" by *Life* magazine, is still pioneering, still very outspoken, and can admittedly "get a little wound up" during a conversation. Even her "full-time" job, WTT, is a competitive coed endeavor.

Much has changed for women in the sport, and King expects and is working toward further changes. In speaking to the Women's Tennis Association earlier this year, King said, "You are living the dream we envisioned 30 years ago. International. Lots of money. Television. And you are celebrated for your accomplishments, not just your looks. That is huge. But it's important to take responsibility and think about how you want to shape the future."

Among today's athletes, King sees Julie Foudy, a WUSA founding player and Women's Sports Foundation president, as a groundbreaker and torchbearer a la King. "I think she is one of the most underrated athletes in our country. She's the glue, she's the spokesperson, she's the voice that got the women to stick together."

Of course, most of those words could be applied to King, whose match in Houston against that bespectacled older guy ■ more than a generation ago still has the power to inspire.

"Usually, it's a parent or grandparent now, which is really scary, telling them the story, and then they go look it up," she says. "I get a lot of requests because they have chosen me to do their book report on as a pioneer."

WORLD TEAMTENNIS

Marilyn Barnett (above) and her palimony suit cost King millions.

lack of attention drove Billie Jean into Marilyn's arms. There was an autobiography in which Billie Jean fully acknowledged the affair, but claimed it had lasted only a year. She implied it was her first homosexual relationship, that she was by no means living a gay lifestyle.

Not much helped. While King won the court case, she spent so much money on lawyers she had to stay on the tour for two more years. Worse, her corporate sponsors all dropped away, including the clothing deal. The progress of World TeamTennis was seriously slowed.

King says she wants to "get beyond tennis." **One plan: a foundation that would concentrate on health and youth issues, including an attempt to stem the rise in suicides among gay and lesbian teenagers.** Her great power now, she says, is that "I get to all those people who can make things happen with a stroke of their pen."

The Prophet Looks Up

"If I ever write another book," she said, "I know what the first line will be: 'Tennis is the best thing that ever happened to me and the worst.' The best because I got to travel, because I really love to hit the ball, it's an aesthetic thing, and because it gave me the chance to make social change, to be the mother of modern sports. The worst because the sport discounted me, its lack of embrace of new ideas that could rejuvenate it, and because there are all those people in tennis who still just don't get it."

Of course, some do. Billie Jean King, who rattled Avery Brundage's cage when she talked about "shamateurism" back in the '60s, was coach of the United States women's tennis team at the 2000 Sydney Olympics. But the horizon of her vision can't be limited to the tennis court, even on a world stage. This prophet looked up. In 1982, she said: "I went to see *E.T.* the other night. I loved it. There was only one thing really wrong with it . . . when the boys soar off into the sky on their bikes, not one girl gets to fly. I kept thinking of all the little girls who were thinking, 'Hey, I want to go on the bike in the sky, too.' "

As prophets get smaller in the rearview mirror, they tend to either grow larger in our minds or disappear. Of this gospel, Avery will probably shrink into a footnote, and Ali will be blown into a Moses, or at least one of the heroes he has invoked for himself, Wyatt Earp or Davy Crockett.

Billie Jean is the one we'll have to struggle to hold on to, because the women who climbed on her shoulders have tended to obscure her. Many of the daughters (now granddaughters) of Title IX seem to think that sports was always a female birthright, that there were always World Cup

IT'S ALL RELATIVE

In 1971, Billie Jean King struck a chord for equality when she earned $100,000 in a year, the first female athlete to do so. Still, it was just a chord, because when she won the U.S. Open that year, her prize money was $10,000 less than Stan Smith, the men's winner.

So King continued her crusade to level the playing field and, two years later, the Open awarded equal prize money to the winners; it's the only major that consistently does so. Of course, that amount is a pittance compared to today's prize monies. In 2001, Venus Williams finished first on the money list with $2.7 million—a 2,600-percent increase over King in '71. Six other players earned at least $1 million. And Slovenia's Tina Krizan—ranked 108th on the list—pulled down about $100,000 without a singles title.

You've come a long way, baby . . . uh, ladies . . . as have other athletes, whose stellar performances paralleled the rapid growth in earning power:

Hank Greenberg

Fred Lorenzen

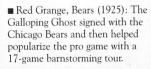

Red Grange

Baseball

■ Hank Greenberg, Pirates (1947): Statistically, this was the worst year for the original Hammerin' Hank, but as a two-time MVP with Detroit, Pittsburgh thought he was worth it.

First to $1M: Nolan Ryan, Astros (1979)

Record to break: Alex Rodriguez, Rangers, $22 million (2002)

NASCAR

■ Fred Lorenzen (1963): Despite racing in only 29 of 55 events, he won six events and had 21 top-5 finishes. He retired at age 33.

First to $1M: Bill Elliott (1985)

Record to break: Jeff Gordon, $10.9 million (2001)

Football

■ Red Grange, Bears (1925): The Galloping Ghost signed with the Chicago Bears and then helped popularize the pro game with a 17-game barnstorming tour.

First to $1M: Herschel Walker, New Jersey Generals (1983)

Record to break: Brett Favre, Packers, $9.7 million (2002)

Hockey

■ Bobby Hull, Blackhawks (1968): The Golden Jet scored 58 goals with 49 assists, the seventh time he led the league in goals.

First to $1M: Hull, Jets (1972) Yes, Bobby was the first million-dollar man. The year he left Chicago, Winnipeg made him the first.

Record to break: Peter Forsberg, Avalanche, $11 million (2001-2002)

Basketball

■ Wilt Chamberlain, 76ers (1966): He averaged 33.5 ppg, 24.6 rpg and 5.2 apg during an MVP season. Coincidentally, the Celtics immediately spiked Bill Russell to $100,001.

First to $1M: Kareem Abdul-Jabbar, Lakers; Moses Malone, Sixers (1982)

Record to break: Michael Jordan, Bulls, $33.1 million (1997-98).

Tennis, men

■ Rod Laver (1969): He won his first Grand Slam in 1962, and in '69 became the only player to accomplish it twice.

First to $1M: Bjorn Borg (1979)

Record to break: Pete Sampras, $6.5 million (1997)

Tennis, women

■ Billie Jean King (1971): Won the U.S. Open, one of her 12 career Grand Slam singles victories, and was ranked No. 2 in the world behind Evonne Goolagong.

First to $1M: Martina Navratilova (1982)

Record to break: Martina Hingis, $3.5 million (2000)

Golf, men

■ Arnold Palmer (1963): He did not win any of his seven majors this year, but played well enough to lead the PGA Tour in earnings.

First to $1M: Curtis Strange (1988)

Record to break: Tiger Woods, $9.2 million (2000)

Golf, women

■ Judy Rankin (1976): She won seven tournaments during the year, but a fine career was cut short due to back injuries.

First to $1M: Karrie Webb (1996)

Record to break: Annika Sorenstam, $2.1 million (2001)

Billie Jean King

Arnold Palmer

Judy Rankin

Bobby Hull

Wilt Chamberlain

Rod Laver

soccer babes whipping off their shirts, that the LPGA never had an "image" lady to de-butch golfers who might scare off the sponsors.

What's the problem?, the girls ask. We're here.

And because they were so frequently misinterpreted, often with their own complicity, one wonders if Brundage, Ali and King will eventually be labeled false prophets. After all, old Honest Ave would do anything so the Games could go on. There was blood on his hands. Ali's selfish early stand against the Vietnam War made it possible for draft-dodgers to feel good about themselves for the wrong reasons. And King often lied to protect her heterosexual image. She was Averian in accepting cigarette sponsorship so the women's tour wouldn't go up in smoke. The end justifies the means.

What kind of role models are these?

Wrong question. They are not role models. They are prophets. The Great Manager stuck them in the lineup to get on base any way they could, and maybe even drive us home.

Right, the once and future King: U.S. Fed Cup team captain Billie Jean gives advice to Venus Williams. "Could I be No. 1 today?" King asks. "With my game then? No way. I'd be like Martina Hingis . . . much more aggressive though."

AYBE *THE GREAT AMERICAN NOVEL* BY PHILIP ROTH ISN'T REALLY THE GREAT AMERICAN NOVEL, BUT IT'S DEFINITELY A STRONG CONTENDER FOR THE TITLE OF THE GREAT AMERICAN SPORTS NOVEL. AND IT'S ONE OF THE LAUGH-OUT-LOUD FUNNNIEST NOVELS EVER WRITTEN ABOUT ANYTHING.

IT'S THE STORY OF THE RUPPERT MUNDYS, A HAPLESS, HOMELESS 1943 BASE-BALL TEAM WHOSE STADIUM HAS BEEN COMMANDEERED FOR USE AS AN ARMY CAMP AND WHO MUST THEREFORE PLAY ALL THEIR GAMES ON THE ROAD, WAN-DERING ACROSS AMERICA'S NEON WILDERNESS AND SINKING DEEPER INTO THE PATRIOT LEAGUE CELLAR. ROTH PLAYS WITH EVERY CLICHE OF BASEBALL MYTHOLOGY—THE ROOKIE PHENOM, THE GRIZZLED VETS, THE GREEDY OWNERS, THE BLOWHARD SPORTSWRITERS—THE WHOLE GRAND AND GAUDY SHEBANG.

by Peter Carlson

FALLEN ANGELS

But the most memorable character of all is Big John Baal, a foul-mouthed, drunken, brawling slugger who is a parody of every bad boy in sports history.

Big John gets busted for gambling—"he'd shot craps after the World Series with the rookie of the year and wiped the boy out with a pair of loaded dice"—so they send him to Sing Sing. But **he plays so well for the prison team that he's released, paroled into the custody of the Mundys' manager, and returned to the show with a new nick-name, "The Babe Ruth of the Big House."**

Funny stuff, but not particularly realistic, right?

Wrong. The book was published in May 1973. That same month, Billy Martin, the foul-mouthed, drunken, brawling manager of the Detroit Tigers, went to Jackson State prison in Michigan to visit an inmate named Ron LeFlore. LeFlore was serving 5 to 15 years for armed robbery, and he was wowing fans on the prison baseball circuit. Martin arranged a tryout for LeFlore, who was paroled, signed and sent to the minors. Within a year, he was playing the outfield for the Tigers. Soon, he was leading the league in—yes, you guessed it—steals.

LeFlore was a delightfully colorful knave. Playing for the Expos in 1980, he bragged to *Inside Sports* magazine about how he'd deliberately spiked Pirate shortstop Tim Foli: "He kneed me in the head and I put him on the disabled list. Spiked him good." He also revealed the secret of his pre-game preparations: "Some guys need amphetamines to get up for a game. For me, sex does it. Baseball is an intense game and an orgasm releases the tensions so you can perform comfortably . . . Getting some just before a game is good for you."

"How close to the game?" the interviewer asked.

"As close as possible," LeFlore replied.

Great stuff. But that's not all. Get a load of this: *The Great American Novel* also proved prescient about the future of bad boys in *football*.

■ The False Gods of Sports

Here's how Roth described Big John Baal: "If he didn't drink, if he didn't gamble, if he didn't whore and cheat and curse, if he wasn't a roughneck, a glutton and a brawler, why he just wasn't himself, and his whole damn game went to pot, hitting *and* fielding."

And here's how Lawrence Taylor, the great New York Giants line-backer, writing in his autobiography, *LT: Living on the Edge*, explained why he ended his post-addiction recovery program in 1986 and went back to a life of drinking, carousing and raising hell: "If I don't come into a game with my eyes red, my ears pinned back and hell in my heart, I'd just be another number in a football suit."

Which just goes to show that when it comes to the bad boys of sport, even the most outrageous fiction is no match for good old reality.

Roth was right: Big John Baal is a great American archetype—the ballplayer as bad boy, as outlaw, as anti-hero.

Ron LeFlore (above) was an atypical fallen angel, in that he fell first . . . and then arose with the Detroit Tigers under manager Billy Martin. Martin resided, on and off, in his own personal hell, like the angels (right) in Luca Signorelli's fresco "The Damned Cast into Hell."

If sport is America's secular religion, then the Baals are its devils, its sinners, its fallen angels. Even the name is perfect: In the Old Testament, Baal is the false god worshipped by the heathen Canaanites. In contemporary America, Baals are the false gods of sports, anti-heroes exalted for their amorality.

There were plenty of Big Johns before Roth invented Baal, and there have been plenty since then. They come in infinite varieties of obnoxiousness and evil.

They are the drunks, the dope fiends, the flagrant philanderers.

They are wife cheaters, wife beaters, accused wife killers.

They are the locker-room vandals, the bat-smashers, the water-cooler trashers.

They are the back stabbers, the backbiters (Hi, Marv!), the ear-biters (Hi, Mike!).

They're the ramblers, the gamblers, the point-shavers and game-throwers.

They're the hotheads, the potheads, the overpaid shitheads who demand that their contract be renegotiated because somebody else is making more.

They're the brawlers, the maulers, the bullies, the thugs, the bar fighters, the umpire fighters, the spike-sharpening sociopaths.

They are the coaches who choke their players, and the players who choke their coaches.

They're the egomaniacs, the dipsomaniacs, the kleptomaniacs, the sex maniacs, the just-plain maniacs who have made the sports pages read like a police blotter.

Sportswriters and hand wringers and professional viewers-with-alarm love to tut-tut about today's Big John Baals, claiming that their dastardly deeds show the decline of morality and sportsmanship. But Big John has always been with us. There never was a golden age of sports innocence.

The Golden Age of Sports Guilt

A century ago, football inspired so much rioting and rowdiness that there was a movement to ban it. And **big league baseball was widely regarded as too uncouth and disgusting for women to watch—a brutal game played by drunks and ruffians who brawled on the field and yelled obscene epithets at opposing players,** a pastime known as "bench jockeying." Even the great Babe Ruth was tormented by bench jockeys. Once, the Babe got irate at being called "niggerlips" and responded thusly: "I don't mind being called a prick or a cocksucker or things like that. I expect that. But lay off the personal stuff."

A century before the O.J. trial, Edgar McNabb, a rookie pitcher for the 1894 Baltimore Orioles, shot and killed killed his mistress, a beautiful blonde actress named Louise Kellogg, during a quarrel in a Pittsburgh hotel room.

Seventy years before Pete Rose was banned from baseball for gam-

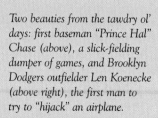

Two beauties from the tawdry ol' days: first baseman "Prince Hal" Chase (above), a slick-fielding dumper of games, and Brooklyn Dodgers outfielder Len Koenecke (above right), the first man to try to "hijack" an airplane.

bling, the 1919 Black Sox were banished—and so was Hal Chase, a slick-fielding first baseman who nonetheless led the majors in errors five times, because he was throwing games for the gamblers who bribed him. They were baseball's version of Judas, betraying the game for 30 pieces of silver—or more, if they could get it.

And here's a neat bit of sports trivia: The first man to try to hijack an airplane was an outfielder for the Brooklyn Dodgers—Len Koenecke. In 1934, he hit .320, but in 1935, he broke curfew so often and raised so much hell that his manager, Casey Stengel, sent him down to the minors. Koenecke got mad. He got drunk. He got on an airplane and, in mid-air, he invaded the cockpit and tried to seize control. In the ensuing fight, the pilot smashed Koenecke over the head with a fire extinguisher, killing him.

So much for the golden age of sports innocence.

The difference between sports then and sports now is not a decrease in morality or sportsmanship. It's an increase in the honesty and realism of sportswriting.

Celebrating the Sordid Detail

In the old days, sportswriting was a form of secular hagiography—writing about saints—and sportswriters felt compelled to portray players as proper heroes for little boys. Consequently, the fans were not informed that Ruth was a gluttonous womanizer, that Cobb was a vicious, psychotic racist, that DiMaggio, a man hailed as the epitome of class, was a regular customer in Polly Adler's famous Manhattan brothel, and later beat his wife, who was Marilyn Monroe.

Things began to change in 1970—at the height of the age of revisionist history—when pitcher Jim Bouton published his baseball diary, *Ball Four*. Bouton wrote about players getting plastered, popping pep pills, and looking up the skirts of female fans during the national anthem—a practice known as "beaver shooting."

Ball Four was pretty mild stuff by today's standards, but Bouton was denounced by baseball commissioner Bowie Kuhn and countless sportswriters for betraying what was routinely called "the sanctity of the game." And Pete Rose, from the dugout steps, hollered out to Bouton his literary criticism: "Fuck you, Shakespeare!"

But the book became a bestseller. Fans enjoyed reading about the players' bad-boy hijinks. It gave the plaster saints some flesh and blood. *Ball Four* made ballplayers seem more human—and a lot more fun.

Within a couple decades, the conventions of sports books had reversed completely: Instead of hiding the sordid details of their lives, ballplayers reveled in them. Basketball great Wilt Chamberlain bragged in an autobiography that he'd bedded 20,000 women. And Chicago Bull Dennis Rodman detailed everything from his suicidal tendencies to his cross-dressing to his night of amour with Madonna: "She wasn't an acrobat but she wasn't a dead fish either."

"Get me rewrite!" After former Yankee Jim Bouton's Ball Four *was published in 1970, nothing about athletes—not even their sex lives—was out of bounds.*

The book—appropriately titled *Bad As I Wanna Be*—soared to No. 1 on *The New York Times* bestseller list.

Meanwhile, sports movies were also changing. Hollywood used to churn out hagiographic flicks about heroic athletes—*The Babe Ruth Story* and *The Pride of the Yankees* and *Knute Rockne, All American* (starring Ronald Reagan as the Gipper). Now, sports movies chronicle the bad boys and psychos of sport—*Cobb* and *Raging Bull* (about brutal boxer Jake La Motta) and *Eight Men Out* (about the Black Sox scandal) and *Any Given Sunday*, which shows fictitious football players snorting cocaine off the naked chests of their groupies.

None of this should be particularly surprising. Americans have always enjoyed rogues and outlaws. Think of the legends of the Wild West: Billy the Kid, Jesse James, Butch Cassidy and the Sundance Kid—thieves and gunslingers, one and all.

In the Depression, John Dillinger, Pretty Boy Floyd and Bonnie and Clyde were folk heroes, particularly when they robbed the banks that were foreclosing on the beleaguered farmers. These days, we love tales of the mobsters, real and fictitious—Don Corleone, Al Capone, John Gotti, *The Sopranos*.

■ We Love Our Outlaws, Detest Yours

Americans enjoy characters who break the rules and get away with it, particularly if they do it with panache. We love a charming con man. We elect some of them to office—Huey Long, James Michael Curley, Edwin Edwards, Bill Clinton. They're much more fun than bland and serious statesmen.

We feel the same way about athletes. We profess to be appalled by the bad boys, but deep in our hearts we prefer the colorful rogue to the bland role model. We admire the saints of sport—the humble, hardworking, hospital-visiting, pre-game-praying choirboys—but when it comes to

Nobody loves a fallen angel more than Americans. Boxer and serial domestic abuser Jake La Motta (above, with wife Vicki after winning the middleweight title in 1949) became the subject of a popular and critically acclaimed movie—Martin Scorsese's Raging Bull, *which starred the great Robert De Niro as La Motta.*

our entertainment dollar, we tend to opt for the sinners.

As Billy Joel sings: "The sinners are much more fun."

America is the land of the second chance. We are a wonderfully forgiving people, particularly when the forgiven keep winning.

"In sports, winning is an excuse for just about any act, no matter how vile," wrote John Feinstein, biographer of Bobby Knight. "You can choke your coach in San Francisco and end up a hero in New York, as long as you make enough clutch jump shots. You can spit on an umpire in Toronto and get a standing ovation five days later in Baltimore, as long as you are batting .321 for the home team."

We like our Big John Baals—but not all of them, and not all of the time. In outlaws, as in everything else, we have our preferences. Frequently, our views break down along predictable lines. Liberals like the free spirits who flaunt the rules and shoot off their mouths. Conservatives prefer the mad-dog coaches who throw chairs at the free spirits who flaunt the rules and shoot off their mouths.

One man's rotten, spoiled sports villain is another man's tragic put-upon sports hero. To one side, Muhammad Ali was a big-mouth, draft-dodging egomaniac; to the other side, he was a charming martyr who courageously defied an evil war. To one side, Pete Rose was a gambling, tax-dodging greedhead; to the other, he was a scrappy blue-collar hero screwed by self-righteous baseball bureaucrats.

But generally our preferences break down to something far more basic—tribalism. We love *our* outlaws, but we detest yours. **We feel about our own bad boys the way Franklin Roosevelt felt about Nicaraguan dictator Anastasio Somoza: "He's a bastard but he's our bastard."**

We feel our team's thugs and dope fiends deserve a second chance, but your team's thugs and dope fiends should be locked up.

And we love arguing about all this. Is Hurricane Carter a murderer or the victim of a racist frame-up? What about O.J. Simpson?

The bad boys and fallen angels of sport give us something to talk about. They're walking soap operas, psychiatric case studies in colorful uniforms. If they didn't exist, we'd have to invent them.

Which is exactly what the lords of professional wrestling did. They knew they needed story lines to perk up their ersatz "sports entertainment" spectacles, so they turned some wrestlers into heroes and others into "heels," which is what they call their bad boys.

Real sports don't have to do that. In baseball and football and basketball and boxing, the bad boys popped up naturally—dandelions thriving in the green Elysian Fields. Their stories are far richer than any fictitious concoction—more tragic, more comic, more delightfully improbable and implausible. They are stories that Americans love and stories that reveal a great deal about who we are.

Let's tell a few.

BY THEIR ENEMIES SHALL YE KNOW THEM

Thanks to the late, great Richard Nixon, all public men who become Fallen Angels must have an Enemies' List. Here's the Top 5 for each of our sporting Fallen Angels (but remember that in all cases, they are/were their own worst enemy):

Ty Cobb
1. Blacks
2. Babe Ruth—their fierce rivalry was laced with hatred
3. Matty McIntyre—bickering with teammate extended to the playing field, once leading to a famous incident where a ball dropped in while they were arguing
4. AL President Ban Johnson—meted out punishment for Cobb's frequent defiance of rules
5. Charlie "Boss" Schmidt—this teammate once beat him up badly

Pete Rose
1. A. Bartlett Giamatti—commissioner who banned him from baseball
2. Tommy Gioiosa—former confidant who turned him in for gambling
3. Bud Selig—commissioner who refuses to reinstate Rose
4. Jim Dowd—attorney who investigated gambling allegations for MLB
5. Kane—nemesis at three WrestleManias

Bobby Knight
1. Indiana President Myles Brand—he fired him
2. Murray Sperber—IU professor who dubbed him "The Emperor of Indiana"
3. Neil Reed—former Indiana player Knight grabbed by the neck, an incident that eventually led to Knight being put on a "zero tolerance" policy
4. Kent Harvey—this student's encounter with Knight led to his firing
5. Sportswriters—a love-hate deal: He hated almost all of them, loved a few, and the feelings were generally mutual

Billy Martin
1. Reggie Jackson—often clashed; once they almost came to blows in the dugout during a game
2. George Steinbrenner—the ultimate love-hate relationship; he hired and fired Martin five times
3. George Weiss—Yankee GM who traded him to Kansas City after the Copa incident
4. Henry Hecht—Martin always believed the *New York Post* sportswriter was trying to turn his Yankee team against him
5. Clint Courtney—their feud began in the minors and led to brawling in the majors

Rubin "Hurricane" Carter
1. Judge Samuel Larner—presided over trial, later denied a new trial
2. Vincent Hull Jr.—prosecutor
3. Alfred Bello—claimed Carter left scene with a gun
4. Arthur Bradley—also said he saw Carter at scene of triple murders
5. Cal Deal—his Web site continues to make the case against Carter

O.J. Simpson
1. Fred Goldman—father of the man Simpson was accused of murdering
2. Denise Brown—sister of Simpson's slain wife
3. Mark Fuhrman—detective accused of planting bloody glove at Simpson's home
4. Marcia Clark—prosecutor in double-murder trial
5. "Kato" Kaelin—former house guest, who "reluctantly" took the stand against him

A Snarling Wildcat

O N CHRISTMAS EVE, 1960, TY COBB STAGGERED THROUGH A cemetery in his Georgia hometown, searching for his grave.

He'd purchased a tomb in Royston, Georgia, by phone from his home in California, and now he couldn't find it. His anger, which simmered constantly, now began to boil.

"Dammit!" he barked. "I ordered the biggest damn mausoleum in the graveyard. I know it's around here somewhere."

He was old and sick and dying, and as he shuffled through the cemetery, he leaned on the shoulder of Al Stump, the sportswriter he'd hired to ghost his memoirs. A light snow fell through the twilight. They walked over a hill and spotted the tomb—an eight-foot-high marble mausoleum with one word, "COBB," carved over the entrance.

"You want to pray with me?" Cobb said.

It was an odd request coming from Cobb, who was always more sinner than saint. In their 10 months of collaboration, Stump had seen Cobb hurl a drink at a bartender, throw a punch at a casino croupier, shoot a pistol at a group of rowdy drunks. Now he knelt with the old outfielder and prayed to God.

Inside the tomb, Cobb pointed out the crypts of his father, his mother and his sister. He'd had them all disinterred from their graves and placed here to wait for him.

"My father was the greatest man I ever knew," he said. "He was a scholar, state senator, editor and philosopher. I worshipped him."

Cobb braced himself against the crypt that would soon hold his corpse. **"My father had his head blown off by a shotgun when I was 18 years old—by a member of my own family!** I didn't get over that. I've never gotten over it."

He didn't tell Stump the rest of the horrific story: William H. Cobb suspected that his wife was cheating on him. He told her he was leaving town on a business trip, then returned late that night and climbed up on the porch roof to peek into the bedroom window. His wife, Amanda, who was alone, heard a noise and saw a man outside her window. She picked up a shotgun and fired twice, blasting her husband's head off.

News reached Cobb the next day, August 9, 1905, in Augusta, where he was playing minor league baseball. His father had disapproved of Cobb's passion for baseball, a game the senator believed was filled with lower-class louts and drunks. Ty was stubborn, and his father finally relented. But he issued a warning: "Don't come home a failure."

Now Cobb came home to find his father dead, and his mother charged with murder. Ten days later, the Detroit Tigers called him up to the big leagues. He had realized his dream, but he couldn't enjoy the moment. All he could think was, "Father won't know it."

Cobb once climbed into the stands at Hilltop Park in New York to attack a crippled fan who had been heckling him, a chaotic event captured in this illustration by Gabe Perillo. Cobb was unapologetic. To him, baseball—and life itself—was "a struggle for supremacy, survival of the fittest."

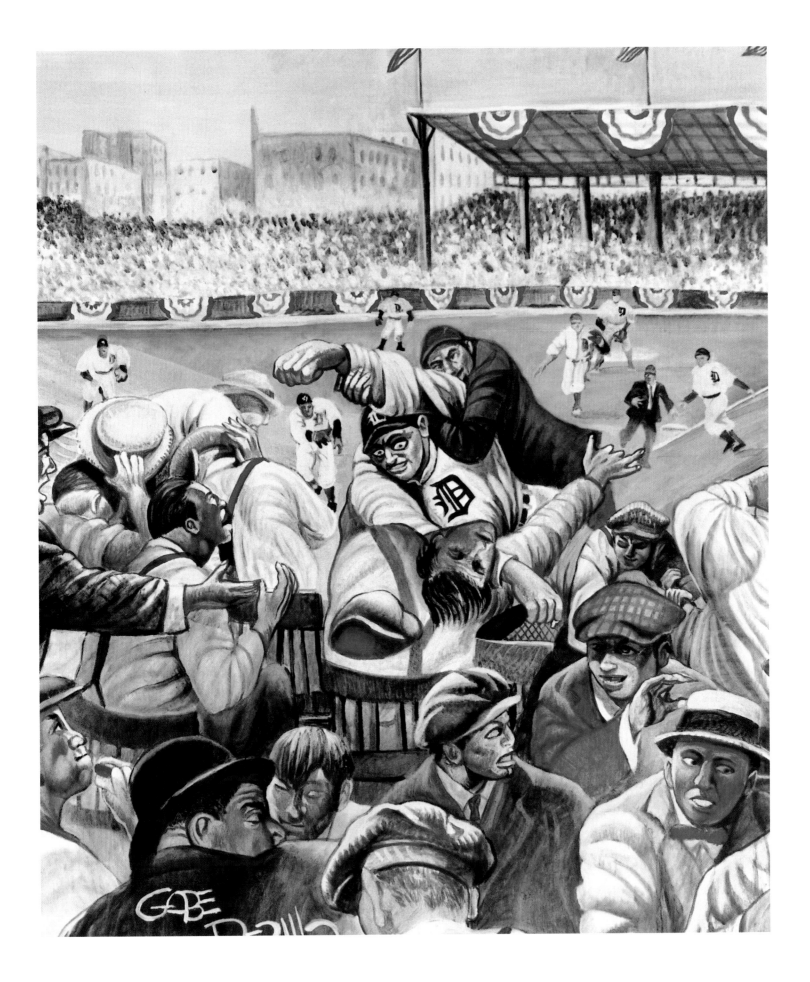

COBB, DETROIT

STATS ON THE COBB

When Ty Cobb retired after 24 seasons, he had set dozens of major league records, including most of the major hitting marks. Now, more than 70 years have passed. His career statistics are still impressive, and many of his records (those marked with an ★) remain intact.

Games, 3,033

At-bats, 11,429

★Batting average, .367

★Highest batting average over three consecutive seasons, .408

★Years batting .400 or over, 3 (ties record)

★Years batting .300 or over, 23

★Years leading in batting average, 11

★Consecutive years leading in batting average, 9

★Years leading in hits, 7

Hits, 4,191

★Five or more hits, one game, 14

Total bases, 5,863

RBI, 1,967

Runs, 2,245

Stolen bases, 892

★Stole home, 54

★Stole home, season, 8

He arrived in the big leagues, a sensitive, high-strung 18-year-old boy in deep psychic pain. His teammates didn't care. They were lower-class louts and drunks, and they delighted in tormenting the rookie, sawing his bats in half, nailing his shoes to the locker-room floor, stuffing his pockets with rotting fruit. They thought it was funny. Cobb didn't. He raged and fought back, earning a broken nose in the process.

"Those old-timers turned me into a snarling wildcat," he said years later.

Fierceness Bordering on Insanity

Propelled by rage—and perhaps by the need to prove himself to his father's ghost—the wildcat soon became the best player in baseball. He won the American League batting championship in 1907, then he won it 11 out of the next 12 seasons. He led the majors in stolen bases five times, RBI four times, total bases six times and slugging percentage eight times. He hit over .300 for 23 consecutive seasons and ended up with a career batting average of .367, a record that will probably never be broken.

Cobb in action: balanced at the plate (far left), unbalanced on the base paths. Though he was involved in many ugly onfield incidents (like the spiking above), he claims he deliberately tried to slash a man only once— Red Sox pitcher Hub Leonard, who made a habit of throwing at Cobb's head.

But numbers can't capture the way Cobb dominated the diamond. He drove pitchers and catchers crazy with his wild baserunning and scared infielders by sliding into bases with his sharpened spikes high. **His intensity went beyond hustle, beyond aggressive competition. He played with a furious rage and a fierceness that bordered on insanity.**

His ferocity did nothing to diminish his popularity. In fact, Cobb was a national hero, hired to advertise everything from cigars and cigarettes to underwear and overcoats and a snake oil pick-me-up called "Nuxated Iron."

"Ty Cobb symbolized America from the turn of the century to World War I perhaps better than any other single figure," wrote baseball historian Lawrence Ritter.

"A Red-Blooded Game for Red-Blooded Men"

It was an era of robber barons and labor wars, a time when John D. Rockefeller Jr. responded to a strike at his Colorado coal mines by hiring a private army to fire Gatling guns at the strikers' tent colony, killing two women and 11 children.

The reigning philosophy of the era was not the loving Christianity preached in churches. It was the pitiless Social Darwinism—the "survival of the fittest"—that was practiced in business. Cobb bragged that his brand of baseball embodied that idea.

"Baseball is a red-blooded game for red-blooded men," he said in an extraordinary interview with sportswriter F. C. Lane. "It's a contest with all that name implies, a struggle for supremacy, a survival of the fittest . . . Baseball is the great American game. It expresses more nearly than any

FIT TO BE TY

■ Long before it was commonplace for athletes to move on to entertainment careers, Ty Cobb made a movie called *Somewhere in Georgia,* a sort of boy-meets-girl, boy-meets-baseball, boy-wins-game, boy-wins-girl flick.

He plays a Georgia bank clerk who joins the Detroit Tigers, leaving behind the woman he loves. After a rough period with his new teammates, Cobb heads home to see his girl, but is kidnapped along the way. He escapes just in time to race to the ballpark, hit a big home run and win the game. The lovebirds are married and live happily ever after.

Cobb was roundly criticized for his lack of passion in the romantic scenes, in which he seemed to barely kiss his girlfriend. And the 1916 release was universally panned. Critic Ward Morehouse called it the worst film he had ever seen.

Insipid smooching notwithstanding, Cobb raked in $25,000 for his film debut, more than he earned for the entire season with the Tigers. Besides a cameo appearance in *Angels in the Outfield* (1951), Cobb left acting behind.

But the entertainment world has not forgotten him, decades after his death.

In 1994, former minor league infielder Ron Shelton directed Tommy Lee Jones in *Cobb,* based on the biography by Al Stump.

In 1996, Soundgarden included a track called *Ty Cobb* on *Down on the Upside.*

In 2000, Kevin Spacey paid money out of his own pocket to keep alive a production of the stage show "Cobb" by the Melting Pot Theater Company in New York. So enamored was he of the play that he had his production company, Trigger Street Productions, arrange a special Off-Broadway run of the show at New York City's Lucille Lortel Theater.

other game the aggressive, fighting American spirit, the determination to succeed . . . Baseball is a grand democracy. The top is within reach of anyone who has ability enough and fights hard enough to get there. But rest assured, it's a fight. It's a fight every step of the way to the top, and a still bitterer fight to keep on the top when you arrive . . . "

Cobb fought to stay on top. He fought opponents, umpires, his own teammates. One day in 1912, a fan in New York heckled him, yelling that Cobb was "half nigger." Enraged, Cobb leaped over a railing, climbed into the stands and stomped the man until he was forcibly pulled away. Later, reporters informed Cobb that the fan was missing all of one hand and part of the other.

"I don't care if he has no feet," Cobb replied.

He was a vicious racist, who regularly attacked black people he deemed insufficiently deferential. He fought a black elevator operator, a black construction worker, a black groundskeeper—and when the groundskeeper's wife protested, he grabbed her by the throat.

Never Forgive, Never Forget

When he retired following the 1928 season, after playing 24 years, he held dozens of records, including highest average, most games, most hits, most runs, most total bases. When sportswriters elected the first five members of the Baseball Hall of Fame in 1936, Cobb received the most votes—seven more than Babe Ruth.

Ruth did not dispute his runner-up status. "Ty Cobb was the greatest I ever saw or heard about," he said.

In retirement, Cobb remained a volatile, violent man. He brawled in bars and was barred from at least one country club for fighting. His temper tantrums, frequently fueled by whiskey, drove away two wives, most of his five children, many friends and countless cooks, nurses, maids, handymen and sportswriters.

Once, at a lunch at the Detroit Athletic Club, former Cleveland catcher Jay "Nig" Clarke confessed that he'd used fake tags to trick umpires into calling Cobb out a few times on plays at the plate. Sportswriters at the table laughed at the story of decades-old chicanery. Cobb did not. "You cost me runs!" he bellowed as he belted Clarke.

By the late 1950s, Cobb was alone and ailing, sick with cancer, heart disease and diabetes, and sinking into paranoia. Afraid of eavesdropping by

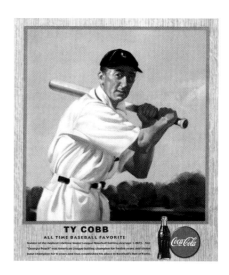

HITTING THE JACKPOT

■ During Ty Cobb's career, he was at or near the top in almost all hitting categories, but the most the Georgia Peach earned in a year was $50,000, a great salary in those days.

However, Cobb was shrewd with his money, following stock market ups and downs as avidly as a fantasy baseball owner combs batting averages. (He was also nuts, sometimes carrying around a brown paper sack stuffed with negotiable securities, which he kept next to his bed . . . along with a loaded Luger.)

Once he purchased 300 shares in a little-known Atlanta-based company called Coca-Cola, and at one time he owned as many as 20,000 shares. Players would look to Cobb for financial advice, since they couldn't retire on their incomes. And, if Cobb liked you, he would offer some tips.

When Cobb died in 1961, he had $2 million in Coke stock plus other investments that brought his estimated worth to $12 million. The $2 million in stock would now be worth more than $486 million had dividends been reinvested, according to Coca-Cola.

He also lent his name to the product, with Coca-Cola regularly using Cobb in newspaper advertisements beginning in 1907. One ad quoted Cobb as saying: "On days when we are playing a doubleheader, I always find that a drink of Coca-Cola between the games refreshes me to such an extent that I can start the second game feeling as if I had not been exercising at all."

And that was after cocaine had been removed from the formula in 1904.

the IRS or divorce lawyers, he disconnected the phone at his lodge in Lake Tahoe, Nevada. He lived for months without electricity at his mansion in Atherton, California, because he believed the Pacific Gas and Electric Company had overcharged him by $16.

In 1960, after firing two previous scribes, he hired Stump to write his memoirs. During their 10 months together, Cobb cursed Stump, threw a booze bottle at him and pulled a gun on him. But Stump stayed on. When the interviews were finally completed, just a few months before Cobb's death in 1961, Stump drove the old wildcat home to Atherton one last time.

"Have you got enough to finish the book?" Cobb asked.

"More than enough," Stump replied.

"Give 'em the word then," Cobb said. **"I had to fight all my life to survive. They were all against me—tried every dirty trick to cut me down. But I beat the bastards and left them in the ditch.** Make sure the book says that."

Before leaving, Stump asked the question he'd avoided for 10 months. "Why did you fight so hard in baseball, Ty?"

Cobb looked at him fiercely. "I did it for my father, who was an exalted man," he said. "They killed him when he was still young. They blew his head off the same week I became a major leaguer. He never got to see me play. But I knew he was watching me and I never let him down."

An astute if somewhat idiosyncratic investor (he often carried a brown paper bag full of negotiable securities around with him), Cobb became wealthy enough after baseball to indulge himself in luxuries like this family trip to Paris in 1929 (above).

SICK FLICKS

America loves sports movies, because they can inspire you and teach you to believe in yourself, if only for a few moments. Of course, there are some notable exceptions. The following are deserving candidates for any Top 10 Worst Sports Movies Ever Made list:

1. *Teen Wolf Too* (1987)
Preposterous plot revolves around a boxer who must decide if he should use his lupine prowess to win a championship.

2. *Johnny Be Good* (1988)
Anthony Michael Hall, the former Brat Pack nerd, is terribly miscast as a hotly recruited high school QB.

3. *American Anthem* (1986)
Can there be compelling drama in a gymnastics flick? Sure, if tension is built around what music to use in a routine.

4. *Cobb* (1994)
Ty Cobb (Tommy Lee Jones) hires a sportswriter to pen a sanitized version of his life story. Only Jones' talent and a few good one-liners make this bearable.

5. *Over the Top* (1987)
In yet another wearisome Stallone vehicle—this time centered around an armwrestling championship—he fights for custody of his son.

6. *Caddyshack II* (1988)
Good guys battle snobs in a winner-take-all golf match in a charmless ripoff of the original.

7. *Space Jam* (1996)
Aliens invade earth! Only Michael Jordan and the Looney Tunes can stop them.

8. *Ed* (1996)
Pitcher Matthew LeBlanc rooms with a baseball-playing chimp.

9. *Gymkata* (1985)
"American Anthem Jr."

10. *Rocky V* (1990)
Punch-drunk boxer loses it all, and the series mercifully ends.

Honorable mention:
Tonya Harding's wedding-night video, *Victory*, *The Slugger's Wife*, *Necessary Roughness*

The Hustler

T HE STORY OF PETE ROSE IS AS STARK AND PRIMAL AS A GREEK myth or a Biblical parable:

He was a mortal, a mere man, but through heroic, superhuman efforts, he raised himself up to Olympus. Then, just as he was about to be enthroned in the pantheon, he committed the one unpardonable sin and was excommunicated, ejected from Eden, banished from the garden.

He is still banished and he still can't quite believe it.

Peter Edward Rose was born in 1941, on the blue-collar west side of Cincinnati. He was the son of a bank clerk who played semi-pro football until he was in his mid-40s.

"You tackle him low, he'd kick you in the face," Pete proudly described his dad. "You tackle him high, he'd stiff-arm you in the face."

Harry Rose preached Ty Cobb's Social Darwinist gospel of toughness, hard work and hustle, and his son was an eager acolyte. In high school, Pete was small and skinny, but that didn't stop him from playing football and baseball. He didn't have extraordinary natural talent, but he was hungry. He wanted it bad. In the off-season, he got a job unloading boxcars to bulk himself up. He worked hard, and he hustled, and he kept moving up—to Tampa, where he hit .331, then to Macon where he hit .330 and led the league in triples.

The Reds summoned him to spring training in 1963, and **he irritated the hell out of the team's veterans with his ostentatious hustle and his constant stream of cheerful infield chatter. In an era of cool, Pete Rose was hot.**

Playing the Yankees one day that spring, the Reds veterans told Whitey Ford and Mickey Mantle about their eager young hot dog, who ran full speed to first on walks. Ford thought that was funny and he started heckling Rose, calling him, "Charlie Hustle."

It was an insult, but Rose chose to take it as a compliment, and he kept on hustling. He doubled in his first spring at-bat and then he doubled

Rose worshipped his father, Harry (far left), so unconditionally that after a single paternal lecture about not hustling to first on a groundout, Rose never again held anything back on the field (right).

2nd BASE
PETE ROSE

FOWL BALL!

■ Pete Rose wae already a two-time veteran of WrestleMania when he appeared again in 2000 to take on his archenemy, the seven-foot Kane. The previous year, Rose had donned a San Diego Chicken costume in an ill-fated ploy against Kane, but this time Rose used it as a decoy. With Kane seemingly fooled, the Real Pete raced up with his favorite weapon, a bat, which he had already hit with more than 4,000 times. But the masked monster just knocked him out "cold" with a Tombstone. Then, his tag-team partner Rikishi went to work using his signature move—the Stink Face. Pete was dragged into the corner of the ring, where the 400-pound Rikishi thrust his giant buttocks into the Hit King's face.

Rose's brawl with Bud Harrelson of the New York Mets (left, top and bottom) led to a bench-clearing melee in Game 3 of the 1973 National League Championship Series. Twelve years later—on September 11, 1985—Rose stroked hit number 4,192 (above right), breaking Cobb's record, after which he bestowed a rare hug on Petey Jr. (right).

again in his second. He beat out veteran second baseman Don Blasingame for the starting job, then he hit .273 and was voted Rookie of the Year.

By then, his pattern was set. He loved three things—baseball, betting and chasing women. One day during that rookie year, he was at the racetrack when he spotted a pretty girl in a short skirt. He walked right up to Karolyn Engelhardt and introduced himself. The next January, they got married. The wedding was on the same day as the Cincinnati baseball writers dinner. Pete said his vows, jumped into his mint-green Corvette and zoomed off to the baseball dinner. He picked up an award, made a short speech, then sped back to his wedding reception.

For Pete Rose, baseball always came first.

He kept hustling, driven, like his hero, Cobb, by a demanding father. Harry Rose attended almost every game and he watched very closely. Once, he took Pete aside and told him he hadn't hustled to first on one groundout. "That's a direct reflection on me," he said.

So Pete kept hustling.

"If he got three hits, he wanted four," teammate Johnny Bench recalled. "If he got four, he wanted five. He was insatiable."

"He played every game like it was the seventh game of the World Series," said teammate Joe Morgan. "I've never seen anyone else do that."

In the 12th inning of the 1970 All-Star game, Rose sprinted home from second on a single, looking to score the winning run, and barreled

KID CONFUSION

What becomes a legend most? Obviously not a well-adjusted son. Over the years, Pete Rose Jr., a baseball player of modest talent—14 at-bats in the Show with the Reds in 1997, a career minor leaguer—has tried to make sense of his self-involved, less-than-sensitve father and his own tangled feelings about being the son of the Hit King. As the quotes below attest, progress has been slow.

■ *On growing up:*
"When I was growing up, my dad was never around. I couldn't talk to him about girls or ask him to borrow the keys to the car. I always turned to my mom."

■ *On following in his father's footsteps:*
"That's the only thing I've ever wanted to do; that's the only thing I ever thought about doing, because I've always wanted to be just like Dad."

■ *On choosing uniform No. 21, instead of Pete's No. 14:*
"One part of me was saying 'Take it, take it.' It's been my number all of my life, but another part of me said, 'No. It's time for me to make my own identity.' "

■ *On his father watching him play in the minors:*
"When I woke up this morning, I looked over at my roommate and said, 'This is going to be a fiasco today, just like it always is.' That's expected when your dad is the Hit King, but sometimes I wish he'd just come in unannounced,

sit in the stands, watch the game, and then go out to dinner [with me]. I'm not into this hoopla, but that's what you get when your dad is Pete Rose."

■ *On making it to the Show:*
"Right now, that's my only goal, but once I get there, what the hell, I'll take a shot at dad's record."

■ *On occasionally playing under the name P. J. Rose to avoid abuse from fans in the Northern League:*
"Don't take it the wrong way. I'm the proudest son anywhere."

■ *On the record-breaking hit:*
"Dad being Dad, Mr. Tough Guy, [I'd] never seen him cry before, never really got a hug before or a kiss before. He told me he loved me. I told him I loved him. That was the night and it was just a special night . . . Dad was always the tough guy; if you cried, you were a sissy . . . When that happened, I think it kind of broke the ice. It was the kind of thing I'll never forget as long as I live."

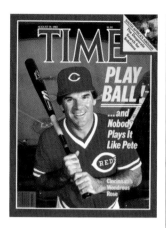

into catcher Ray Fosse so hard that he ended Fosse's career. When sports-writers squawked that the shot was unnecessarily vicious, Rose's reply sounded like Cobb: "Nobody told me they changed it to girl's softball between third and home."

Later that year, Harry Rose suddenly died of a heart attack at 57. The man who had driven his son to greatness was gone. After that, Rose make a pilgrimage to his father's grave at the end of every season to tell the Old Man how he'd done.

He was baseball's Peter Pan—the boy who wouldn't grow up, a kid with boundless energy and endless exuberance. In an era of overpaid grumblers and spoiled sulkers, he was refreshingly enthusiastic and America loved him.

When his Reds contract expired, he traveled the country shameless-ly hustling himself to the highest bidder. The Phillies made him the offer he couldn't refuse—four years for $3.2 million—making him the highest-paid player in baseball.

"That's so much money," he bragged, "that if you stacked up all the cash, a show horse couldn't jump over it."

Rose loved the money, and he flaunted it outrageously, dressing in Gucci loafers, gold chains, a diamond Rolex, a fur coat and pants so tight you could see the thick roll of bills he stuffed into the pocket. He was tacky but charming, and he embodied one of the cliches of what Tom Wolfe called the Me Decade: *If you got it, flaunt it.*

He also flaunted his philandering, draping his mistresses in diamonds and buying them Porsches and new, improved breasts. One girlfriend got a necklace inscribed, "To My Rookie of the Year." Another hit him with a paternity suit.

Finally, in 1980, his wife got fed up and divorced him, dishing all the nasty details of his sex life to reporters. It got ugly. At one point, the first Mrs. Pete Rose ripped a necklace off the throat of the former cheerleader, Carol Woilung, who would soon become the second Mrs. Pete Rose. But the fans didn't care because he was baseball's Peter Pan and boys will be boys and, besides, he led the Phillies to their first World Championship ever, ending the Series with a lunging grab of a foul pop-up.

■ A Glutton for Excitement

After that, it was Rose against the record book, as he marched obsessive-ly up the all-time hits ladder. After he got 3,000, he wrote 3,631 on all his bats—that was Stan Musial's NL hits record. When he passed Musial, he wrote 4,000 on his bats. When he passed that, he wrote 4,191, which was Cobb's all-time record.

On September 11, 1985, he passed Cobb with hit number 4,192. As he stood on the field, basking in a long standing ovation, he saw his father and Ty Cobb in the sky, sitting together, and he began to weep. His broth-er said it was the first time he'd ever seen Pete cry.

Rose married Carol (left) after a contentious and highly public divorce from his first wife, Karolyn, the mother of his two oldest kids, Fawn, now 36, and Pete Jr., now 31. He was also hit with a paternity suit, which didn't help any. Rose always said his father was a better person than he was, "because my father never got divorced, or any of that stuff."

That was the best night of his life, the happy culmination of all his endless hustling. But when it was over, he had no more goals to chase, no more big numbers to write on his bat. He managed the Reds, but managing wasn't nearly enough action for Rose. He needed more excitement so he'd sit in front of his satellite TV, watching any sporting event he could find, calling in bets to his bookies—$1,000 a game, $2,000 a game. That cranked up the adrenaline a few notches.

But he hated losing, and he didn't always pay his bookies, and one of them ratted on him, telling *Sports Illustrated* that Rose bet on baseball while managing the Reds.

The lords of baseball hired lawyer John Dowd to investigate. Dowd examined Rose's phone records and interviewed his associates and issued a scathing 225-page report. It concluded that Rose had bet on baseball games, including at least 52 Reds games (always with the Reds to win) while he was managing the team.

Rose admittted betting, but he denied betting on baseball. "I'd be willing to bet you if I was a betting man," he said, "that I never bet on baseball."

On August 23, 1989, Commissioner Bart Giamatti summoned Rose to a meeting. They were a mismatched pair. Giamatti was a Yale intellecual who wrote ethereal essays comparing baseball to Homer's *Odyssey*. Rose was an uneducated ballplayer who knew nothing about Homer, except

that he'd never hit very many.

When the meeting was over, the man with more hits than anybody in history had signed an agreement that banned him from baseball forever, but allowed him to apply for reinstatement after a year.

He figured he'd be in exile for a year or two and then come back. He figured wrong.

Things kept getting worse. In 1990, he went to prison for five months for evading taxes on $354,698 he'd earned signing autographs.

Then, in 1991, the Hall of Fame announced a new rule: Any player banned from baseball was ineligible for admission. It was a rule designed solely to keep Rose out. And now the most prolific hitter in history could not take his place beside Ty Cobb in the Hall of Fame.

Rose was crushed. The Hall of Fame is baseball's pantheon—the home of the gods, the temple of the immortals. To be enshrined there is to gain a form of eternal life. Rose had spent his life fighting for admittance to the Hall, and now he was barred, banned, banished. All his hard work, all those head-first slides, all that endless hustling—it was all for nothing.

"I know it's eating him up inside," said his old Reds teammate Frank Robinson. "Baseball—that's all he ever wanted to do, that's all he ever talked about. I'm sure that's all he ever dreamed about when he slept—baseball, baseball, baseball."

Baseball's Peter Pan

Exiled from baseball, Rose hustled money signing autographs and running a restaurant and hosting a talk show—talking mainly about himself, and how he ought to be allowed back in baseball.

The polls showed that most fans agreed with him. They still loved baseball's Peter Pan. They figured he'd suffered enough, and they were

---

NO SUCH THING AS A SURE THING

America is a country of bettors—from office pools to the racetrack to casinos to lotteries—but nothing riles the fans, the guardians of the games and law enforcement officials quite like headlines about point-shaving or dumping, or incidents of gambling by those who play in or coach/manage the games. Punishment can be severe.

Major League Baseball

■ Eight Chicago White Sox players are indicted in 1920 for conspiracy to defraud the public by fixing the 1919 World Series, which the Sox lost. Although all—forever after to be known as "The Black Sox"—are acquitted in court, Commissioner Kenesaw Mountain Landis bars all eight from baseball for life, including potential Hall of Famer Shoeless Joe Jackson.

■ In 1920, Hal Chase, considered by some to be baseball's most dishonest player ever, is banned for attempting to fix a game while with the New York Giants.

■ Dodger manager Leo Durocher is suspended for the 1947 season by Commissioner Happy Chandler for consorting with gamblers.

■ Denny McLain, the Tigers 31-game winner in 1968, is suspended for half the 1970 season for consorting with gamblers.

■ In 1989, Commissioner Bart Giamatti bans Reds manager Pete Rose from baseball for life (also, in effect, barring him from the Hall of Fame) for gambling on major league games.

College Basketball

■ The sport's biggest point-shaving scandal brings down many of the game's biggest stars, including Ed Warner and Ed Roman (they confess to dumping three games during the 1950-51 season) of CCNY, the only team ever to win the NCAA and NIT titles in the same season; Sherman White of LIU, possibly the greatest college player of that era; and former Kentucky All-Americans Alex Groza and Ralph Beard (they are accused of dumping the Wildcats' NIT game against Loyola of Chicago in 1949, and both are barred from the NBA for life). All-American center Bill Spivey is also barred from playing any sports for Kentucky.

■ Former NBA player Jack Molinas—he was banished from the league in 1954 for gambling—is arrested in 1962 on charges of fixing games, a scheme involving 37 players from 22 schools. Molinas is convicted and sentenced to 10-15 years in prison, and is later murdered. Connie Hawkins, though never charged with a crime, is booted out of Iowa and effectively barred from the NBA for five years merely for associating with Molinas.

■ In 1981, Former BC forward Rick Kuhn and four others are found guilty of conspiring to fix BC games during the 1978-79 season. Kuhn serves 2½ years.

Boxing

■ In the ring's most infamous case, Jake (Raging Bull) La Motta takes a dive in his 1947 match with Billy Fox in exchange for a shot at the middleweight title.

Pro Football

■ In 1946, Giants QB Frankie Filchock and running back Merle Hapes are suspended indefinitely for gambling.

■ Green Bay halfback Paul Hornung and Detroit defensive tackle Alex Karras are suspended for the entire 1963 NFL season for betting on league games.

■ Colts quarterback Art Schlichter is suspended in 1983 by the NFL for betting on league games; he is reinstated 14 months later. Schlichter, whose gambling addiction will keep him in legal trouble for two decades, is currently incarcerated in an Indiana state prison for forgery, theft and probation violations.

Soccer

■ In 1980, Juventus star Paolo Rossi is charged with taking bribes to fix Italian Serie A league games. Rossi is banned from competition for life. Reinstated after two years, Rossi leads Italy to the '82 World Cup title.

willing to forgive him. They voted him onto baseball's All-Century Team and gave him a standing ovation at the 1999 World Series.

Bill Clinton, a man who knew a thing or two about forgiveness, agreed. "I just think everybody ought to get a second chance," the president said. "I'd like to see it worked out, because he brought a lot of joy to the game, and he gave a lot of joy to people, and he's paid a price—God knows he's paid a price."

Baseball's Peter Pan is in his 60s now, but when he talks about his banishment from the garden, he sounds like a petulant teenager trying to talk his way out of getting grounded by Dad.

"I didn't kill anybody," he says. "I didn't *kill* anybody."

Despite his many legal troubles (Rose is escorted by a federal marshal to his 1990 sentencing on tax evasion charges, above left)—or perhaps because of them—he remains stunningly popular with the average fan. At the introduction of baseball's 30-player All-Century Team before Game 2 of the 1999 World Series in Atlanta (right), the Hit King got a 55-second standing ovation, the longest of any living team member. Hometown hero Hank Aaron, by comparison, was cheered for only 40 seconds.

The General

NRAGED, THE STUDENTS MARCHED ON THE HOME OF THE university president, chanting obscenities. Along the way, they stopped traffic, tore down light posts, vandalized the sign on the campus art museum.

Two thousand strong, they stormed the president's front lawn and burned him in effigy until cops in riot gear moved in, squirting mace.

Why were the students so angry? Was it Vietnam? Racism? Apartheid?

No, it was an issue far more important to the average American student—intercollegiate sports. This wasn't Berkeley in the '60s, it was Indiana University on September 10, 2000, the day president Myles Brand fired basketball coach Bobby Knight.

The students were outraged: How could a mere college president remove a living legend?

In 29 years at Indiana University, Knight had led the Hoosiers to 661 wins, 11 Big Ten championships, three NCAA national championships.

He was a brilliant coach, but he was also a raging, foul-mouthed bully who'd made headlines for punching a player, fighting a cop, throwing a fan into a trash can, tossing a chair onto the court in the middle of a game.

Needless to say, the winning outweighed the bullying. And Bobby Knight became a god in Indiana. Five months earlier, when he got in trouble for choking a player, students marched with signs that read: "The Lord Is My Shepherd and Knight Is My Coach."

The religious language is telling: The Knight controversy was a classic example of a curious American phenomenon—the cult of the coach.

For many Americans, a coach is a king, an emperor, an imperial ruler. In hundreds of American towns, the high school coach is better known, more respected and frequently higher paid than the high school principal—or even the mayor. In scores of American colleges, the coach is far more powerful than the president, who is, after all, just a glorified professor.

In America, sport is the moral equivalent of war—a nonviolent means of conquering one's neighbors—and a winning coach has the status of a victorious general. It's a tough job that calls for a tough man. If he can win, the coach is not held to normal standards of conduct. He is expected, even encouraged, to be foul-mouthed, hot-tempered and brutal—a

After Bobby Knight was fired in September 2000, Indiana U. students went ballistic, setting fires and wreaking campus-wide havoc (above). Twenty-five years earlier, as his team was losing an NCAA Mideast Regional final to Kentucky, the 1975 AP Coach of the Year went ballistic (right), hurling a towel to the floor.

drill instructor imposing iron discipline. Tales of his nastiness only add luster to his legend.

America's legendary coaches are stern, angry Olympian figures who become the objects of worshipful cults. George Blanda once described famous football coach Paul "Bear" Bryant thusly: "That must be what God looks like."

It's odd: In democratic America, we are suspicious of authority. We demand that senators and even presidents obey the rules and act like regular guys. But coaches are encouraged to be arrogant, megalomaniacal tyrants. They seem to fulfill our secret inner need for a dictator.

■ Following in Woody's Footsteps

But sometimes the little generals go too far. Or they stop winning. Or both. And then their imperial reign comes tumbling down. Bobby Knight should have known that. He watched it happen to one of his heroes—Woodrow Hayes.

Hayes was a brilliant football coach at Ohio State, Knight's alma mater. In 28 years of coaching the Buckeyes, Hayes won 13 Big Ten championships and five national championships. He was nicknamed "Woody," but he ran his team like a general, and he loved to discourse on military history. "He never really forgave the world for making him a football coach instead of a field marshal," wrote sports columnist Jim Murray. "Woody always hankered to capture Paris or destroy Carthage or cross the Alps on

Although his luck would improve as a coach (he was named Indiana head man in 1971, right, after modest success as Army's honcho), Knight's choice of a college was most unfortunate. At Ohio State (above, far right), he never cracked the starting lineup, mostly because (from second left, above) Jerry Lucas, Larry Siegfried, Mel Nowell and John Havlicek were all so good they would later play in the NBA.

an elephant. When he couldn't, he'd settle for beating Michigan."

Hayes had a hot temper and quick fists. Over the years, he punched reporters, players, a cameraman, an assistant coach, a goal post. Then, in the Gator Bowl in 1978, he punched a Clemson player named Charlie Bauman who had the audacity to intercept a Buckeye pass in the final minutes of a close game.

That was too much. Like Truman confronting MacArthur, the president of Ohio State demanded his coach's resignation. Hayes refused to give it. "That would make it too easy for you," he said.

So the president fired him.

A few months later, at the College Football Hall of Fame, Hayes was given an award for his "outstanding contribution to character building."

Maybe Bobby Knight couldn't see his future in Hayes's downfall but *The Indianapolis Star* did. **In 1997, the newspaper ran a cartoon that showed Knight gazing into a mirror only to see Woody Hayes staring back at him.**

Knight was raised in Orrville, Ohio, the only child of a railroad freight agent and a teacher. At 6-foot-4, he was the star of his high school team, but when he got to Ohio State, he couldn't crack the starting lineup of the Buckeyes' championship team, which was led by future Celtics star John Havlicek. He hated sitting on the bench, and he complained so much that his coach, Fred Taylor, dubbed him "The Brat from Orrville."

He got a job coaching basketball at West Point and he whipped his cadets into winners, compiling a record of 102-50 in six seasons and beating Navy every year. But his hot temper made him controversial. "Even people at West Point would say, 'He's too tough on the cadets,' " he recalled later. "But why the hell shouldn't we be? I mean, you're watching Army playing in Madison Square Garden, you ought to think these guys are going to be able to go out and protect the country, too."

Indiana's basketball team was awful before Knight arrived, but he changed that quickly. He booted the spectators out of practices and ran his players through intense drills that left them gasping for air. He'd roll a ball on the floor and have three players dive for it. He'd toss it against the backboard and have three players fight for it.

It worked. The Hoosiers finished 17-7 in Knight's first year. In his

THE MOTHER OF ALL MENTORS

Bob Knight may not fit the image of the perfect coaching mentor, but his proteges' accomplishments are irrefutable. Several of today's most successful Division I head coaches have direct ties to him. Though most have had rocky times with Knight, they still respect him.

■ Mike Krzyzewski, Duke
Record: 637-227 (career); three national championships.
  Coach K is Knight's prize pupil. He was recruited by Knight at West Point and assisted him at Indiana. Their relationship became strained after Duke defeated Indiana in the 1992 Final Four. In fact, Knight did not acknowledge Krzyzewski at the postgame press conference. The thaw began after Coach K picked Knight as his presenter for his induction into the Basketball Hall of Fame in 2001.

■ Don DeVoe, Navy
Record: 499-346 (career); 10 NCAA tournament appearances.
  He was an assistant to Knight at Army and a teammate on national runner-up Ohio State in 1962. They have been friends for 40 years, sort of. Said DeVoe, "We don't talk that often—you only talk with Coach Knight when he wants to . . . if there was ever anything I needed help with, though, he would be one of the first people I would call."

■ Steve Alford, Iowa
Record: 212-121 (career); two NCAA tournament appearances.
  He always seems to be in Knight's corner, even if the feeling isn't mutual. In 1987, Alford helped Knight win his last national title, but when he took over at Iowa as coach, Knight didn't call.

At Alford's first Big Ten media day (for the 1999-2000 season), Knight didn't talk to Alford. However, Alford defended Knight after he was fired, although he was a top candidate to replace him. During a winter 2002 call made by Alford, the two mended what differences they had.

■ Mike Davis, Indiana
Record: 46-25, in two seasons; two NCAA Tournament appearances and one Final Four.
  He had been one of the least criticial of Knight's former assistants, until the media got hold of Davis' comments in a deposition he made in former IU assistant Ron Felling's case against Knight. Davis called Knight a bully and criticized his communication methods toward anyone who disagreed with him.

■ Dave Bliss, Baylor
Record: 512-314 (career); 11 NCAA appearances.
  A member of Knight's original staff at Indiana, Bliss can thank Knight for his first job as head coach at Oklahoma in 1975. The two have only met once on the court—in the 2002 season when Texas Tech defeated Baylor—so perhaps that's why their relationship has endured. Bliss has likened Knight to two of the most controversial figures in U.S. military history, Douglas MacArthur and George Patton.

second, they went 22-6 and won the Big Ten title. In 1975, the team finished 31-1, but that wasn't good enough for Coach Knight. He hung a sign in the locker room: "Kentucky 92-Indiana 90. Our Defense Was Responsible For This." The next year they went 32-0 and won the NCAA championship.

After that, Bobby Knight was a god in Indiana.

But he was a vengeful god, a butt-kicking Old Testament-type god, quick to anger and eager to punish. He became at least as famous for his temper tantrums as he did for his championships.

In 1975, he threw a chair across the court during a loss to Purdue.

In 1977, he took off a shoe and banged it on the scorekeepers' table like Khrushchev at the UN.

In 1979, at the Pan American games in Puerto Rico, he got into a fistfight with a cop.

In 1981, he grabbed a heckling fan in a hotel lobby and threw him into a trash can.

Would he or wouldn't he? You could never tell with the General. At top right, he demonstrates on assistant coach Mike Krzyzewski how he reacted to a San Juan policeman at the Pan American Games in 1979. At center, he literally yanks guard Jim Wisman out of a game against Michigan in 1976. At bottom, he ponders a question at a news conference at the NCAA tourney in Philadelphia in 1981 about an altercation with an LSU fan.

The WIZARD of ODD

In 1993, when his son Patrick made a bad pass in a game against Notre Dame, Knight yanked him off the court, pushed him into a chair and kicked him.

In 1994, he pulled an errant player out of a game against Michigan State, stood over him, screaming, and then head-butted him.

"My Critics Can Kiss My Ass"

There were other incidents, too, plenty of others. Knight never apologized. He never explained. He responded to all criticism with attacks on the critics. In 1994, at a pre-game ceremony honoring his seniors, he recited a poem for the fans:

> "When my time on earth is done and my activities here are past
> I want them to bury me upside down and my critics can kiss my ass."

Knight's aura of invincibility began to crack in March of 2000, when CNN aired a devastating documentary on the coach. It showed former Hoosier players describing how Knight had booted the college president out of a practice and how he'd once chastised his team by emerging from a bathroom with his pants around his ankles, wiping his butt with toilet paper, then showing the soiled paper to his team, saying, "This is how you guys are playing." Even worse, a former Indiana player named Neil Reed charged that Knight had choked him during a practice.

A week later, president Brand announced that he was launching an investigation of the coach. That brought Knight's critics out of hiding. A former assistant coach claimed that Knight had punched him. A university secretary recalled that he'd once thrown a potted plant against an office wall in a fit of temper, splattering her with shards of glass. And somebody leaked a vidoetape of the practice session in which Knight had choked Reed.

LITERARY CRITICISM

■ Remember Murray Sperber? You know, the English professor at Indiana University and outspoken critic of Bobby Knight's behavior (example: choking Neil Reed), who took a leave of absence after being threatened by the General's devoted fans. He returned to Bloomington for the 2001 spring semester, where he has been teaching for more than 30 years.

Knight is now in his second season coaching at Texas Tech; his Red Raiders went 23-9 in 2001-02, but were eliminated in the first round of the NCAA Tournament.

Knight's success—on court— came as no surprise to Sperber, the author of *Beer and Circus: How Big-time College Sports Is Crippling Undergraduate Education*, who said: "Bob Knight is winning at Texas Tech—a place where no other basketball coach has won very much—and the fans are hungry for a winner. Not surprisingly, they are turning out to see him and his team. I'd be amazed if they didn't. It wouldn't be college b-ball then. Universities will tolerate outrageous behavior from coaches, as well as their outrageous pay demands, as long as they win.

"Knight is not an individual, aberrant case, but a caricature [above, left] of what many coaches do. He yelled louder and with more profanity, and also yelled at the media louder and with more profanity, than other coaches do. I think that his legacy will be as an exceptional coach . . . exceptionally good with the X's-and-O's and exceptionally loud, profane and even violent at times toward his players and everyone else with whom he had contact."

That was enough for Brand. In May, he suspended Knight for three games, fined him $30,000 and announced a "zero tolerance" policy on future misbehavior.

Four months later, Knight misbehaved again. On September 7, 2000, Kent Harvey, a freshman standing in line to buy football tickets, spotted the famous coach and called out, "Hey, what's up, Knight?" At that point, according to Harvey and his friends, **Knight grabbed the freshman by the arm, dragged him aside and said, "Show me some fucking respect. I'm older than you."**

Knight claimed that all he'd done was gently touch the lad's elbow and offer some sage advice on the proper use of honorific titles: "My name to you is Coach or Mr. Knight, and you should remember that when you're dealing with elders."

Brand summoned Knight to a meeting. Knight said he couldn't make it—he was scheduled to fly off on a fishing trip. Brand fired him.

After that came the protests and the riot on the president's lawn.

The controversy seemed to break down on ideological lines. Right-wing talk show hosts Rush Limbaugh and Oliver North defended Knight. Former presidents Bush and Ford sent him letters of support. Meanwhile, liberal cartoonist Garry Trudeau mocked the coach and his supporters in *Doonesbury*. And Bill Walton, the leftist former NBA star, wrote that Knight "psychologically terrorizes his players."

But none of that hindered his search for employment. Quite the contrary. In March of 2001, he was hired to coach basketball at Texas Tech.

As Vince Lombardi used to say: "Winning isn't everything, it's the only thing."

Yes, the volatile Knight has a wife, Karen (at a rally after he was fired by Indiana, right). They've been married for 14 years, which attests to her otherworldly patience with a man who, when asked in an NBC interview with Connie Chung how he handles stress, can say, "I think that if rape is inevitable, relax and enjoy it."

Billy the Kid

ILLY MARTIN LOVED WESTERN MOVIES AND LOUIS L'AMOUR novels. He wore a cowboy hat—a black one—and he called himself Billy the Kid. He told his son that if he'd lived back in the Wild West, he would have been a sheriff or a gunfighter.

That sounds about right. Billy was the baseball equivalent of the Wild West gunslingers hired as unlikely lawmen by city fathers who figured they needed a rough, tough bad boy to clean up their towns. Baseball owners hired Billy when they figured they needed a tough, feisty manager to fire up a tepid team.

He did it, too. He was a genius at turning losing teams into winners—at least, for a while. But then the teams would fall apart, and Billy would lose his temper and pick a fight with somebody, and end up getting fired. It happened again and again. **He was a gunslinger who specialized in shooting himself in the foot.**

Billy was possessed by demons that caused him to rage and curse and fight the world for no real reason. But to thousands of his countrymen, he was a hero, a courageous little underdog, a David battling an endless succession of Goliaths. Born in 1928, Alfred Manuel Pesano grew up poor in a tough neighborhood in Berkeley, California. His father left when he was

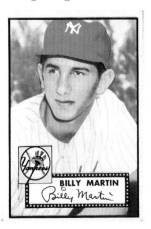

a baby. His mother gave him some advice: *Don't take any crap from anybody.* He never did.

He was a skinny, scrawny, funny-looking kid with a big nose and jug-handle ears, and he'd eagerly fight anybody who pointed that out. He was a scrappy little guy who played the infield well enough to make the New York Yankees back in the glory years of the 1950s, when Yankee Stadium was Olympus and the Yankees were a pantheon of gods.

On a team of giants, he was the little guy, the slap-hitting second baseman who worked harder than anybody else and was always the first guy out of the dugout for a bench-clearing brawl. On a team of heroes, Billy was the hero once: In the 1953 World Series, he hit .500, including two triples and two homers. It was glorious. Being a Yankee hero almost made up for all the indignities of his youth. Almost, but not quite.

In the Yankee dugout, he sat at the right hand of Casey Stengel, learning the art of managing. He loved Casey like the father he'd never had. And Casey, who never had a son, loved Billy and taught him the fine points of strategy. Unfortunately, in 1957, a bunch of Yankees, including Mickey Mantle and Yogi Berra and Martin, got into a barroom brawl at the Copacabana nightclub in New York. It was all over the papers and the

Martin (kicking dirt on rookie ump Dallas Parks during a 1979 game, right) was a man-in-blue's worst nightmare—and, of course, his own. In 1981, he was suspended indefinitely after charging ump Terry Cooney, knocking him backward, then kicking and throwing dirt on his back. "It was like a freight train ran into me," Cooney said. "I've never been run into that hard in my life, not even in college, where I played football."

Yankee brass was embarrassed. Somebody had to be banished from Olympus, and it sure as hell wasn't going to be Mantle or Berra. Casey broke the news to Billy: He'd been traded to Kansas City.

Martin was devastated. He loved being a Yankee and he knew that gods didn't live in Kansas City. He blamed Casey and refused to talk to him. Casey kept calling, but Billy would never come to the phone. He wandered in the wilderness for the next four years—Detroit, Cleveland, Cincinnati, Milwaukee, Minnesota—and his most memorable feat of slugging came when he sucker-punched Cubs pitcher Jim Brewer, shattering his cheekbone and ending his season. Brewer sued Billy and won $10,000.

■ The Pugnacious Skipper

In 1969, Billy became a big league manager, leading the Minnesota Twins to a division title. That year, he punched his ace pitcher, Dave Boswell, outside a bar, blackening his eye. When the season ended, he got fired. That set the pattern for his managing career—first victory, then violence, then good-bye.

He lasted three years in Detroit, winning a division title in 1972. Fired a year later, he went to Texas, taking a terrible team to second place.

Billy knew how to manage. He'd learned it at Casey's right hand. In

He may have looked innocent posing as a young Yankee (above, left) and an angel (to the delight of manager and father figure Casey Stengel, above right), but Martin was born and bred to battle. As sportswriter Red Smith once wrote, "Ever since [he] was a street kid in Oakland, getting into fights under his square name of Alfred Manuel Pesano, he has been characterized by what Joseph Conrad called 'an open, generous, frank, barbarous recklessness.'"

ONCE A HERO

■ Not surprisingly, the play bore Billy Martin's signature pluck, and it happened in one of the World Series' most memorable games. The scenario:1952 Series, Game 7, the Yankees leading the Dodgers 4-2 in the seventh inning.

With one out and the bases loaded, Bob Kuzava retired Duke Snider on a pop-up. The next batter, Jackie Robinson, hit a 3-2 pitch—a high, windblown tricky pop-up that froze the infield.

Said Kuzava to the *Bergen (N.J.) Record*: "Yogi was hollering for (first baseman Joe) Collins, the people were hollering, then here comes Billy."

Martin, playing deep at second, raced in and made a lunging knee-high grab. Two Dodgers had already crossed the plate and the third would have likely scored, if not for Martin's play.

And the Yankees won 4-2, claiming their fourth straight World Series title.

fact, he'd be named Manager of the Year three times.

In 1975, Billy was hired to manage the Yankees. He was thrilled: After 18 years of wandering in the wilderness, he had finally returned to the Promised Land. In 1976, he led them to their first pennant in 12 years. In 1977, he led them to their first World Championship in 15 years. In 1978, however, he couldn't lead them anywhere. He got drunk one night and insulted owner George Steinbrenner and slugger Reggie Jackson, and when Steinbrenner demanded his resignation, Billy left in tears.

In the off-season, he punched a sportswriter in a Reno bar.

In 1979, Steinbrenner brought him back to manage again, but the Yankees finished fourth. In the off-season, Martin punched a marshmallow salesman in a Minnesota bar. A few days later, Steinbrenner fired him.

He was becoming a folk hero—the scrappy little guy who won't take crap from anybody. Chicago columnist Mike Royko, the great champion of the underdog, defended Billy in his battle against evil bosses and obnoxious marshmallow salesmen who pester people in bars. "What Martin really did was strike a blow for civilization and against anarchy," Royko wrote. "And for that he lost his job. It just shows that in the age of jerkism, which we're in, the jerks are winning."

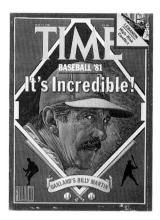

HOW I INVENTED "BILLYBALL"

PHOENIX — THE ONLY ONE OF ITS KIND. AT THE END OF A CERTAIN NUMBER OF YEARS, IT WAS SAID TO MAKE A NEST OF SPICES, SING A MELODIOUS DIRGE, FLAP ITS WINGS TO SET FIRE TO THE PILE, CONSUME ITSELF IN THE ASHES, BUT COME FORTH WITH NEW LIFE TO REPEAT THE FORMER ONE.

HEY, THIS IS KINDA FUN... TOASTIN' MARSHMALLOWS

■ Billy Martin was volatile, confrontational, the more violent the better, and he was also a superior tactician in the ways of winning a big league ball game. As to whether or not he was also certifiable, well, in the long run, aren't we all?

Martin, shunned by his beloved Yankees, who had won two World Series in '77 and '78 with him managing, came in to manage the Oakland A's, or, the "Triple-A's," as they had become known at the time in the San Francisco Bay Area. Martin infused the A's with an aggressive style of sign- and base-stealing, unleashing Rickey Henderson, who stole 100 and 130 bases in separate seasons, and pitched his starters until their arms fell off.

Much in the manner of the business, this aggressive style was given a nickname by a tyro sportswriter in Oakland. The style was called "Billyball;" the writer, *moi*.

In 1980, I had a sports column at *The Oakland Tribune*, and my editor, Bob Valli, sent me to spring training. Right out of the box, I wrote that Billy was a different breed. Being a sometime boxing writer, I also mentioned Martin was said to have a cute little right hand. There was a marshmallow salesman in his future who should've read that.

None of this endeared me to Martin. He said, "I'm complaining. And I'm watching you." Fair enough. I planned on watching him as well.

After watching the A's win four of five spring games, I wrote, "Billy Ball"—later "Billyball."

Billy never complained about that, though he tried to manipulate me to think one of his outfielders was gay. Billy was generally a good source, even as his life came crashing down, but not before the A's won the 1981 divisional title.

Martin left Oakland to go back to New York to coach the Yankees, the tyro sportswriter left Oakland to go to New York to write for *Sports Illustrated*, Al Davis left Oakland to go to Los Angeles and move the Oakland Raiders, which is another story, but somehow fits. Thought I'd mention it.

The last time I saw Billy Martin, it was in the manager's office of the home team at Yankee Stadium. I was having trouble finding an apartment with a new wife and infant son on my hip. Billy suggested I go over to Woodbridge, New Jersey, and look. I did, and rented an apartment there, and that was how Billy had his revenge.

—*Ralph Wiley*

HE SAID, HE SAID

Both Billy Martin and George Steinbrenner were intense, stubborn and pugnacious, and they couldn't resist mouthing off to newspaper reporters and anyone with a microphone. And since the Boss hired Billy Martin five times, only to fire him each time, they said some things about each other that attest powerfully to the love-hate relationship that inevitably resulted.

Martin on Steinbrenner

■ During spring training 1977: "You fat bastard. I don't care what you say!"

■ In July 1978, on Reggie Jackson and the Boss: "One's a born liar, the other's convicted."

■ In October 1981, prior to the ALCS between the Yankees and Billy's A's, he spoke on George's attempts to catch Billy's pitchers throwing spitballs: "Steinbrenner's power and dollars and influence end at the white lines. If necessary, my pitchers will walk to home plate, hand the umpire the ball, take off their clothes and demand to be frisked. We don't cheat and we won't be intimidated again."

■ Prior to the 1988 season, upon being hired for the fifth time: "George wants a winner, and I'm going to give him one. I do know that whatever I decide, George will back me and that I'll never step down, only up. George likes me and is a generous man." Billy lasted only until June before the relationship once again soured and Billy was canned.

■ On June 1988: "If they want to fire me and think it's the best thing, then fire me. If they want me and my pitching coach to go, then we'll go home tomorrow. But I won't ever come back as manager." (Martin was fired later that month and though he never managed the Yanks again, rumors were swirling at the time of his death that he and George had been discussing a sixth pinstriped tour of duty for Billy.)

Steinbrenner on Martin

■ On rehiring him . . . again . . . as manager of the Yankees: "It's like a child doing something bad at the dinner table. You send him to bed without dinner, but he's back down for breakfast in the morning."

■ "Billy said many things in many places under the influence of many things—his drinking or his anger or whatever. Billy was a warrior. And I appreciated that."

■ "Now, in the case of Billy Martin—I loved Billy. I never knew a better manager in baseball. But Billy was sometimes the cause of the firings. At least three of the five times I hired him and fired him, things had happened that prevented me from keeping him on."

■ On Martin's fight with the marshmallow salesman: "When Billy hit this guy, he fell down inches away from one of those huge metal andirons. If the guy hits his head on that, he's dead. Wouldn't that be something, the manager of the Yankees on trial for murder?"

Martin vs. Steinbrenner

■ After a spring training loss to the Mets, they got into one of their frequent shouting matches:
George: "Do you want to be fired right now?"
Billy: "You do whatever you want, but don't yell at me in front of my players."

Despite a seemingly endless series of self-destructive and hostile acts, like this punchout while a Cincinnati Reds player with Cubs pitcher Jim Brewer (left), the Phoenix-like Martin never lacked for managerial opportunities (above, left). He was hired and fired five times by George Steinbrenner alone (with Martin in a beer commercial, far right).

In 1980, Billy went to Oakland and lit a fire under the Athletics. He got them running and stealing and winning. They called it "Billyball," and it was thrilling. The A's won the division title, and Billy made the cover of *Time*.

But after a few years of fun, **the A's crashed to the ground and Billy went into his office and locked the door and started punching the walls, and when he came out, he had a bloody, broken hand.**

He got fired. Mike Royko did not write a column saying that Billy's war against office walls was a blow for civilization.

In 1983, Steinbrenner summoned Billy back to manage the Yankees for the third time, but it didn't work out well.

In April, he was suspended for kicking dirt on an umpire. In May, he got in a fight in a California bar. In June, he smashed a urinal in the clubhouse in Cleveland and cursed out a female sportswriter in the locker room in New York. I happened to be in Yankee Stadium that night, reporting another story, and I saw Billy after the game. He looked gaunt, drawn, pale, his eyes filled with terror—a whipped dog awaiting another beating.

The Yankees finished third. Billy got fired.

Sociopath with a Chip on His Shoulder

He no longer seemed like a folk hero or a scrappy underdog. He seemed like a mean drunk, a sociopath with a chip on his shoulder. "To be around him," wrote columnist George Vecsey, "was to constantly suck in one's breath, fearful that he might start something."

But in 1985, Steinbrenner brought him back for the fourth time. It was crazy. It was an insane soap opera, with George as the ultimate evil boss and Billy as his tormented slave. Billy was drinking heavily, showing

up late, looking like hell. On September 20, he got into a fight in a bar in Baltimore. The next night, he got into another fight in the same bar, this time with one of his pitchers, Ed Whitson. Whitson whipped him bad, breaking Billy's arm. After the season, Billy got fired again.

In 1986, Steinbrenner did not hire Billy. Instead, he announced that August 10 would be Billy Martin Day, and his number would be retired and he'd be honored with a plaque in the pantheon of Yankee greats out past the centerfield fence. **Yankee Stadium was packed that day with fans who saw Billy as a David battling the loathsome Goliath that was George.** They gave Billy a standing ovation and his eyes filled with tears.

But even on that triumphant day, Billy's demons were on view. At a press conference, he was asked: If you could change anything in your life, Billy, what would it be? And Billy said, If he could change one thing in his life, he'd find a certain sportswriter he hated, and he'd kick the man's ass.

Maybe he was kidding. Maybe he wasn't. By then, it was hard to tell.

In 1988, Steinbrenner brought Billy back for the fifth time and the soap opera degenerated into a sad farce. On May 6, Billy threw a tantrum and kicked dirt on an umpire and was fined $300. That night, he got into a fight with two guys in the men's room of a topless bar and was beaten so

In the end, he was his own worst enemy. He wept while reading a statement after resigning as manager of the Yankees—his dream job—in July 1978 (above) after feuding with Steinbrenner and star slugger Reggie Jackson. Few wept—and fewer were surprised —at his funeral in December 1989, which was attended by many other fallen angels, including Steinbrenner, Mickey Mantle and disgraced ex-President Richard Nixon (right).

badly he had to be hospitalized.

On June 2, Billy went into a rage and threw dirt on another umpire and was suspended for three days. Fed up, the umpire's union announced that he would henceforth be ejected as soon as he stepped out of the dugout.

On June 21, the Yankees blew a five-run lead in the ninth and Billy got into his last fight. Let the record show that he won it: He kicked the hell out of the buffet table in the Yankee clubhouse.

Two days later, he was fired again.

"Always an Interesting Show"

By then, Billy the Kid was 60 years old. He and his fourth wife, Jill, bought a country retreat, 148 acres in upstate New York. Jill hoped the change of scene would mellow Billy, keep him out of bars and bar fights.

They were there at the country place on Christmas Day 1989. Billy and a buddy went out that morning about 10 to celebrate the birth of Jesus Christ in a nontraditional way—by bar-hopping. At dusk, they drove home. The streets were snowy. They skidded and crashed. Billy wasn't wearing a seat belt. He flew through the windshield and broke his neck. He was 61.

In his eulogy, Bishop Edwin Broderick paid Billy the ultimate compliment for a tabloid age: "He was always, one must admit, an interesting show." St. Patrick's Cathedral was packed for his funeral and the overflow filled the sidewalks for blocks. Mickey Mantle was there. So were Ron Guidry, Don Mattingly and Phil Rizzuto. And so was another scrappy, hotheaded Californian who'd spent his life in a long battle against the world—Richard Nixon. When the funeral ended, Bishop Broderick said, "May he rest in peace."

That was a good idea. Too bad Billy hadn't tried it earlier.

Hurricane

AYBE WE'LL NEVER KNOW IF RUBIN "HURRICANE" CARTER IS A murderer or a martyr, and maybe it doesn't matter anymore, because Carter is no longer a mere man. He has become a symbol.

Hurricane is a symbol of every innocent black man ever railroaded into prison by racist cops and judges. He is a symbol of black resistance to white oppression. He is a symbol of every evil man who ever entered the hell of prison, only to emerge redeemed, his soul saved by the purifying fires.

Hurricane is a symbol now. And symbols trump facts every time.

But before Rubin Carter became a symbol, before he became a Bob Dylan song, before he became a Denzel Washington movie, he was just a human being, born in 1937 in Clifton, New Jersey. (He would fight out of the nearby decaying old mill town of Paterson, a city made briefly famous by a textile strike that was starved into submission back in 1913.) Rubin Carter was born with a speech impediment that made him stutter, which caused others to mock him, which caused Rubin to lash out in anger.

"When people laughed at me," he said years later, "the only sound they'd hear in reply was the sound of my fist whistling through the air."

He was small but ferocious, a child seething with rage, a thief and brawler well known to the Paterson police. As a kid, he was sent to reform school for breaking a bottle on a man's head during a robbery. As an adult, he served four years in prison for a series of muggings and purse snatchings.

"I was mean as a rattlesnake," he said.

■ Burning with Hatred

In the early '60s, he channeled his rage into boxing, where it brought him money and fame. He would climb into the ring in a long robe, his face hidden beneath a black hood so that when he shook hands with his opponent, all the man would see was two dark eyes burning with hatred. When the bell rang, he charged across the ring, swinging wildly, like an enraged angel of retribution.

A boxing writer said he fought like "a human hurricane," and Rubin took the metaphor for his name. He liked to project an air of evil. He shaved his head and grew a goatee and spouted angry racial rhetoric. **He carried a personal arsenal, and he once shot a cow in a pasture near his training camp, just for the hell of it.** He told a reporter that he wished he'd taken his guns to Harlem after a riot there so he could have shot a few cops—"I know I can get two or three before they get me."

Hurricane blew through the middleweight ranks like a whirlwind, winning most of his fights by knockout, including hammering ex-champ Emile Griffith to the canvas in the first round. In December 1964, he got a shot at the middleweight champion, Joey Giardello. As usual, Hurricane came out swinging. He hit Giardello with his best shots, but the champ

Carter (on the old death row at Trenton State Prison in New Jersey in 1974, right) never stopped fighting, even in prison. Upon entering Trenton, he refused to give up his watch and ring, to shave his goatee, to work at any prison job, to wear prison clothes, to submit to a psychiatric evaluation— in short, to let his spirit be broken in any way.

didn't go down. Giardello hung in there, out-boxing Hurricane and winning a unanimous decision.

Guilty as Charged

After that, Hurricane was never quite as intimidating. He kept fighting, but he won only seven of his last 15 fights, and he dropped from the ranks of contenders. He was 29 years old and headed for obscurity, when he was arrested for a triple murder.

It's a complicated case, with almost every fact in dispute, but here is what is known:

On June 16, 1966, a black bartender was shot dead by a white man in racially polarized Paterson. News of the killing spread fast. At 2:30 the next morning, two black men entered a white bar called the Lafayette Grill and opened fire with a shotgun and pistol, killing the bartender and a customer. A second customer, Hazel Tanis, was severely wounded and died 28 days later. The shots awoke Patricia Valentine, who lived above the bar. She told the cops she saw two black men flee in a white car with distinctive butterfly-shaped taillights. Ten minutes later, the cops stopped a white car with butterfly-shaped taillights. There were two black men inside—John Artis and Rubin Carter. The cops found a shotgun shell and a bullet in the car. Interviewed separately, the two suspects gave conflicting accounts of how they'd spent the evening.

Indicted for three murders, Carter and Artis went to trial in 1967. The main witnesses against them were Valentine and two white thieves, Alfred Bello and Arthur Bradley, who testified that they were burglarizing a building nearby when they saw Carter and Artis leave the bar, Carter carrying a shotgun, Artis with a pistol. The all-white jury reached a verdict: guilty as charged. The judge sentenced both men to life in prison.

Rubin Carter did not go quietly. He warned the guards that if they touched him, they'd better kill him quick, because otherwise he would kill them.

They put him in solitary confinement. They figured that would break his spirit. They were wrong.

"I sat in prison in solitary confinement," he said, "eating hate like it was a succulent morsel of buttered steak."

He kept to himself. He rarely spoke to anyone. He sat in his cell, a boxer with an eighth grade education, writing his autobiography. It took him seven years, but he did it, and *The Sixteenth Round* was published in 1974. It was an eloquent cry of black rage, and it sparked new interest in his case. *The New York Times* reporter Selwyn Raab located Bello and Bradley, and they told him they'd lied about Carter and Artis in exchange for leniency in their own cases.

Their recantation made the front page of the *Times*. In post-Watergate America, people found it easy to believe that Rubin Carter had been framed.

NAME THAT TUNE

"Now all the criminals in their coats and their ties
Are free to drink martinis and watch the sun rise,
While Rubin sits like Buddha in a ten-foot cell,
An innocent man in a living hell."

Some, like Bob Dylan's "Hurricane" (1975), are stirring. Others are fond tributes, still others light-hearted. When lyrics invoke famous sports names, you'd expect irreverency, as is true of many of these songs that are named for or include the names of well-known athletes.

"Slide Kelly Slide," Maggie Cline, 1889 (Mike "King" Kelly, a Hall of Famer, was renowned for his baserunning exploits)

"Joltin' Joe DiMaggio," Les Brown and His Orchestra, 1941

"Let's Go Joe," Cab Calloway and His Orchestra (Joe Louis), 1942

"Did You See Jackie Robinson Hit that Ball?" Buddy Johnson, 1949

"Say Hey (The Willie Mays Song)," The Treniers, 1954

"Mrs. Robinson," Simon & Garfunkel (DiMaggio), 1968

"Van Lingle Mungo," Dave Frishberg, 1970 (This Brooklyn Dodgers All-Star pitcher of the '30s was known for his tempestuousness)

"Let It Flow (for Dr. J.)," Grover Washington Jr., 1980

"Talkin' Baseball," Terry Cashman (Mays, Mickey Mantle, Duke Snider), 1981

"Centerfield," John Fogerty (Mays, Ty Cobb, DiMaggio), 1985

"I Think I Can Beat Mike Tyson," DJ Jazzy Jeff and The Fresh Prince, 1989

"Magic Johnson," Red Hot Chili Peppers, 1989

"We Didn't Start the Fire," Billy Joel (DiMaggio, Mantle), 1989

"Vogue," Madonna (DiMaggio), 1990

"Scenario," A Tribe Called Quest (Bo Jackson), 1991

Intro to *"Eat the Rich,"* Aerosmith (Babe Ruth), 1993

"Ty Cobb," Soundgarden, 1996

"I-76," G. Love & Special Sauce (Maurice Cheeks, Julius Erving, Darryl Dawkins, Bobby Jones, Andrew Toney, Moses Malone, Charles Barkley, Larry Bird, Jerry Stackhouse, Allen Iverson), 1997

"Lie To Kick It," 2Pac (Michael Jordan, Tyson), 1997

"Michael Jordan Returns," Space Jam soundtrack, James Newton-Howard, 1997

"Tyson Bites," John Landecker and Legends, 1997

"Sweet Beatrice," Adam Sandler (Guy Lafleur, Robert Parish), 1997

"Gettin' Jiggy Wit It," Will Smith (Shaquille O'Neal, Muhammad Ali), 1997

"What Would Brian Boitano Do," "South Park: Bigger Longer & Uncut" soundtrack, DVDA, 1999

"Loaded," Ricky Martin (Sammy Sosa), 2000

"Michael Jordan," Five For Fighting, 2000

"Mighty Healthy," Ghostface Killah (Derek Jeter), 2000

"That's How I Beat Shaq," Aaron Carter, 2000

"5Gether," 2Gether soundtrack (Tiger Woods), 2000

"Live From the Streets," Angie Martinez (Latrell Sprewell), 2001

"Run Yo Shit," Foxy Brown (Jeter), 2001

KO IN COURT

■ Joey Giardello wanted his day in court, too.

On December 14, 1964, Rubin Carter, 27, had his title shot, when he took on the 35-year-old Giardello for the undisputed middleweight crown.

Although Carter lost a unanimous decision, he did bloody the champ's eye in the fourth round, and caught him with his powerful left hook in the sixth. Carter moved in for the knockout both times, but Giardello tied him up.

The outcome wasn't controversial, though the 1999 movie, *The Hurricane*, starring Denzel Washington, portrayed the decision as racially motivated.

In the real world, Jerry Izenberg, who covered the fight for the *Newark Star-Ledger*, scored it 10-5 in favor of Giardello, and sportswriter Jesse Abramson noted that the ringside press agreed with the result by a 3-1 ratio.

So Giardello filed a defamation suit against the film's producers, alleging that the movie had fictionalized the fight. The suit was settled out of court for an undisclosed figure. "I beat Carter fair and square," Giardello told the *Philadelphia Daily News.* "I just wanted to set the record straight, and I think it has been."

Carter lost the two biggest fights of his life—for the middleweight title against Joey Giardello (above right); and his trial on triple murder charges (at bottom right, he leaves the Passaic County courthouse after sentencing with co-defendant John Artis, at left in photo). Folksinging legend Bob Dylan, who believed that at least the second fight was fixed, wrote a song about the case, "Hurricane."

Bob Dylan wrote a protest song about the case:
Here comes the story of the Hurricane,
the man the authorities came to blame
for somethin' that he never done . . .

Muhammad Ali led a protest march. Celebrities flocked to Carter's cause—Burt Reynolds, Bill Bradley, Stevie Wonder, Candice Bergen.

When a New Jersey judge ordered a new trial, Ali put up Hurricane's bail.

The prosecutor offered Carter a deal: If he passed a lie detector test, they would drop the charges. Carter refused. He said he didn't trust lie detector tests.

So, in 1976, there was a second trial. **This time, the defendants had high-powered attorneys. This time, there were two black people on the jury. This time, the world was watching.**

Again, the prosecution put Bello on the stand. He recanted his recantation. He said he'd changed his story because Carter's lawyers promised him money. He swore he saw Carter and Artis leave the Lafayette Grill carrying guns. He wasn't the only witness to recant. Three of Carter's alibi witnesses from the first trial testified that they had lied to help Hurricane.

Carter declined to testify in his own defense. He said he feared the prosecutors would grill him about the angry racial rhetoric in his book.

In the end, the integrated jury came back with the same verdict as the all-white jury: guilty as charged.

The celebrities went back home, and after nine months of sweet freedom, Rubin Carter went back to prison. Devastated, he cut off all communication with his supporters and his lawyers and even with his wife and children. He sat in his cell all night long, living on soup he heated with an electric coil, reading philosophy, mysticism, metaphysics.

After 19 Years . . . Freedom

One day in 1980, Carter opened a letter from Lesra Martin, a 17-year-old black kid from Brooklyn who had been adopted by a group of white leftists living in a commune in Toronto. Inspired by *The Sixteenth Round*, Martin wanted to meet Hurricane. Carter agreed and the boy visited. So did the leader of the commune, Lisa Peters. Later, Peters and other communards moved to Jersey to work as researchers for the lawyers preparing Carter's appeal.

In 1985, Judge H. Lee Sarokin granted the appeal and reversed Carter's conviction, ruling that it had been based on "an appeal to racism rather than reason."

This time, the prosecutors opted not to try Hurricane again. After 19 years, Rubin Carter was finally free.

He joined the commune and married Peters. But he chaffed under the group's strict discipline, and he quit the commune and divorced Peters

DEAF, DUMB AND BLIND JUSTICE

Rubin Carter was imprisoned for 19 years before he finally gained his freedom. In the past century, there have been several other high-profile cases in which there were serious reservations about the accused party's (or parties') "guilt."

■ Eugene Debs: In 1920, the labor organizer and Socialist Party candidate ran for U.S. president from jail; he had criticized the government's prosecution of persons charged with sedition. He was released by presidential order in 1921; his citizenship, which he lost when convicted of sedition in 1918, was restored in 1976.

■ Nicola Sacco and Bartolomeo Vanzetti: The two Italian immigrants/anarchists (above), were arrested for the murder of a paymaster and his guard. They were sentenced to death in 1927 and were executed despite massive public demonstrations throughout the world. In 1977, Massachusetts Gov. Michael Dukakis signed a proclamation stating that they had not been treated justly, thus clearing their names.

■ The Hollywood Ten (producers, directors and writers, including Ring Lardner Jr. and Dalton Trumbo): In 1947, they refused to answer questions from the House Un-American Activities Committee regarding possible communist affiliations. After spending six months to a year in prison for contempt of Congress, they were blacklisted by studios for years. Some were able to work under pseudonyms, while others never worked in the industry again.

■ Alger Hiss: In 1950, the former U.S. State Department official was convicted of perjury for his communist links and acts of possible espionage, and served 44 months in jail before he was released. He maintained his innocence for the rest of his life.

■ Dr. Samuel Sheppard: He served 10 years for the 1954 murder of his wife, only to be freed when the Supreme Court ruled that he did not have a fair trial. In 1998, genetic tests provided "conclusive evidence" of his innocence.

■ Leonard Peltier: An activist in the American Indian Movement, he has spent 26 years in prison for the murder of two FBI agents. Peltier was at the scene of the crime, but his supporters contend that evidence was tampered with.

■ Mumia Abu-Jamal: The former Black Panther, radio journalist and prison author is serving a life sentence (a federal judge in 2001 voided his death sentence) for the 1981 murder of a police officer, a crime for which he—and his many supporters—has maintained his innocence.

■ Wen Ho Lee: The former Los Alamos nuclear scientist was accused of spying for China and spent nine months in solitary confinement in 2000. He was finally freed after being cleared of most charges.

and told a reporter that they'd used him as their "trophy horse."

Hollywood bought his story and turned it into a movie starring Denzel Washington, who'd already played two black martyrs, Steve Biko and Malcolm X.

In the movie, Carter didn't go to reform school for a mugging, he went for defending a playmate from a molester. In the movie, he didn't lose to Giardello, the fight was stolen by racist judges. In the movie, he was an innocent man framed by the same racist cop who had railroaded him into reform school as a kid. When Washington won a Golden Globe award, he brought Hurricane up on stage and said: "This man right here is love. He is all love."

There was some protest. A few reporters pointed out that Carter's car was seen at the Lafayette Grill that night, that a bullet and a shotgun shell were found in it, that he'd been found guilty twice. The daughter who watched Hazel Tanis die 28 days after she was shotgunned said that her mother was certain that Carter was the killer. A woman who'd worked on Carter's defense team during the second trial said he got drunk one night and beat her so badly that she was hospitalized.

But none of it mattered. **Rubin Carter was no longer merely a man. He had become a symbol. And symbols trump facts every time.**

He spoke at the White House. He spoke at the United Nations. He spoke of love and peace and forgiveness. He set up a foundation to free the unjustly imprisoned. He took up gardening. He seemed mellow, gentle, almost saintly.

"I would not change one thing in my life, not one single thing," he told an interviewer. "Everything that went before has made me what I am today. And today I am deeply and seriously in love with myself."

Superstar actor Denzel Washington (above, with Carter) played the ex-boxer in a movie—The Hurricane—that many critics excoriated for the liberties it took with historical accuracy in the name of drama.

America's Greatest Living Hero

IT'S HARD TO REMEMBER NOW, AFTER ALL THAT HAS HAPPENED since, but not so long ago, O.J. Simpson was an affable angel of integration, a sweet-smiling symbol of how easy racial reconciliation could be.

Now, after the brutal murders and the televised trial, he is the symbol of precisely the opposite—of how enduring and intractable America's racial divide remains.

Thanks to CNN, O.J. Simpson is the most famous bad boy in American sports history. Indeed, he is one of the most famous human beings on the planet, his face recognizable to millions of people who could not tell you what position he played—perhaps not even what *sport*. He will be forever famous not as one of the greatest running backs in football history, but as the star of the most widely watched murder trial in human history.

Orenthal James Simpson was born in 1947 in Potrero Hills, a poor black section of San Francisco. He had rickets as a child and hobbled along on homemade braces. But he recovered and he grew strong and fast. He excelled in sports but frequently got into trouble for joyriding in stolen cars. A mentor who recognized his potential—and his problems—arranged for him to have dinner with Willie Mays. The giant of the Giants told O.J. that he could be a star if he just stayed out of trouble, and the boy took the lesson to heart.

At the University of Southern California, O.J. was an awesome combination of size, strength and speed. On the track team, he ran on a record-breaking relay. On the football team, he set 19 individual running records. In 1967, he led his team to a 21-20 victory over rival UCLA in what might have been the greatest college football game ever played, scoring the winning touchdown on a beautiful 64-yard run. The following year, he gained 1,709 yards, scored 22 touchdowns and won the Heisman Trophy.

"Simpson was not only the greatest player I ever had," said his coach John McKay, "he was the greatest player anyone ever had."

Drafted by the dismal Buffalo Bills, his talents were wasted for two years as a decoy in a pass-oriented offense. But when coach Lou Saban took over in 1972, he gave Simpson the ball and cut him loose, and the Juice responded by winning the NFL rushing title—the first of four times in five seasons. The next year, O.J. broke Jim Brown's single-season rushing record by scoring 2,003 yards—200 of them in the unforgettable season finale against the Jets in a raging snowstorm.

But the numbers don't tell his story or capture his glory. He was a joy to watch, banging his way through the line like a bull, then gliding down the field with the grace of a gazelle. The Juice was a glorious hunk of humanity with the physique of a classical sculpture and the face of a matinee idol. He had a bright smile and a sunny disposition. And in an era of racial

If ever an American sports star led a schizoid existence, it was Simpson (kissing then fiancée Nicole Brown at Dodger Stadium in 1980, right; and booked for her murder 14 years later, left).

JUICE ON THE LOOSE

The Juice's records after he finished playing for USC in the Pac-10 and retired from the NFL are impressive, especially considering his NCAA stats were for only two seasons, and most of his pro seasons consisted of 14 games, compared with the 16 played today. Many of his records have been erased, but he still has a foothold in the record books (designated by "★").

Pac-10

SEASON
Rushing yards, 1,709 (NCAA record)
Carries, 355 (NCAA record)
★ Rushing touchdowns, 22
(tied with three others)
Points, 138
CAREER
Rushing yards, 3,423
★ Yards per game, 164

NFL

GAMES
★ Consecutive, 200-yard rushing, 2 (tied)
SEASON
Rushing yards, 2,003
100-yard rushing games, 11 (tied)
200-yard rushing games, 3
CAREER
★ 200-yard rushing games, 6

tension, he wasn't angry or militant or sullen.

O.J. wasn't like other black athletes. He wasn't like Muhammad Ali, who joined a religion that was vehemently anti-white and who refused to be drafted to fight in Vietnam. O.J. wasn't like Tommie Smith and John Carlos, the sprinters who celebrated their Olympic triumph by raising their clenched, black-gloved fists in the air during "The Star-Spangled Banner."

O.J. wasn't interested in protest. Harry Edwards, the radical academic who served as political guru to Smith and Carlos, tried to recruit O.J. into the movement. So did Jim Brown, the militant ex-running back. But they got nowhere. "It wasn't in me to do it," O.J. explained. "Everybody can't be Martin Luther King."

O.J. was a black man who white folks found appealing, and that proved to be a very lucrative talent. In 1975, O.J. became the first black man to star in a national TV ad campaign—scooting through airports to promote Hertz rental cars. Those ads were so successful—and O.J. was so appealing—that he was hired to hawk Chevrolet cars, Firestone tires, RC cola and Foster Grant sunglasses. Meanwhile, his popularity led to movie roles and a brief part in TV's *Roots*.

In 1976, a poll of fifth graders, conducted by the *Ladies' Home Journal*, named him "America's greatest living hero."

His private life was, however, less than heroic. He philandered as flagrantly as any other superstar, divorced his childhood sweetheart and married Nicole Brown, a blonde he'd begun dating when she was barely out of

O.J. was the ultimate runner: first, as a star back with USC and the Buffalo Bills (above left); then as the first major "crossover" national TV endorser (running through airports for Hertz, above right); and finally from the police in a white Bronco on that surreal day in June of 1994.

A PARTIAL—AND PAINFUL—FILMOGRAPHY

O.J. Simpson's films, commercials and TV appearances may have helped pave the way for other Afro-American athletes in Hollywood. But at what cost to the viewing public? For his performance in Naked Gun 33 1/3: The Final Insult, *he "won" a 1994 Razzie for worst supporting actor from the Golden Raspberry Award Foundation. This, of course, was not Simpson's only forgettable performance:*

The Towering Inferno (1974)
Plot: Cheap wiring in the world's tallest skyscraper causes it to go up in flames.
Role: Security chief Harry Jernigan.
Showstopper: When the monitors signal trouble, he says "Something's screwed up." Later, as a fireball engulfs a man, Jernigan yells, "Call an ambulance for this man ... Dammit, man! Get on the ball! Call an ambulance!!"
Epilogue: Atypically, O.J.'s character survives, and saves a cat.

The Cassandra Crossing (1976)
Plot: Terrorists try to spread a disease on a luxury train.
Role: Inspector Haley goes undercover as Father Haley.
Showstopper: To one impatient passenger, he says, "Better one day late in Paris than 20 years early in Heaven."
Epilogue: Haley is killed by a bullet in the back.

Hambone and Hillie (1984)
Plot: Family film about an old woman and her lost dog trying to find each other.
Role: Tucker the Trucker, who befriends the dog on the East Coast.
Showstopper: When he notices the dogtags are from L.A., he says, "Jeez Louise, you're really out of the ballpark." He fancies the dog as a driving companion, discards Hambone's tags, and tells the pup, "Better get rid of this collar, boss. One thing I've learned . . . 'you gotta bury the past.'"
Epilogue: The dog abandons Tucker at a truckstop.

Naked Gun series (1988, '91, '94)
Plots: The misadventures of L.A.'s Keystone Kops led by Lt. Frank Drebin (Leslie Nielsen).

Role: Simpleminded Det. Nordberg, who in *From the Files of Police Squad*, takes on a roomful of drug dealers alone and is shot countless times but manages to survive.
Showstopper: In *Final Insult*, after a rough day, George Kennedy's character, Ed Hocken, asks Drebin if he needs anything. Nordberg chimes in: "Like Dr. Kevorkian's home phone number!"
Epilogue: Do cops protect their own? In 1996, Nielsen was asked by the *Chicago Sun-Times* about O.J. appearing in another *Naked Gun*: "O.J. would just be too controversial to be in it."

CIA: Code Name Alexa (1992)
Plot: B movie king Lorenzo Lamas stars in a microchip caper.
Role: Nick Murphy, a maverick machine gun-toting cop, who wants to avenge his partner's death.
Showstopper: The video was reissued two years later, after Simpson had been charged with double murder. It was given free as a sales incentive to video stores that bought the sequel, *CIA II: Target Alexa*. The timing was coincidential, and Simpson did not appear in the sequel.
Epilogue: Murphy is killed as he pursues the terrorists.

No Place to Hide (1993)
Plot: Cop Kris Kristofferson protects Drew Barrymore from the bad guys who killed her sister.
Role: A wheelchair-bound former football player named Allie Wheeler who tries to help.
Showstopper: Though he fights valiantly with a sledgehammer, Wheeler is killed by hitmen.
Epilogue: A *Washington Post* review stated it's "so bad it's not even any good."

high school. He cheated on her, too, and pummeled her so badly one night that she called 911, yelling, "He's gonna beat the shit out of me!" That 911 call would become famous years later. But that night, when the cops arrived at the Simpsons' house, they didn't arrest O.J., they asked him for his autograph. Such is the power of celebrity.

More ugly scenes were followed by a painful divorce, and then, on the night of June 12, 1994, someone stabbed Nicole Brown Simpson and her acquaintance, a waiter named Ron Goldman, to death outside Nicole's door.

The police charged O.J. with murder, and he fled down the freeway in his white Bronco with a pal and a pile of cash. **It was a long, strange, low-speed chase, witnessed by millions on television and hundreds who gathered on the roadway to cheer O.J. on as if he were running for another touchdown.**

Imprisoned for seven months awaiting trial, O.J. spent his time signing autographs, which earned him nearly a million dollars. He spent the money on a legal "dream team"—a gaggle of famous lawyers who attacked every bit of the prosecution's evidence from every conceivable angle.

The angle that worked best was race. The attorneys for one of white America's favorite black men selected a predominantly black jury and then demonized a nasty white cop named Mark Fuhrman as a bigot who hated blacks enough to frame O.J.. That scenario seemed preposterous to most

FIRST CAME JACK JOHNSON

■ Think Muhammad Ali on a larger scale, and you start to form a mental picture of Jack Johnson, who became the first black heavyweight champion in 1908.

Johnson held the title when race relations weren't even a discussion; he cared little what others thought and lived life to its fullest.

Johnson loved to prove his skeptics wrong, too. He won the title from Tommy Burns, and during the match was reported to have told him, "You're white, Tommy —white as the flag of surrender."

Sportswriters and boxing insiders couldn't accept the fact that Johnson was the best, so they begged former champ Jim Jeffries to come out of retirement and take the heavyweight crown away from Johnson. Author Jack London in the *New York Herald* asked The Great White Hope to "remove the golden smile from Jack Johnson's face." London didn't get his wish; on July 4, 1910, Johnson, who taunted Jeffries throughout the match, won when Jeffries' corner threw in the towel in the 15th round. The victory set off race riots in many cities.

Johnson lived in an era when a black male could be lynched for dating a white woman, but he married three and lived with the last one for the final 14 years of his life.

In 1912, Johnson was charged with violating the Mann Act, which outlawed the transporting of women across state lines for immoral purposes, and he was sentenced to a year in prison. (It didn't matter to the jury that the woman in question, Lucille Cameron, was now Johnson's wife.)

He evaded the police, made his way to Canada and then to Europe, where he lived for several years before he went to Havana for a title defense against Jess Willard in 1915. Willard won in the 26th round, but not without controversy; Johnson claimed in his autobiography that he agreed to "lie down" for an additional $50,000, which he said he never received. He came back to the U.S. in 1920 and served eight months in prison at Leavenworth, Kansas.

Johnson also claimed, "There are few men in any period of the world's history who have led a more varied or intense existence than I." Few would argue the point.

He died in a car accident in 1946; he was 68. A year later, O.J. Simpson would be born. Later in life, as a defendant himself, Simpson would benefit from a more enlightened view on fair and equal legal representation, thanks, in part, to Jack Johnson.

whites—*hadn't the LA cops always treated O.J. more like a celebrity than a minority?* But black folks in Los Angeles had been harassed and brutalized so often by white cops that it seemed perfectly plausible to them.

After eight months of trial, the jury deliberated for four hours and then found O.J. not guilty.

When the verdict was broadcast live on TV, millions of people gathered to watch it and photographers across America snapped pictures of blacks rejoicing and whites groaning at the verdict. Those photos were grim, depressing reminders that—even 30 years after the great victories of the Civil Rights movement—America remained profoundly divided along racial lines.

Even O.J. recognized the irony of those images. "I was one of the least racial-issue people in history," he said later, "and all of a sudden I was in the middle of this big racial issue."

■ ## "Bad Boy" Love

There was a second trial, a civil case brought by the relatives of the murder victims. This time, the jury was predominantly white, and it found O.J. liable for the "wrongful deaths" of Nicole Simpson and Ron Goldman and awarded their relatives $33.5 million. The court ordered the auction of O.J.'s belongings, including his Heisman Trophy, which was purchased for $255,500 by a sheet metal dealer who said he wanted to impress his girlfriend. But O.J. had a $300,000 annual pension that the victim's relatives couldn't touch, and he supplemented his income by signing his name on photos and footballs and helmets for $10 a scribble.

In Manhattan one morning in the summer of 2000, he made $10,000 just writing his name—the media age equivalent of the Midas touch.

Polls showed that 80 percent of Americans thought he was guilty of

TOTAL MAKEOVER

In the history of American celebrity-hood, nobody's image ever changed as totally after a single event as O.J. Simpson's after his double murder trial. Consider, as admissible evidence, the following quotes:

Before:

"Simpson is already an actor, an excellent one. A natural one."
—*acting teacher Lee Strasberg*

"(Simpson) can walk into a room and suddenly everyone in it is smiling and feeling amiable. True, celebrities always cause a crowd's pulse to quicken, but O.J. seems to make people glow."
—*writer Lawrence Linderman, (Playboy Interview)*

"There were guys who could have taken O.J., but he had a way of manipulating people, of making them like him, of getting them to do what he wanted."
—*childhood friend Joe Bell*

"He (is) one of the most effective sports figures ever to endorse a product. He prompted Americans to say they were 'pulling an O.J. Simpson' each time they ran through the airport to make a departing flight."
—*Newsday*

After:

"Nobody will ever think of him as a football player again. Clearly what has taken place since 1994 will forever be Simpson's legacy and whatever he did in a sporting sense becomes totally secondary."
—*sportscaster Al Michaels*

"The O.J. of June 12, 1994 is gone. The outgoing personality the public knew, that's gone."
—*lawyer Leo Terrell, one of his staunchest public defenders*

"O.J. is guilty 15 times . . . he won't do any movies; any producer that employs him, I'll be sure, is painted with a big 'S' for 'Shame' . . . O.J. served 16 months for two murders."
—*former Rep. Bob Dornan, R-California*

"O.J. Simpson is in the news. He said he voted in Miami. Finally a voter down there we know can stab through a piece of paper."
—*comedian Jay Leno*

murder, but when he walked down the street, he was greeted with smiles and waves and friendly salutations. Such is the power of celebrity.

He left LA and bought a $625,000 house near Miami, where the laws protected more of his income from his creditors. For a while, he dated a 25-year-old waitress named Christie Prody, but she filed a complaint charging that O.J. had broken into her home in the middle of the night to erase a message on her answering machine. Despite that incident, and despite the fact that he may have killed two people, he found that women—sometimes five or six a day—slipped him their phone numbers.

Why did they do that? Was it his fame? His money? His looks? His reputation? He pondered those questions. He concluded that it had something to do with America's enduing love of bad boys and women's age-old love of dangerous men.

"There's this thing that, historically, all the most gorgeous models and stuff are attracted to the bad-boy rock-and-roll guys," he told writer Anthony Haden-Guest. "So I tried to understand it in those terms. **Someone who doesn't know me, who's never had a conversation with me—why would they be willing to come to my house and have sex with me?** Obviously, part of it has to do with fame. And then there's a certain fear. These girls fall in love with the bad boys. They marry 'em. Two or three years later, everybody is feeling sorry for the Pamela Lees or the whoever, *because the bad boy did exactly what attracted them to him!*"

O.J. Simpson has learned a lot about the dark side of the American psyche. He may understand us better than we understand ourselves.

Will the real O.J. please stand up? He is skewered in Doonesbury (above, far left) during his double-murder trial, in which he was found not guilty. An angry crowd greets him after his civil trial in LA in 1997 (above), in which he was found liable in the deaths of his wife, Nicole, and her friend, Ron Goldman. In less complicated times, he gives his son Jason, then 2, a piggyback ride in Buffalo in 1973 (below).

Hollywood

S O MANY FALLEN ANGELS, SO LITTLE SPACE.

The Big John Baals of American sport have been with us for decades, and they just keep on coming, an endless array of Dickensian rogues, knaves and fools, each with a story fit for a tabloid headline or a soap opera.

There's Sonny Liston, who was a thief, ex-con and head-breaker for the mob before knocking out Floyd Paterson to win the heavyweight championship in 1962. Liston was a surly, nasty bully, but plenty of boxing fans and sportswriters preferred his sullen viciousness to the young Cassius Clay's ebullient braggadocio. In their 1964 title fight, thousands rooted for Liston to shut the bum's mouth. But Sonny couldn't do it. Clay pummeled Liston, who promptly quit, losing his title by sitting on his stool. Six years later, he died of a heroin overdose.

There's Mike Tyson, who admired Liston enough to lay a wreath on his grave a few days before fighting Evander Holyfield for the heavyweight title. Tyson was a ghetto guttersnipe who was adopted by the saintly boxing manager Cus D'Amato, who treated him like a son and set him on the path of righteousness. But then D'Amato died and Tyson went astray, serving time for rape and later for assault. Like Liston, he was a thug who got frustrated when he couldn't win easily. Finding himself losing to Holyfield, Tyson bit off a piece off the champion's ear. Apparently, that didn't satisfy Tyson's taste for human flesh, because he later told heavyweight champ Lennox Lewis, "I want to eat your children . . . "

There's Tonya Harding, who rose from a trailer park childhood to becomes one of the little princesses of American sport—a champion figure skater. **A chain-smoking, beer-drinking, truck-driving, pool-shooting kinda gal, Tonya showed that the "ladies" of skating could be just as nasty as the bad boys of sport.** After her bodyguard and ex-husband hired a friend to kneecap chief rival Nancy Kerrigan, Harding admitted that she'd withheld information from the cops, and she pled guilty to a felony count of "hindering prosecution."

After that, her life became an absurd soap opera: She sold her wedding-night videos to *Penthouse*. She became a national joke, a symbol of the only minority group it was still permissible to mock—the Redneck.

When she attempted a comeback, the crowd booed so loudly she could barely hear her music. She drove her car into a tree one night and claimed that she'd been kidnapped by a "bushy-haired" man. She tried another comeback, saying that she'd grown up, matured by blissful domesticity with her new love, Darren Silver.

"I'm a lady now," she said. Six months later, she was jailed for hitting Silver with a hubcap.

There's Darryl Strawberry, the great, graceful outfielder with the sweet, sweet swing, who became another human soap opera. First he got busted for threatening his wife with a gun. Then he went into rehab for alcoholism. Then he became a born-again Christian. Then he was arrested for hitting the woman who would later become his second wife. Then he got busted for tax fraud. Then he went back into rehab, this time for cocaine addiction. Then he failed a drug test and was suspended from baseball. Then he was diagnosed with colon cancer and underwent surgery. Then he was busted for possession of cocaine and soliciting an undercover policewoman for prostitution. Then he and his wife wrote an inspirational book about how he'd beat cancer and addiction. Then he failed another drug test and was suspended again. Then his cancer returned. Then he was busted for smoking crack. Then . . .

There's Rae Carruth, the Carolina Panthers wide receiver convicted of conspiracy to commit murder for hiring a hit man to murder his pregnant girlfriend.

There's Ray Lewis, the Baltimore Ravens linebacker who was busted for a double murder on the night of the 2000 Super Bowl game, pled guilty to obstructing a police investigation, and then went on to earn the MVP at the 2001 Super Bowl.

There's . . . but wait. Hold it. Stop right there. I could go on listing fallen angels forever, but that's enough. We all know dozens of these stories by heart, the way earlier generations knew Bible stories. And, like Bible stories, they are cautionary tales that teach moral lessons to the young: *Don't do that, son, or you'll end up like Darryl Strawberry.*

These days, the rise and fall of sports heroes has itself become a kind of spectator sport. The scenes on TV are so familiar they've become cliches: The fallen hero led away by cops, his head bowed in shame . . . His fellow players urging that he be given a second (or third, or fourth) chance . . . The fallen hero emerging from the courthouse, announcing that he wants to "put this behind me" and "get on with my life" . . .

If we loved the fallen one, we root for him to overcome his troubles and rise again. If we hated the bum, we gloat at his comeuppance. Either way, we get an opportunity to feel superior: *No way I'd be dumb enough to throw away a million-dollar job and a beautiful wife for a toot of coke and a cheap floozy!*

In a perverse way, these bad-boy athletes can be as inspiring as the good boys. Watching Michael Irvin, the Cowboys wide receiver, make a leaping, spinning catch at full speed with a defender on his back, you think, "I'll never be that good," which is kind of depressing. But watching Michael Irvin, husband and father of two, get caught in a hotel room with cocaine, marijuana, sex toys and two women who describe themselves as "self-employed models," you think, "I'll never be that bad," and you feel kind of virtuous. (Or maybe not. Maybe you think: *Boy, there's a guy who really knows how to have fun.*)

The self-destructive fall of a sports hero is great theater, full of low comedy and high tragedy. But it is more than that. It is the playing out,

Fallen angels and their favorite body parts: Mike Tyson took a healthy bite out of Evander Holyfield's ear (left); Tonya Harding (above, at left) went after Nancy Kerrigan's kneecaps (above, at right); and Darryl Strawberry found his wrists in handcuffs for the umpteenth time (right), after violating conditions of his probation on drug charges in early 2002.

over and over again, of the three great mythic narratives of American democracy.

The first narrative is the rags-to-riches story—Lincoln rising from the log cabin to the White House, Booker T. Washington's *Up from Slavery*, the Horatio Alger stories. American sports history is full of tales of humble lads rising from the orphanage or the farm or the ghetto to superstardom. We love these stories, because they show that anybody can make it in America if they have talent and work hard.

The second narrative is the fall of the mighty. This is the reverse of the rags-to-riches story, but it is equally democratic. It's the tale of the powerful destroyed by their own hubris or folly—Custer at Little Bighorn, Nixon in Watergate, the fall of countless hypocritical preachers and pols. In sports, this is the story of the fallen angels—Rose brought down by his greed, Strawberry ruined by his addiction, Cobb and Knight destroyed by their rage. We love these stories, because they show that the people at the top are no better than the rest of us, and that they, too, must pay for their sins.

The third narrative is redemption. It's the story of second chances, of being born again—the fallen sinner saved by the grace of God or the love of a good woman or the magic of the Betty Ford Clinic. This story is at the heart of such enduring American institutions as the revival meeting and Alcoholics Anonymous: The sinner confesses and repents and is redeemed. We love this story, because it shows that nobody is too wretched to be saved. And it explains why Strawberry kept getting second chances (he confessed and repented) and why Rose didn't (he refused to admit he'd bet on baseball).

These narratives are as powerful as Greek myths or Bible stories. They are how we Americans explain ourselves to ourselves.

And sometimes all three of these mythic narratives come together in one incredible story. Such is the amazing tale of Hollywood Henderson—which just might be the sports bad-boy story to end all sports bad-boy stories.

■ From Rags to Riches to Rags

Thomas Henderson was born in 1953 in a tough ghetto neighborhood on the east side of Austin, Texas, with "illegitimate" stamped on his birth certificate. His mother scrubbed floors and his stepfather pumped gas. There were seven kids and not enough beds, so he slept with his brothers and awoke perfumed with urine. He was a terrific high school linebacker, but no college seemed to want him, except Langston University, an obscure black school in Oklahoma. He was great there, too, and the Dallas Cowboys grabbed him in the first round of the 1975 draft.

He was quick on his feet, a star linebacker for the legendary Cowboy team that went to the Super Bowl three times. He was quick with his tongue, too. The man gave good quote, like the line about how Steelers quarterback Terry Bradshaw was so dumb he couldn't spell cat if you spotted him the "c" and the "a." Henderson ran his mouth like Muhammad Ali

No Rays of sunshine: Former Carolina Panthers wide receiver Rae Carruth (above) was found guilty of conspiracy to murder his pregnant girlfriend; Ray Lewis (right), All-Pro linebacker of the Baltimore Ravens and MVP of the 2001 Super Bowl, pled guilty to obstructing justice after two men were stabbed to death on the night of the 2000 Super Bowl.

Hollywood Henderson (right) overcame a lot to make it with the Cowboys—deserted by his father at birth, poor, illegitimate, poorly educated, unrecruited by major colleges, self-destructive and, eventually, addicted to coke. During the coin toss for Super Bowl X, Henderson, captain of the special teams, remembers thinking, "Here I am, this dysfunctional black bastard in the biggest game in the world, and if they really knew me, they'd throw me out of here."

QUOTE MACHINE

Whether he was up or down at the time, Hollywood Henderson always had something to say—often funny, occasionally poignant, on very rare occasions wise.

■ A child of big-city poverty, Henderson wound up playing football at Langston University in Oklahoma, where it was his custom to suit up and dash into the opponents' locker room an hour before the game and say, "I'm Thomas Henderson, and you better touch me now, 'cause when the game starts you won't get near me."

■ He assessed his prospects in 1979 as follows: "I'm tall, talented, neat in the waist, cute in the face, and they call me 'Hollywood.' How can I lose?"

■ He once explained his nickname, given to him by teammates in his junior year at Langston, this way: "Hollywood was sort of an alter ego of drug addiction and women. Hollywood never played football. He was hanging out with Marvin Gaye and doing wild things."

■ The man knew he gave good interview, once explaining: "I could talk a hungry cat off a fish truck."

■ On his own hitting ability: "I hit Archie Griffin so hard, I knocked the Heisman Trophy off his dresser at home."

■ On his own place in the hierarchy of great linebackers: "People can talk about Lawrence Taylor all they want. I believe, to this day, I was the best all-around linebacker to ever play the game."

Guys like Lawrence Taylor were defensive ends calling themselves linebackers. They couldn't cover Terry Metcalf one-on-one, couldn't cover Chuck Foreman one-on-one and couldn't cover O.J. one-on-one like I could."

■ On his frequent and massive use of "recreational" drugs . . . before they ruined his life: "Don't think I was loaded all the time. But that natural ebullience, sometimes it wasn't just the champagne. At Super Bowl XII, a guy gives me an ounce (of cocaine) for two tickets. I go into the john, come out and the press is talking to me. I suddenly got a lot to say."

■ On the effect of his arrest on one count of sexual assault and two counts of false imprisonment after he said he had smoked crack with two teen-age women in his apartment: He said he could not pursue an acting career because "(my) starring role as a crack addict would not allow me to audition for other parts."

■ On how his addictions are always with him, even the night he found out he hit the lottery for $28 million: "Man, this physical strain came over me. I felt like the weight of the world was on me that night. I felt the fear. Y'know, could I handle it? Could I stay sober? Because it was a great moment for champagne. It was a great time for some cocaine."

and strutted his stuff in Superfly suits and a calf-length beaver coat. Pretty soon they started calling him "Hollywood."

That was the first narrative, the rags-to-riches story.

Hollywood became rich and famous. He made a ton of money but he blew it all on clothes, women, whiskey and cocaine. Particularly cocaine.

By 1978, he was playing with a Vicks' inhaler full of coke hidden in his uniform. By 1979, after a wretched game against the Redskins—he stunk on the field, then made a fool of himself on the sideline, mugging for the TV cameras—the Cowboys cut him.

The 49ers gave him a second chance. The Oilers gave him a third chance. But the coke gave him no chance at all. By 1981, he was gone—washed up and strung out. In November of 1983, he hit bottom: He was busted in Long Beach, California, for trading crack for sex from two teenage girls, one of them in a wheelchair.

That was the second narrative—the fall of the mighty.

He spent 28 months in jail, but he came out clean and he stayed clean. He married a woman he met in rehab and moved back to Austin. He started running his mouth again, this time as a motivational speaker, preaching against drugs for $7,500 a speech. He earned enough money to buy a nice house and a Mercedes. Then he decided to do something for his old East Austin neighborhood. He spent his own money transforming a run-down, abandoned high school football field into a fancy sports facility, complete with lights and a scoreboard. After that, Hollywood figured that East Austin needed a track-and-field facility, too. So he announced that he was going on a hunger strike until he raised enough money to build it. He pitched a tent on a ghetto street corner and he moved into it, living on water spiced with red pepper, maple syrup and lemon juice.

And it worked. He raised $250,000 and he built the track. Hollywood had become some kind of ghetto Gandhi.

That was the third narrative—redemption, the sinner born again. It was amazing! It was uplifting! It was downright inspirational!

But wait. There's more.

A Wealthy Clairvoyant

Hollywood bought lottery tickets—hundreds of them, *thousands* of them—because he knew he was going to win. He just *knew* it. And then, in March of 2000, he *did* win. He hit the big one—worth $28 million over 20 years. But Hollywood didn't want the money over 20 years. He wanted it now. So he cashed the ticket in for a lump-sum payment of $10.7 million. He gave 10 grand to the guy who sold him the ticket, and then he announced that he would spend a million bucks building low-cost housing in East Austin.

Incredible! **It's one of these stories that's so unbelievable that it has to be true, because nobody could possibly make it up. Hollywood's life was more Hollywood than anything ever created by Hollywood**, more bizarre than anything in *The Great American Novel*.

No self-respecting writer would ever end a story with the hero hitting the lottery for 10 million bucks and then giving a million away. It's too corny. Too unbelievable.

Hollywood Henderson's story is too bizarre to be written by a mere mortal. It could only be created by the Great Narrator in the Sky—He Who Has No Editor.

Which makes you wonder: Maybe God loves these fallen angels as much as we do.

Not even Hollywood could have imagined this Hollywood. Even before hitting the lottery for $28 million in March of 2000 (he took $10.7 million instead in a lump-sum payout), Henderson had donated and gone on a hunger strike to raise the $250,000 to build this track-and-field facility in Austin, Texas. During his hunger strike, "one woman brought her grandchildren, these two little white girls who were running and playing with no idea that they might get mugged or propositioned or worse. I'm watching her watching them. Then she walks over and puts a thousand-dollar check in my jug."

THERE ARE

CERTAIN LIVES IN SPORT SO BRIEF AND DAZZLING THAT THEY CAST A LIGHT THAT LINGERS LONG AFTER ITS SOURCE HAS BEEN EXTINGUISHED. IF THE TIMES AND PLACES THEY LIT WERE DARK, THE INTENSITY OF THEIR SUDDEN FLARING LEAVES AN AFTERGLOW THAT STAYS FOR LIFE UPON THE RETINAS OF THOSE WHO SAW THAT TIME AND PLACE TRANSFIGURED.

THE MIND'S EYE IS INDELIBLY MARKED, AND THOSE WHO CARRY THE MARK ARE BOUND TO ONE ANOTHER BY AN EXCLUSIVITY OF EXPERIENCE THAT CANNOT BE TRANSMITTED. YOU HAD TO BE THERE.

SAINTS

by Le Anne Schreiber

For those who were there, the mere mention of a name or season—Kinnick, Fidrych, Iowa '39, Detroit '76—is invocation enough. Nothing more elaborate is needed to stir the flame—a flame less of memory than of pure feeling, an exaltation unlike any experienced before or since. The rest of us must resort to story and statistic, to old photographs and news clippings, grainy film footage or latter-day Web sites, just to get a glimpse of what fills their field of vision. We can bring the athletes themselves into view, fathom the extraordinary nature of their achievement and character. What eludes us is the felt experience of context, the specific circumstances of time and place that so tightly bound these athletes to their fans, and the fans to one another.

There are now, have always been, and will always be many extraordinary athletes, honored, admired, besieged in their seasons of glory by adoring fans. But few have inspired the intense, intimate sense of connection between athlete and fan that gives rise to a lasting cult. That intensity is born of brevity. **These athletes seem to explode out of nowhere to brighten their fans' lives with a burst of athletic fireworks so spectacular and unanticipated that it defies belief.** And then, just as suddenly and incredibly, they are gone. The double shocks of gain and loss, following so closely upon one another, plunge fans into a state of unbelief so disorienting that it becomes its opposite, a belief that they have experienced something very like transcendence.

The word cult has been sullied in recent decades, tarnished by association with the demonic and destructive. But stripped of these acquired overtones, a cult is simply a group of people united in their devotion to a particular person or idea. Among historians of early Christianity, the word cult is applied to the sudden and widespread rise of devotion to the saints at the turn of the 4th century. In early church history, the "cult of the saints" was, by definition, a "cult of the martyrs," and its rise met a need engendered by specific historic circumstances.

■ Cult of the Saints

In the latter half of the 20th century, we became so used to athletes vying for their place in a commercially debased cult of celebrity that it is hard to imagine athletes uniting fans in a spirit that more closely resembles "the cult of the saints." But under certain conditions, in certain times and places, they have. This is not to say this rare subset of athletes are saints, or that abbreviated glory constitutes martyrdom, but that in a few rare instances, historical circumstance collided with the individual fate of an athlete in such a volatile way that it exposed a vein of unlikely affinity. Under the right conditions, 20th-century fans have more in common with 5th-century Christians than one might suspect.

Beginning with the conversion of Emperor Constantine in 312 and ending with the birth of the Holy Roman Empire c. 800 A.D., Christianity was transformed from a church persecuted to a church with imperial

Emperor Constantine ("The Battle between Constantine and Maxentius" by Piero della Francesca) did for the Catholic Church what Pete Rozelle did for the NFL—turned it into an imperial power.

power, authority and wealth. When martyrdom became history rather than prospect, when the threat of persecution had been replaced by the threat of opportunistic conversion, "the cult of the martyrs arose as an essential link to the heroic past of the church."

In *The End of Ancient Christianity*, religious historian R. A. Markus documents how communities of believers began erecting shrines and staging festivals at the burial sites of their local martyrs. Communities disenfranchised from a direct connection to the heroic past by the lack of their own martyrs began making pilgrimages en masse to the holy sites. Eventually, the practice of exhuming martyrs and distributing relics of their mortal remains allowed every town to erect shrines, stage festivals and host pilgrims. The map of Europe became a network of roads linking shrine to shrine, binding disparate communities of believers through pilgrimages. The church calendar, "which had taken little note of martyrs until the 4th century, became filled with festivals of the martyrs, especially during summer, when there were long spells without any event in the life of Christ to celebrate." Local martyrs became saints of the Empire.

■ Industrial Revolution to the Rescue

The years 1880-1930 marked a watershed in sports history, when, as sports historian Allen Guttmann has documented, the industrial revolution spawned changes in mass transportation and communications that first allowed American athletes to be organized for regional and national competition, and then to have their exploits broadcast simultaneously to millions of fans. Between 1881 and 1913, the first national organizations for tennis, track and field, rowing, bicycling, swimming and football were founded. Though national in name only, baseball's National League had been formed in 1876 when the railroads of the Northeast had been completed. By the turn of the century, daily newspapers had inaugurated regular sports sections, and on July 2, 1921, radio broadcast one of its first sports events—the Dempsey-Carpentier fight. A month later, listeners exercised their imaginations in a new way when KDKA Pittsburgh invented play-by-play announcing for a Pirates-Phillies game at Forbes Field. By 1927, 50 million listeners tuned in to the blow-by-blow of a Dempsey-Tunney bout.

Railroads and radio gave birth to the American Empire of Sports, transforming local heroes into national icons, forging discrete pockets of spectators or isolated readers of sports pages into a mass audience of fans who could experience the rise or plunge of their emotions simultaneously. Radio made possible the kind of spontaneous city-wide celebrations that sent fans rushing into the streets, or the less visible, more dispersed euphoria that erupted whenever Joe Louis triumphed over yet another white opponent.

Much was gained, including a steadily increasing level of competition which would ultimately allow legitimate claims of "national champions" or "the world's greatest." The foundation had been laid for a national and,

WAGNER, PITTSBURG

TOPPS 206

AUTHENTIC GAME-USED BAT

A 2001 version of Honus Wagner's original baseball card (the original, which came out during the first decade of the 20th century, is worth nearly $1 million) is at left; the copy contains a sports relic, a piece of one of Wagner's game-used bats. Fortunately for Wagner, he arrived during a watershed period in sports history. Unfortunately for St. Apollonia (right), she arrived during a watershed period in martyrdom.

soon enough, international "cult of celebrity," but the intimate link between a community and its athletes had been attenuated. Like a 5th-century Christian, who saw his local martyr exhumed and his bones dispersed for worship across the Empire, the 20th-century fan was torn between claiming pride of origin and fearing loss of a more exclusive, favored connection to his local heroes.

Local Bonding

At the beginning of the 5th century, Bishop Maximus of Turin found it necessary to reassure his congregation of their continuing special bond with their local martyrs: "Though we should celebrate, brothers, the anniversaries of all the martyrs with great devotion, yet we ought to put our whole veneration into observing the festivals especially of those who poured out their blood in our own hometown. Though all the saints are everywhere present and aid everyone, those who suffered for us intervene for us especially. For when a martyr suffers, he suffers not only for himself, but for his fellow citizens . . . With these we have a sort of familiarity: they are always with us, they live among us."

The doctrine that a martyr was actually still present at his burial site, linking heaven to earth, always available to listen, bless and intercede for favors on behalf of those who visited him there ensured a kind of local favoritism no matter how far his fame spread. For the 20th-century fan, there were, of course, no such reassurances that a great athlete would remain bound in flesh or spirit to the community that gave rise to him.

Only accidents of fate could forge such a permanent bond.

Iowa's Golden Boy

ERHAPS THE PUREST, MOST EXEMPLARY CASE OF SUCH A BOND is the one forged between Nile Kinnick and the state of Iowa in 1939. Nile Kinnick was so uniquely the right man at the right place at the right time, that if he hadn't existed, Iowans would have had to invent him. In 1939, Kinnick became Iowa's first (and to this date last) Heisman Trophy winner. More tellingly, in a year that saw Joe DiMaggio lead the Yankees to a championship and Joe Louis successfully defend his boxing title against four heavyweight contenders, Kinnick was named Athlete of the Year by the Associated Press.

The nation honored him, but Iowans worshipped him. "He captured the imagination of this state the way nobody ever has since," said George Wine, former sports information director of the University of Iowa, where in 1939 Kinnick not only led a football team out of Big Ten's basement to national prominence, but was class president and a Phi Beta Kappa scholar. "All the cliches fit Nile," teammate Al Couppee told a *Sports Illustrated* reporter in 1987. "He was Jack Armstrong and Frank Merriwell rolled into one. He was the smallest—only about 5-foot-8, 170 to 175 pounds—and the slowest of all our backs. . . . But in a game, you knew he'd do something in the last minute, find a way to pull us out. In my 66 years, I've never met anyone who had the self-discipline that 21-year-old had. There was just an aura about him."

Part of the aura—and many of the cliches—emanated from his broad, smiling, square-jawed, dimple-chinned face. **He looked the part of poster boy for everything Iowans wanted to believe of themselves—that they were honest, healthy, wholesome, hardworking, modest, friendly, persevering people, and would be well-rewarded sooner or later for being so.** Dubbed the "Cornbelt Comet" by sportswriters, he looked like the heroic American innocent many thought him to be, but as Paul Baender, the editor of Kinnick's diary and letters, warns us: "Let no one invoke the cliche about 'simpler and more innocent times.' Kinnick lived in a time of terror, desperation and complexity beyond charting."

■ The Worst of Times

In 1939, Iowa was still suffering the effects of an economic depression that had begun not a decade earlier, as it had in the rest of the nation, but two decades earlier, when the end of World War I had meant the end of federal price supports for farm products. In 1920, grain prices plunged to 50 percent of what they had been during the war, and many farmers who had taken mortgages to buy high-priced land during more prosperous years faced foreclosure. Between 1921 and 1929, there were 457 bank suspensions in Iowa, and that was before the Great Depression hit the entire

TESTAMENT

Wayne Duke retired in 1989, following 18 years as the Big Ten commissioner and eight as the Big Eight commissioner. He was raised about two hours from the Iowa campus.

■ Nile Kinnick was a statewide hero, particularly to kids like myself. Iowa never had a great record in football. But the Ironmen, with Kinnick as the Heisman Trophy winner, brought Iowa to the fore. As a kid growing up in Burlington, who was as interested in sports as I was, that was it. I watched him play in 1939 when I was 11 years old, when he threw two touchdown passes in the last quarter and drop-kicked an extra point to upset Minnesota, 13-9.

In that game the line for tickets extended clear around the north end of the stadium. I can remember breaking the line with my brother Jack; we ran along with the adults, got up to the front and were able to get into the game in the knothole (25-cent) section. I watched my first Iowa game when I was four years old. My dad was a fire chief; he wrapped me in a rubber coat and I became a Big Ten fan, and even more so, watching Kinnick play. And, as kids do, we'd go home and start a scrub football game. Everybody wanted to be Nile Kinnick, which I always wanted to be and never was.

Yes, I'm choked up. Yep. It's a great tradition. Sorry to be so corny; we Iowa guys are corny.

Kinnick transcended sports, as this editorial cartoon from the news section of the Chicago Herald American *attests.*

HE SURE DID, BUTCH!

"If George Sisler can improve baseball umpiring, as he proposes," writes Jack House of Birmingham, "he played all those years or nothing to get into the Hall of Fame." There's more truth than poetry in the Alabaman's remarks.

HERALD CHICAGO AMERICAN

★ FRIDAY, NOVEMBER 24, 1939 23

FIRST BOWL GAME

JUNEAU, Alaska, Nov. 24.—(P)—An ambulance, Red Cross nurses and doctors were on the sidelines yesterday as the continent's "Bowl" season got under way. The Alaska Sourdough's football team defeated the Baranoff Bears, 6 to 0, in the first Gold Bowl game. Only one player was injured.

HAWKEYE HERO

By Burris Jenkins Jr.

WITH KINNICK IN THERE, IOWA HAS ONE OF THE BEST COLLEGE TEAMS OF THE YEAR -- WITHOUT HIM IT WOULD BE ANOTHER STORY ---

WHEN THEY LOST DAVEY O'BRIEN, T.C.U. DROPPED FROM A STAND-OUT TEAM TO A MEDIOCRE ONE --

WHEN EVASHEUSKI, THE GREAT BLOCKING BACK, WAS HURT MICHIGAN LOST THE NEXT TWO GAMES -- EVEN WITH HARMON - !

IOWA ISN'T A ONE-MAN TEAM BUT NILE KINNICK IS THE HEART AND SOUL, THE KEY PLAYER AND THE INSPIRING FORCE OF THE OUTFIT THAT HAS AMAZED AMERICA --- WITHOUT HIM THE TEAM WOULD BE ORDINARY.

TO BE AT THEIR BEST, IT IS NECESSARY TO KEEP THE GREAT LITTLE 170 POUND KINNICK IN THE HAWKEYE LINE FOR A FULL 60 MINUTES OF EVERY GAME.

REMEMBER HOW THAT YALE TEAM WOULD "LIFT" WHEN BOOTH CAME ON THE FIELD ? -

THOUGH HE LACKS SPEED, KINNICK CAN RUN FOR IMPORTANT YARDS WHEN HE HAS TO.

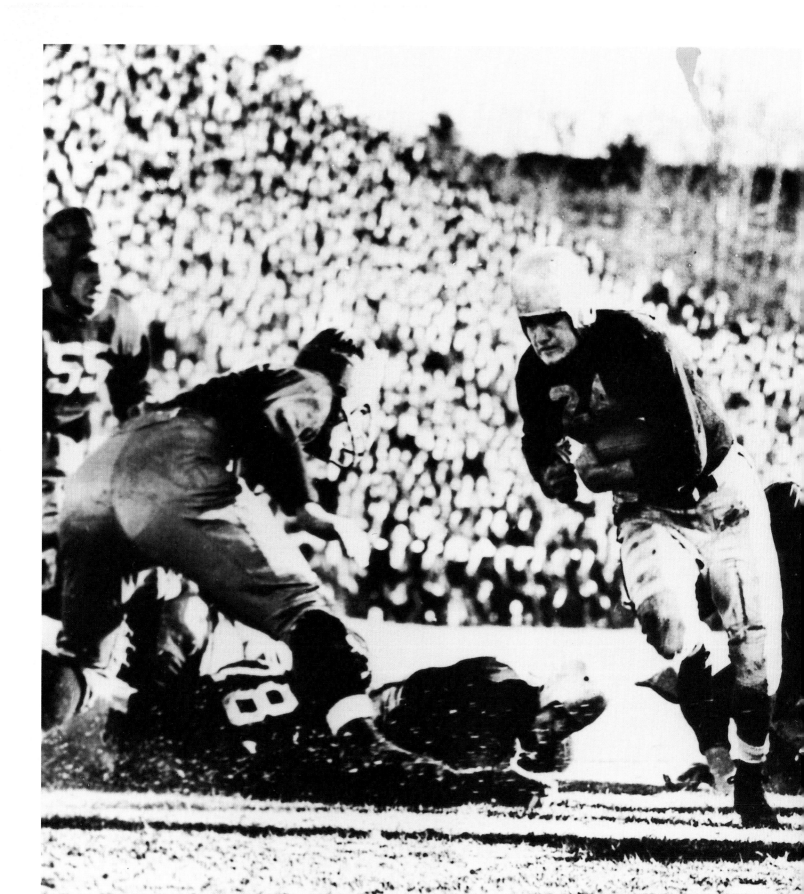

On November 11, 1939, Iowa stunned second-ranked and unbeaten Notre Dame, 7-6, as Kinnick ran for Iowa's TD. He also kicked the game-winning extra point.

country. Between 1926 and 1932, there were close to 25,000 farm foreclosures in Iowa, and the symbiotic relation between town and country in Iowa ensured high rates of bankruptcy and unemployment in non-farm businesses as well.

Conditions were so dire that some Iowa farmers, traditionally renowned for their forbearance in adversity, became militant. In 1931, several hundred angry farmers, incensed by government testing of their cattle for bovine tuberculosis, converged on a state veterinarian's car, slashing tires, cutting the gas line and smashing windows. The next day, the governor called out the National Guard to escort the vets in a convoy along roads bristling with machine guns. In 1932, the Farmers Holiday Association (their name an ironic twist on bank holidays) organized a farmer's strike. In one incident, strikers trying to stop produce from reaching markets intercepted a truck carrying butter and spread its contents over a 200-yard stretch of Highway 75. "I came along in my car and went into the ditch," one Iowan remembered. "Every time you hit a slick place, off you'd go, just like that."

In March 1933, farmers carrying pitchforks stormed the state capitol in Des Moines while the Iowa legislature was in session and threatened to hang a state senator over a railing in the rotunda. The senator retreated to safety in the capitol's golden dome, but the following month a county judge in northwest Iowa was less fortunate when farmers invaded his courtroom to protest a foreclosure proceeding. The judge was pulled from his bench, dragged and kicked down the courthouse steps, and taken several miles out of town, where he was threatened with mutilation and lynching if he did not promise to stop signing foreclosure decrees. He agreed, and was spared. The governor declared martial law in the county.

Only a small minority of Iowa's farmers resorted to such violence, and yet it was their actions that garnered national headlines, delivering a blow to Iowa's image of itself that only compounded its other miseries. The violence stopped in November 1933, when the Agricultural Adjustment Act of 1933 offered the relief of loans to beleaguered farmers. The relief

As a child, Kinnick was never far from sports equipment—or his little brother, George.

proved short-lived, however, because in 1934 and '36, Iowa was hit with extreme droughts and economic conditions worsened. I have seen the before-and-after pictures of my own grandfather: the handsome, proud, mustachioed Edwardian gentleman in his high-collared suit, and the same man in 1937, his Iowa farm foreclosed, his eyes shadowed under the brim of a Texaco hat as he pumps gas in town.

It was in this dispiriting context that Nile Kinnick enrolled at the University of Iowa in 1936. Although Nile had been born and raised in the small town of Adel, Iowa, where he led his high school football team to an undefeated season in 1933, and then scored more than a third of the basketball team's points in the spring, he transferred to Benson High School in Omaha, Nebraska, for his senior year. The Kinnicks had been forced to liquidate their family farms near Adel, and Nile's father found salaried work as a farm appraiser for the Federal Land Bank in Omaha. "We left Adel with nothing but our furniture and a firm belief that we were being cared for adequately," Nile's father told his son's biographer D.W. Stump.

Opposites Attract

After a senior year, in which he won Nebraska all-state honors in football and basketball while earning straight As, he decided to return to Iowa for college. Some say the university's dismal football record was part of the lure, that he wanted to go to a school that was down so he could help lift it up. Others say that Kinnick was equally interested in the University of Minnesota, which was enjoying a reign at the top of Big Ten football, but Minnesota's coach thought Kinnick was too small and too slow for his team. **Whichever the case, in 1936 Kinnick decided to play for the University of Iowa when its football team was at low ebb—and about to get worse.**

In 1936 and '37, Iowa did not win a single Big Ten game. In '38, Iowa's lone victory was over the University of Chicago, which was about

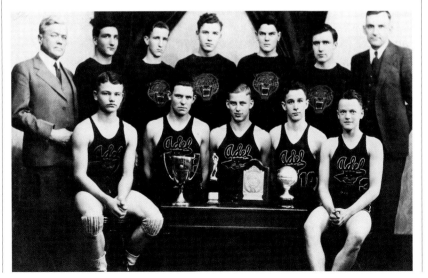

Kinnick not only delivered for his high school basketball team (first row, far left)—during the 1933-34 season he scored 36 percent of the team's points and led Adel to the district finals— he even delivered newspapers at the age of 9. Work meant a lot to Kinnick. Years later, he wrote a letter to his brother George detailing the first jobs he had, including "$1.00 a day scything weeds for 'Simon Legree' Bice (his uncle)."

TESTAMENT

D. W. Stump, a cousin of Kinnick and the author of
Kinnick: The Man and the Legend *(1975), recalls one of his favorite
"snapshots" of Nile, an afternoon spent in the early '70s in Cedar Rapids,
Iowa, with Otto Kohl, the coach of Adel High School
teams while Nile was there.*

■ Kohl urged Nile to enter speech contests and drama activities in order to learn communication skills for his post-athletic years. Nile's first oratorical venture occurred during his grade school days when his parents once found him in the bathroom, standing on the commode, studying his gestures in the mirror while delivering Lincoln's Gettysburg Address.

Later on, with Kohl's encouragement, Nile made it to the state finals in oratory, scheduled the same night as the state district basketball tournament. Nile sought the coach's advice about the conflict. Kohl told him that it was his personal decision, much as he would like to have him with the basketball team. Nile decided to go with the basketball team.

Someone who later played football with Nile (Carl Vergamini) at Iowa saw him in action that night. "He was a sight to behold. I had never seen a basketball player of his ability up until that time. He was so impressive that to this day it remains vivid in my memory. His dribbling with either hand (Nile could pass the football equally well with either arm) and all-round ballhandling ability were uncanny, to say nothing of his accurate shooting."

Nile's talents and his uncanny awareness of everything that was happening on the field naturally fitted him for the position of quarterback, but he had one deficit—humility that bordered on shyness. Said Coach Kohl, "Nile would never take the glory for himself, he'd give it to a fumbler. He made me crazy. He used to pass the football around like a cake at a birthday party!"

Kohl recalled a conversation with Frank Carideo, an assistant coach at Iowa who refined Nile's kicking skills, taught him in childhood by his father, who was a quarterback and kicker for Iowa State. Carideo told Kohl that Nile could get rid of the ball in two seconds. Nile also was taught how to curve the ball and to punt it 70 yards and then make it jump out of bounds in either direction.

Coach Kohl attributed a great part of Nile's courageous and seemingly carefree playing style to his Christian Science upbringing. "There was a close connection between mind and matter in Nile's playing style. He knew no bodily defeat. He would get hit, get up, shake himself like a woolly dog and go on."

Nile had a dry sense of humor. Kohl remembered once when Nile was knocked out during a game. "I ran out on the field and just as I got to Nile, he was opening his eyes. He looked around a bit and asked me how all those people had gotten back into the stands so quickly."

to drop its football program entirely (an 85-0 loss to Michigan the next year was Chicago's death knell). Despite Iowa's pitiful record, Nile had gained sufficient attention as a sophomore halfback to be named to the AP's 1937 Big Ten All-Star team. As a junior, however, he injured, perhaps broke, his ankle in the first game of the season. Nobody is certain about the precise nature of the injury, because Nile, a Christian Scientist, eschewed medical treatment, but it was serious enough to hamper his performance for the entire season. There were no all-star honors for Nile in '38.

Creating Men of Iron

Then came '39. Iowa hired a new head coach—Edward N. Anderson, M.D.—a former Notre Dame All-American who had directed Holy Cross to 47 wins in six seasons. **He introduced a regimen of brutal conditioning, hoping to turn his best players into a first string of "ironmen" who could play offense and defense for a full 60-minute game.** Privately, Anderson nurtured great hopes for a team built around a healthy Kinnick, but Iowa's fans had little reason to expect much from a team reconstituted from last year's losers.

In the first game of the season, the Hawkeyes stunned the Iowa City crowd by defeating South Dakota, a non-conference opponent, 41-0. Nile scored the first touchdown of the season on a 65-yard run, completed two other touchdown runs, threw two touchdown passes, and drop-kicked five conversions in five attempts. The next week, in the opening Big Ten game,

Iowa football fans, with little else to root for, got a boot out of Kinnick, whether practicing drop kicking in real life—he was one of the last great practitioners of that arcane art—or appearing in the pages of local newspapers.

NILE DEVELOPED INTO A FINE DROP-KICKER THIS YEAR BESIDES BEING ONE OF THE NATION'S LEADING PUNTERS

ALL-CONFERENCE IN 1937, KINNICK LAST YEAR WAS HAMPERED BY A BAD ANKLE

A BRILLIANT STUDENT... CANDIDATE FOR PHI BETA KAPPA WITH HIS 3.5 GRADE AVERAGE... PLANS TO ENTER LAW SCHOOL... A CAGE STAR TILL HE QUIT TO CONCENTRATE ON STUDIES...

NILE KINNICK
IOWA'S GREAT HALFBACK

...ALWAYS A GOOD PASSER, KINNICK HAS BECOME A TOUCHDOWN-TOSSER THIS SEASON, HAVING THROWN SEVERAL OF THEM FOR TOTAL GAINS OF OVER HALF THE FIELD... AS A BALL-CARRIER, HE IS AVERAGING ABOUT SIX YARDS PER TRIAL... TO HIS PUNTING AVERAGE OF OVER 42 YARDS FOR THE LAST TWO YEARS, HE HAS ADDED ACCURACY IN 1939 WITH HIS "COFFIN-CORNER" KICKS... NILE IS A SENIOR, WEIGHS 170, IS 5'8" TALL ... BORN IN ADEL, IA., LIVES IN OMAHA...

WHEN YA GOTTA GOAL, YA GOTTA GOAL -- NILE SENT ME - DO I ROLL!

THE PIGSKIN

DEB THOMPSON—11

a last-minute touchdown pass by Kinnick brought Iowa its first victory over Indiana since 1921—and its first victory at home in six years against any Big Ten opponent.

As they charged through the first five games of the season, toppling Wisconsin and Purdue, Iowa's short roster of players was seriously eroded by injury, but its record was marred by only one loss—to Michigan. Iowa's long-suffering football fans couldn't believe such unanticipated good fortune. "There's no way to tell—or let anyone in on—how it felt to be witnessing this," Iowa sportscaster Tait Cummins recalls. "We had been beaten so many times by so many people . . . You didn't even have to buy a seat. You could follow the team up and down the field, and you wouldn't run into any customers."

Now the stadium was filled with 50,000 ecstatic fans for every home game, and the rest of Iowa was tuning in on the radio. "Afterward," writes Kinnick's biographer D.W. Stump, who was a child in '39, "we raced across the road to the side yard of the village church to re-enact the game. As often as possible, I managed to 'be' Nile Kinnick at left halfback. What a thrill that season was. The memory of it has remained with me all my life."

■ ## An Almost Inconceivable Upset

On November 11, when Iowa faced undefeated Notre Dame, ranked second in the country, the whole country tuned in, and news of Iowa's almost inconceivable 7-6 upset flashed all night on the marquee in New York's Times Square. Eight of Iowa's "Ironmen" had played every minute of the game against Notre Dame's deep reserves. Kinnick, playing the full 60 minutes for the fifth consecutive game, had crashed through the formidable Notre Dame line for a second-quarter touchdown and then kicked the extra point. **The following week, when Kinnick passed for two touchdowns in the fourth quarter and then safeguarded Iowa's 13-9 win over top dog Minnesota by intercepting a Gopher pass in the last minute of the game, a homecoming crowd of 50,000 ecstatic fans flooded the field, and the country nearly drowned in a gusher of purple prose.** "There's a golden helmet riding on a human sea across Iowa's football field in the twilight here," wrote James Kearns of the *Chicago Daily News*. "There's a boy under the helmet which is shining like a crown on his head. A golden No. 24 gleams on his slumping, tired shoulders . . . The boy is Nile Clarke Kinnick Jr. . . . leading a frenzied little band of Iowa football players to a victory which was impossible. They couldn't win, but they did."

A more restrained version of the game ran in another Chicago newspaper: "Nile Kinnick 13, Minnesota 9; tersely, that's the story of the most spectacular game in modern Big Ten history." Readers of *The Des Moines Register* understood why veteran sportswriter Bert McGrane began his account with this confession: "A grizzled observer wiped a tear of admiration off his leathery cheek." In delivering Iowans "another amazing victo-

Kinnick was a superhero in Iowa, and like all good superheroes he had his own comic book feature, which, unfortunately, was not published until after his death.

STILL CRAZY ABOUT HIM AFTER ALL THESE YEARS

Nile Kinnick's presence emanates from the northwest corner room, second floor, 363 N. Riverside Drive in Iowa City. Since he roomed there during his sophomore year, it has served as a touchstone for achievement at Phi Kappa Psi. But keeping his spirit alive has proved much easier than preserving his earthly possessions.

■ A 1994 fire left only the house's exterior walls standing. It was rebuilt at the same site, but Kinnick memorabilia—pictures, a helmet—were destroyed. Now, there are only a few photos of Kinnick in the pool table room. "Three years ago on eBay, I saw one of Nile's flight logs from WWII, and it went for $800," says Tim Evans, the fraternity president in 2000. "But we didn't have the money."

■ Only a 100-pound, 16-inch-high bronze bust of his head, cast circa 1950, survived the fire: The bust, which is valued at $5,000, has been snatched three times since the early '90s—first recovered in Des Moines, then at an Iowa City park by a woman and her dog and, most recently in November 2000, on the University of Illinois campus. The last incident got big media play in the area, and the local newspaper ran a large-type, missing person–style bulletin with its news story.

■ The frat pays homage to Kinnick in a number of ways, including a late-night Kinnick Run to his stadium when the pledge education program is completed. Says Evans, "Once we get out there, usually the field is lit up enough to set the mood and make it look cool. We have older members talk about what it means to be a Phi Psi and why this stadium is so special to us. We talk about what made Nile so special and how humble he was, and how he decided to bypass pro football to fight for our country. This is what exemplifies who a Phi Psi really is."

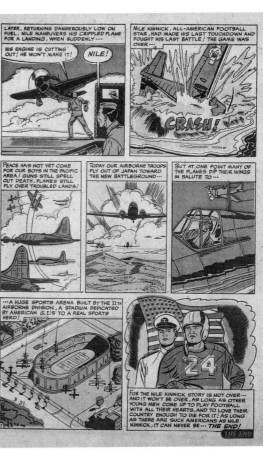

ry against colossal odds," Nile offered a deliverance that extended far beyond the football field. He restored pride to a battered state, and perhaps more important, he reinvigorated faith in the quintessential Iowan virtues of patience, hard work and unflagging endurance. "The whole state seemed uplifted," remembers Jerry Anderson Jr., coach Anderson's son.

Iowans' response to Nile Kinnick may have been sentimental, but it was not escapist. When "Nile for Governor" signs began to sprout around the state, it was not a matter of misplaced hero-worship. The persevering "against colossal odds" nature of his feats made Iowans feel he represented what was best in them, that he provided not only a link to Iowa's "heroic past," but perhaps a link to a longed-for heroic future. Here was a man who was not the fastest, not the biggest, not the luckiest, and yet by sheer dogged effort, he made himself the best.

The best by far. At season's end, Nile had broken 14 University of Iowa records, including most touchdowns, most points after touchdown, longest scoring pass (71 yards), most punts, best punting average, longest punt (73 yards), most punts returned and most kickoff returns. By passing, running or kicking, Nile was involved in 107 of Iowa's 130 points in the miraculous season that elevated Iowa from the Big Ten basement to a No. 9 national ranking in the Associated Press poll.

■ A Heisman Speech for the Ages

On December 6, 1939, he was awarded the Heisman Trophy as the nation's best college football player. In his brief, unrehearsed acceptance speech, broadcast nationwide from the Downtown Athletic Club in New York, he redoubled his fame. After giving Coach Anderson and his teammates due credit for Iowa's season, he continued: "I thank God I was warring on the gridirons of the Midwest and not on the battlefields of Europe. I can speak confidently and positively that the players of this country would much more, much rather, struggle and fight to win the Heisman Award than the Croix de Guerre." The Associated Press account of the event describes the New York audience responding with a whistling, cheering, standing ovation "for Nile Kinnick, typifying everything admirable in American youth."

Six decades later, Kinnick's Heisman speech is frequently misconstrued as an expression of patriotic humility, a tip of the helmet to the boys fighting overseas. But this was December 1939, before the United States had entered the war, and Nile was in fact expressing a popular isolationist sentiment that he would soon rethink. The larger point is that Kinnick showed himself to be considerably more than "the kid from the corn country," as the AP had described him, more than the nation's best college football player. He saw his life in a larger context.

Two days before accepting the Heisman, Nile had written to his mother to ask her what direction she thought he should pursue after college. "I feel that pro ball is not the right direction—I have no desire to play

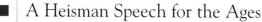

Photos, comics, newspaper illustrations, even sculpture (above right)—Kinnick images were omnipresent in Iowa during his lifetime. This wore on Kinnick. While in the military, he wrote, "Am experiencing a greater degree of anonymity here than at any other time for the past three years . . . it is not unpleasant. In fact, in many ways it is downright enjoyable."

Kinnick (in his induction photo, above) loved to fly. One of his service diary entries read: "Did my first solo spin today . . . Got a faint idea of what a dive bomber's perspective is by nosing my plane straight down . . . it is great fun." Long after Kinnick's death in a training accident, Forest Evashevski, a one-time foe and later a Hall of Fame coach, wrote a letter (right) to the people of Kinnick's hometown, Adel, extolling Kinnick as "a template for the youth of America."

nor hesitancy about passing up the money, though I suppose it will look awfully big in a few years." In another letter to his mother, written closer to graduation, he discusses various job offers and confides that "what bothers me about going into business is, could I do people more good somewhere else—I think that is the main point, naive as it may seem." In a postscript, he returns to the question on his mind, "What is a man's obligation to society?"

The naivete was superficial, but the idealism ran deep in Nile Kinnick. In his commencement address as class president, delivered May 29, 1940, Nile warned his fellow graduates what to expect of life beyond the university, where so many recent "events of terrible and ominous significance have taken place." "Here," he said, "our ideals are lauded, appreciated and protected—the development and expression of a social consciousness has been easy. But you know and I know that this period of easy idealism is now at an end."

Nile entered Iowa Law School that fall, but as the year progressed and the war in Europe intensified, he became more convinced the United States should enter it. During the summer of '41, he enlisted in the Naval Air Corps Reserve, and he reported for active duty on December 4, 1941, three days before Pearl Harbor. On June 2, 1943, during a practice flight from the carrier U.S.S. Lexington, Ensign Nile Kinnick's fighter plane lost all its engine oil and he was forced to crash into the waters of the Gulf of Paria, between Venezuela and Trinidad. His body was never recovered.

■ Only the Good Die Young

Among Iowans of Kinnick's generation, it is common to remember where they were, and what they were doing, when they heard the news of his death. "The only thing I can compare it to is JFK," one contemporary of Kinnick's recently told an ESPN interviewer. "Just thinking about it now, it's devastating," said another. At a time when many were mourning privately the loss of their own sons at war, Nile's death became an occasion to mourn collectively.

The pang of wondering what might have been, "if only he had lived," persists today. Among Iowans who knew him, the presumption that he would have been governor or U.S. senator verges on certainty. Even Iowa Senator Tom Harkin, who should know how hard such futures are to predict, says, "I think he could have been president of the United States, I really do."

There are clues about what kind of man he might have become in his letters and in the diaries he kept during his time in the Navy. Shortly before enlisting in the Navy, Nile read Winston Churchill's collection of speeches, *Blood, Sweat and Tears,* and confided to his parents, "It makes my spine tingle just to read those lines over to myself. I'd rather write a speech like any one of those than do anything I can think of." There are repeated references in Kinnick's diaries to Churchill, to his unyielding defense of

RAISING THE PLANE

■ There were the Kinnick faithful, and then there was Al Couppee, his friend and a sophomore quarterback on the 1939 team. Couppee, now deceased, organized reunions and would never let anyone say anything negative about Kinnick, even in jest. He would get chided at parties for telling stories about how perfect Kinnick was. Once, he even guaranteed that Kinnick never had sex.

So when the most ambitious plan yet to glorify Kinnick was proposed—raising his Grumman Wildcat from the Gulf of Paria in the Caribbean and bringing it to campus—Couppee took the lead, along with Richard Tosaw, a retired FBI agent and lawyer whose brother played at Iowa in 1938.

Couppee, never one for half measures, and teammates George Frye and Erwin Prasse (captain of the '39 team) hoped to recover and restore the fighter and set it atop a pole at Nile Kinnick Stadium. A fund-raising drive was launched, and D.W. Stump, Kinnick's biographer, was the treasurer. Said Stump, "The committee thought that it might be inspiring, similar to the feelings about raising the Titanic."

Hundreds of checks were received totaling thousands of dollars. Tosaw contacted British marine salvage expert Martin Woodward, who thought that he had found the crash site. He believed the plane rested in mud under about 100 feet of water. Said Stump, "In my mind's eye, I could see Nile's plane gleaming in the sun and inspiring teams and students after the ideals of my cousin."

But some of those in the group began to have second thoughts. What would be the condition of the plane? Shouldn't Kinnick be allowed to rest in peace? The group decided to forego the salvage. Even an attempt at retrieving just the propeller was rejected. Said Prasse, "At first we thought it was a good idea. But, when you think about it, I think Nile would have liked it the way it is and so would his parents."

Forest Evashevski
1432 Bay View Heights Drive
Petoskey, Michigan 49770

To the People of Adel, Iowa —

I have been informed you are planning to honor Nile Kinnick during your 150th birthday. Having known Nile and competed against him, I would like to pass along a few of my feelings.

In our game against Iowa, we took advantage of some breaks and handed Iowa its only defeat. During the fourth quarter with the game lost, Nile was competing with a vigor that would indicate a tie ball game. And after the game, he rose above his deep disappointment and congratulated every player on the Michigan team. He trotted off the field and — robbed a team whose dream of a national title was gone. His leadership le— Iowa to a big ten title and for Nile, th— Heisman Trophy.

Were this all I knew about Nile, th— letter would not be written. In the Uni—

Forest Evashevski
1432 Bay View Heights Drive
Petoskey, Michigan 49770

of Iowa Hospital, during my Navy duty at Iowa Pre-Flight, I was with two doctors when word came that Nile had been killed. Both doctors cried and one said, "He was the finest young man I ever knew". If memory serves me correctly, one of the doctors name was Dr. Irwin.

In a day when athletic success takes precedence over morality, reverence, kindness, and academic curiosity, we must preserve the qualities which constitute the whole man. I am confident the great coaches of our time: the Staggs, Rocknes, Warners, Yosts, Zupples, Jones and so many other coaches who contributed so much to the great american game of football dreamed of coaching a Nile Kinnick who would serve as a template for the youth of america.

May you honor this dream

Forest Evashevski

TODAY'S KING—TOMORROW'S PRESIDENT.

KEEPING THE LEGEND ALIVE

The celebrity of many great athletes is generational, and even Hall of Fame status does little to guarantee a legacy or expand it. But almost 60 years after his death, Kinnick's life continues to tug at the heartstrings, as old memorial tributes live on and new ones are still being created.

■ Former Big Ten Commissioner Bill Reed (1961-71) ordered the minting of the "Kinnick flipping coin." Said Dave Parry, the supervisor of Big Ten officials for the past 13 years, "When you come into the Big Ten your rookie season, we give you one as a good luck token." In years past, the captains on the field for the toss would receive one. They also have been fashioned into jewelry for administrators' wives. Kinnick's likeness is heads, tails shows the names of the Big Ten schools, except for Penn State, and provides a place for inscribing the matchup and score.

■ Kinnick Stadium, formerly Iowa Stadium, was renamed in 1972. The change would have happened years earlier, but Kinnick's father initially thought it inappropriate to honor only his son when so many others had died during the war.

■ "No matter what it's named (Days Inn, Clarion Hotel or Holiday Inn), it will still be known as the Ironmen Inn," said manager Nick Holke. It's located in Coralville, right outside Iowa City, and many of the Ironmen reunions were held there. On the inside, the memorabilia might remind one of a booster club's: a football signed by the Ironmen, a '39 letterman jacket, framed clippings, team photos and an oil rendering of Kinnick scoring the winning TD against Notre Dame.

■ Eighth Street in his hometown of Adel, Iowa (pop. 3,500) was renamed Nile Kinnick Drive. (Bob) Feller/Kinnick Park is the town's largest. Preliminary plans for a new library include a Kinnick motif along its corridors.

■ More than 500 students attend Nile C. Kinnick High School at the Yokosuka, Japan, navy facility about two hours from Tokyo.

■ The No. 2 track on the "Go Hawkeyes: Iowa's Greatest Hits" CD (2001) is an excerpt of Kinnick's Heisman acceptance speech.

principle, his incomparable power as an orator. At times, Nile seemed to be rehearsing for the day he might deliver such speeches.

Traveling through the South on his way to the Pensacola Air Force Base, Nile saw rural poverty of a kind he had never seen before, which prompted him to write this diary entry on March 12, 1942: "The inequities in human relationships are many, but the lot of the Negro is one of the worst. . . . Nearly everyone, particularly the southerners, seem to think the only problem involved is seeing to it that they keep in their place, whatever that may be. We supposedly are fighting this war to obliterate the malignant idea of racial supremacy and master-slave relationships. When this war is over, the colored problem is apt to be more difficult than ever. May wisdom, justice, brotherly love guide our steps to the right solution."

High-minded, smitten by rhetorical power, Nile, at 24, a month before his death, was also an astute pragmatist. "How can any political candidate be really free and independent in thought and policy when he is dependent on wealthy backers for campaign funds? Is there any practical remedy for this seemingly inescapable situation?" Early death precluded our ever knowing what answer Nile Kinnick might have found to that question, or to the more fundamental question that underlay it and consumed the better part of his last years: "What is a man's obligation to society?" That lost future gave rise to a cult in which Iowans who were there, in that particular time and place, worship an idealized image of their best selves in the form of "a boy under the helmet which is shining like a crown on his head."

Iowa Rises Again

The Depression was Iowa's time of persecution, when its rural virtues were severely tested by economic and social dislocations on an unprecedented scale. **Kinnick, a son of foreclosed farms and hope, arose from that time to restore faith in the "possibility of victory."** That last phrase is borrowed from religious historian R. A. Markus, who wrote, "The martyr stood for the possibility of victory: over death, our victory over the frailty of our bodies, over the waywardness of our labile wills, the instability of our resolve . . . "

Nile Kinnick died, but Iowa rose again. In the economic equivalent of one of Kinnick's last-minute saving interceptions, Iowa joined in the country's more general recovery from the Depression during the war years, when the state's farmers rallied to the national motto, "Food will win the war and write the peace." There would, of course, be other periods of trial, of drought, of depressed prices. There always are in a farm state. And no one knows what part Nile Kinnick might have played in helping Iowans meet those challenges if he had lived. But in death, he was always present as "the boy in the golden helmet," summoning the faithful to rally once again against the scourge of despair.

The Des Moines Register-Tribune *(far left) thought Kinnick would make a heck of a president, which Iowa Senator Tom Harkin once said was a real possibility. To this day, some Big Ten games start with a flipped Kinnick coin (left).*

The Bird Was the Word

EW REGIONS OF THE COUNTRY HAVE SUFFERED AN ECONOMIC decline as steep and prolonged as that of Iowa in the 1920s and '30s. There have been other regional victims of agricultural devastation or industrial obsolescence, but seldom have their trials matched the scale and duration of Iowa's Depression. And seldom has an athlete met the challenge of raising spirits that had plunged so low. In postwar America, perhaps the most undisputed case of comparable hard times, creating a comparable challenge, was what befell Detroit in the 1970s. Civic pride and social cohesiveness, though tested in earlier decades by labor and racial strife, had reached their lowest ebb, and no one, it seemed, could bring the divided city together again.

In the early '70s, Detroit was still reeling from the impact of the 1967 civil disturbances—called "race riots" by the white population that fled to the suburbs and "rebellions" by the black population that stayed behind in neighborhoods ravaged by fire, looting and disastrously misguided urban renewal policies. Whole swaths of the city were bulldozed to rubble, and the flight of white residents, the most extensive among the nation's cities, was accompanied by the flight of businesses.

"In a few weeks of 1972," Emma Rothschild writes in *Paradise Lost*, her 1973 study of the automobile industry, "two machine-toll plants were moved from Detroit to western Michigan and Ohio, metal-spring operations moved to the South and Canada, and the North American Rockwell Corporation decided to close an axle and forge plant it had operated in Detroit since 1912." Even Motown left Detroit in 1972.

Then came the Arab oil embargo of 1973, knocking the flat-footed Detroit auto industry to its knees. Its failure to respond quickly enough to consumers' changing preferences for smaller, more reliable, more gas-efficient cars resulted in plummeting sales of American cars and massive layoffs. **The collapse of Detroit as Motor City was so extreme and prolonged as to become virtually permanent.** The city that made half the world's cars in 1950 made one car in every 1,000 in 1990.

"The scale of decline now seen in Detroit goes far beyond past American experience," Rothschild wrote. Another economic historian writing two decades later arrived at the same conclusion: "No American city ever fell as far or as fast as Detroit," Julia Vitullo-Martin wrote in the summer 1995 volume of *City Journal*.

In the late '30s, when Iowa was down and Motor City was up, *The New York Times* had described Detroit as "a world capital . . . more fascinating to the outlander than New York, more influential than Washington, or even Hollywood." During the 1970s it became, in the words of *Michigan Quarterly Review* editor Laurence Goldstein, a "national emblem of racial crisis and urban decay."

THE BIRD: A PANCULTURAL ROCK 'N' ROLL THROWBACK

■ "Fidrych is a certified flake, in the grand tradition of a double-talking Casey Stengel, Lefty Gomez (who used to halt games to gaze up at airplanes flying overhead) and Jimmy Piersall, whom fear almost struck out."

"Although he was clearly the biggest star baseball had known since Mickey Mantle retired, his effect was not on the way the game was played . . . Fidrych operated with the most basic and ancient pitching skill of all: the ability to throw low, hard fastballs precisely. Maybe that was revolutionary around the turn of the century when Walter Johnson hit the scene. Not now. No, The Bird cult was built on personality; talent just kept it alive."

"Fidrych embodied rock & roll by being a throwback. Ten years ago, the sporting establishment would never have accommodated his nervy mannerisms, much less his attire and hair. But before (long before) rock & roll, ballplayers were the great eccentrics: Babe Ruth screwing and eating his way through the front pages like a behemoth Keith Richard; Joe DiMaggio as moody as any platinum-record prima donna; Ty Cobb ripping and slashing his way down the base paths like Ted Nugent in spikes. . . ."
—from Dave Marsh's "The Tale of the Bird," the cover story for the May 5, 1977 Rolling Stone

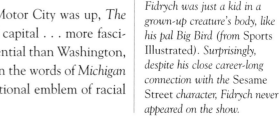

Fidrych was just a kid in a grown-up creature's body, like his pal Big Bird (from Sports Illustrated). Surprisingly, despite his close career-long connection with the Sesame Street character, Fidrych never appeared on the show.

TESTAMENT

*On June 28, 1976, Mark Fidrych pitched in a nationally
televised game and beat the Yankees. Rusty Staub, who was a teammate
for three and a half years, can vividly recall the night
The Bird became a household name.*

■ As we came off the field, people were screaming, "We want The Bird! We want The Bird!"

I was one of the last ones in the clubhouse. He had his uniform top off and was excited, talking. I told him to put his top back on.

He said, "Are you crazy? The game's over."

I said, "No, you have to put the top back on, now."

Finally, he realized I was serious. I said, "You have to come with me."

He said, "Why?"

I said, "Just trust me on this."

So we went back down the runway, and I said, "Can you hear those people?"

This is seven, eight minutes after the team was off the field. Ninety-eight percent of the crowd is there. They are screaming as loud as they can, beating on the stadium, "We want The Bird!"

I said, "You are going out on that field and wave to the fans."

He goes, "No way, no way. I cannot do that!"

I said, "You're not going back in the clubhouse, you're going out on that field."

He said, "You're going to come out with me, you hit a home run."

I said, "They ain't saying, 'We Want Rusty!' they are saying, 'We Want The Bird!' Take your hat and use it like a clock. Bow your head and go around the clock, stop about five places, bow, then you can come back."

Well, he probably did it a little too quickly that day. But it was incredible. The fans went berserk. It became a ritual that he had to perform every time he pitched at home. He refused to do it on the road, and he refused to do it when he lost. But, in that one instant, he created something I never saw in baseball and have yet to see again.

I remember going to Minnesota. They were drawing about 3,500 on a good day; he had 35,000 people, and not many of them over 25.

He just caught the imagination of the youth of America, because he was real. It was not contrived. To be that unique and have those little idiosyncrasies on the mound and to be able to perform as he did was an incredible combination.

And it was fun.

Fidrych's signature crowd-pleasing moves were talking to the ball before pitches (left) and manicuring the mound on his hands and knees (right).

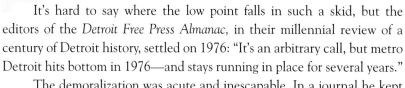

T shirts, bumper stickers, too
Fidrych draws fans and scalpers

TIGERS
MARK FIDRYCH   PITCHER
★ A.L. ALL-STARS ★

It's hard to say where the low point falls in such a skid, but the editors of the *Detroit Free Press Almanac*, in their millennial review of a century of Detroit history, settled on 1976: "It's an arbitrary call, but metro Detroit hits bottom in 1976—and stays running in place for several years."

The demoralization was acute and inescapable. In a journal he kept during 1975, poet Lawrence Joseph captured the mood of the city. "Last night, after dinner, a long drive through the eastside. The constant blight—Van Dyke, Harper, Gratiot, Vernor, Mack Avenue: whole blocks as if bombed during an old war, never rebuilt . . . This morning my past in this city swelled again in me, its strife part of my body, part of my nature."

Wherever he looks, Joseph sees only "how much has been lost." The temptation is to stop looking, to forget, but he believes that the city's survival depends on trying to "remember, at any cost, what is crucial and good. The act of memory becomes an act of faith; if whatever is good is to be revealed (and, therefore, exist) we must remain vigilantly capable of recognizing it, and accepting it." Intentionally or not, Joseph was echoing Detroit's motto, inspired by a catastrophic fire in 1805. Speramus meliora. Resurget cineribus. (*We hope for better things. It will rise from the ashes.*)

The Rookie from Nowhere

For Lawrence Joseph, the means of finding good rising from the ashes of Detroit was poetry. "Write poetry that has value, has the power to counteract oppressive power, that speaks directly to others with love," he urged himself in the pages of his journal. From that impulse, Joseph produced the work included in his first prize-winning volume of poetry, *Shouting to No One* (1982).

Others, unblessed by the gift of poetry, had to look elsewhere for goodness, and many of them found it in The Bird. No, not in the mythical phoenix rising from the ashes, but in a rookie pitcher named Mark Fidrych, nicknamed The Bird, who rose out of nowhere to lift Detroit's spirits in the summer of '76, the summer Detroit had "hit bottom."

Detroit desperately needed something to smile about in 1976, but there was little reason to believe it would be provided by their boys of summer. The Tigers had ended the previous season with the worst record in the majors. Writing a week before the '76 season began, *Detroit Free Press*

Fidrych is an All-Star

Adoring fans turned out in droves wherever he went. More than 5,000 lined up to get his autograph at the Worcester Center Galleria, the forerunner of the outlet mall, during an off-season event. Once, when not scheduled to pitch in Anaheim, he sat in a giant cage and signed autographs for hours.

CROWD PLEASER

The lore of Mark Fidrych's 1976 season will always include his endearing quirkiness, but the spike in attendance when he pitched was equally remarkable.

■ The average attendance for his 18 home starts (more than 33,600) was comparable to what the 1984 World Series–winning team averaged per home game—the highest totals in Tiger Stadium history.

■ Home and away, the Tigers averaged more than 31,000 for each of his 29 starts, with the Tigers' total increasing by 40 percent over the previous year.

■ After his rehab from knee surgery, more than 44,000 fans came to Tiger Stadium to watch Fidrych's first start in 1977.

■ Even during his '79 comeback from an arm injury, his four starts drew average crowds of more than 33,700.

■ Since a Fidrych start could fill any ballpark, opposing teams carefully charted Detroit's pitching rotation, in order to promote his appearances.

■ Noting the "underwhelming" Comerica Park attendance in 2000, Lynn Henning of *The Detroit News* said, "What fans are saying this spring is that it takes more than a new ballpark to draw them away from all the other elements in their lives. It takes either a good team, or an individual who is irresistible—a Mark Fidrych."

■ The downside of a Fidrych start? Concession sales might lag as fans refused to leave their seats. Said Commissioner Bowie Kuhn after seeing Fidrych's curtain calls, now "a baseball game is not just a contest, it's a happening."

columnist Joe Falls warned his readers that "our guys don't look much better than a year ago. They are still a pretty poor excuse for a ball club . . . They probably won't lose a hundred games again, because that doesn't happen too often to anyone—just twice, in fact, in the 75-year history of the Tigers. But it's difficult seeing our lads getting out of last place."

Hope Is the Thing with Feathers

The view from spring training camp was "bleak," one of "weaknesses everywhere, especially on the pitching mound." The "only hope in camp," Falls wrote, "is that one of the kid pitchers will come out of nowhere and give the club an unexpected lift. You must wonder who this will be though."

Perhaps Mark Fidrych took that season-opening column, in which hope crept in despite the near-universal presumption of defeat, as his cue. As a non-roster player who made the team after spring training, despite losing his only decision, the 21-year-old Fidrych was definitely a kid pitcher from nowhere. He had been pumping gas in Northboro, Massachusetts, only two years earlier, so he was happy enough just watching games from the bullpen, which is where he sat out the first five weeks of the season. Then on May 15, the scheduled starting pitcher went down with a bad case of the flu.

Nine short innings later, after giving up only two hits, Fidrych had the first win of a season that catapulted him from nowhere to the center of Detroit's universe. By season's end, he led the league in ERA (2.34), fielding (1.000) and complete games (24). He had won more games (19)

'The Bird' to help Zoo mark 50th birthday

TESTAMENT

Jim Hawkins is a sports columnist for The Oakland (Mich.) Press *and co-author of* Go Bird Go!, *a 1976 biography of Mark Fidrych. He covered the rise and fall of The Bird as the baseball beat writer for the* Detroit Free Press.

■ Mark (The Bird) Fidrych was perched on a stool in front of his cubicle at Philadelphia's Veterans Stadium, spraying underarm deodorant into the one pair of socks he had brought with him on his brief 1976 All-Star Game road trip, when Secret Service agents ushered Gerald R. Ford into the room. One of the dark-suited agents approached Fidrych, who had twice been held back in grade school, and asked the energetic, kinetic, frizzy-haired pitcher if he would autograph a baseball to the President of the United States.

"I've got a game to pitch," grumbled The Bird.

When the presidential procession reached Fidrych's locker, Ford exclaimed, "You're The Bird! How are you?"

Nonplussed as usual, Fidrych—who in a few minutes would pitch in the biggest game of his all-too-brief career—inquired into the love life of the President's son, Jack, who was dating tennis star Chris Evert at the time.

"Come to Washington, and he may fix you up," suggested Ford.

The '76 All-Star Game afforded the national media its first up-close glimpse of The Bird. Several reporters noted with surprise that Fidrych had brought with him three baseball shoes for his right foot—and only one for his left. But then he was The Bird, the flaky, free-spirited right-hander who turned in an expense voucher in spring training after someone in the Tigers' minor league camp ordered him to get a haircut, and worried about the high cost of answering his growing pile of fan mail.

"Ten letters a day times 13 cents a stamp is a lot of money," groaned Fidrych, who was packing ballparks every time he pitched and making the minimum

$16,500 salary. On his way through airports, often in the wee hours of the morning, he would poke his finger into the coin return slots of the pay phones that lined the walls in the hope some hurried traveler had forgotten to reclaim his dime.

At Tiger Stadium, Fidrych's fan mail included cash offerings from as far away as San Francisco and Portland, Maine. One envelope contained a blank cashier's check, made out to "Mark Fidrych," and duly signed by a bank official. All Fidrych had to do was fill in the amount—any amount—and cash it. In Hell, Mich., fans passed the hat and collected $103 for their beloved Bird.

Fidrych didn't bother to have a phone installed in his sparsely furnished suburban Detroit apartment. Instead, he used a pay phone in a supermarket down the street. "Whenever I want to talk to somebody," he explained, "I put in a dime and call collect."

When an enemy batter managed a hit off him, Fidrych would discard that ball and demand a new one. "It's in my mind that that ball has a hit in it," Fidrych explained. "I want that ball to get back in the ball bag and goof around with the other balls. I want him to talk to the other balls. I want the other balls to beat the 'bleep' out of him. Maybe that'll smarten him up so when he comes out the next time, he'll pop up."

Late in the season, the Tigers' wives gave Fidrych his first haircut in two months, then auctioned off his curly locks for charity. The freshly-shorn Bird was asked if he was familiar with the story of Samson and Delilah.

"Goliath, you mean?" responded Fidrych. "Samson and Goliath? No, I never heard about them."

than any Tiger rookie in the previous 68 seasons. Among the 19 wins was an eight-game streak with two back-to-back 11-inning complete games. The statistics accounted for his being named American League Rookie of the Year, and Man of the Year by the National Association of Professional Baseball Leagues. But statistics alone did not make Fidrych the most beloved player in Detroit history.

And between Detroit and Fidrych, it was love at first sight. Mark Fidrych was no Nile Kinnick, but like him, he radiated an aura of unspoiled American innocence. Styles of innocence, like the styles of everything else, had changed with the eras, so his was not the clean-cut, square-jawed innocence of earlier decades, but a mop-headed, goofball innocence that made one think maybe the Beatles might get back together after all. Though his arena was baseball, Fidrych had the kind of crossover appeal that landed him on the cover of *Rolling Stone* as well as *Sports Illustrated* that summer.

He was a gawky 6-foot-3, 175 pounds, with a toothy grin and a fast, floppy, loose-limbed walk, more of a running lope, really, that made his arms flap and his long curly blond locks bounce with every stride. (The nickname Bird was inspired by his resemblance to *Sesame Street*'s Big Bird.) **The first time he went to the mound, and most times thereafter, he didn't walk, he ran, and when he got there, he fell to his knees and began smoothing out the dirt to his liking.** Before each windup, he bent his head close to the ball and talked to it, out loud. When teammates backed him up with good fielding, he would run around the field cranking hands in what looked like spontaneous outbursts of genuine gratitude. He was, in *Sports Illustrated*'s words, "the most refreshing eccentric to enter baseball since Dizzy Dean."

"Too Good to Be True"

That such exuberant gawkiness could then concentrate itself into fiercely controlled fastballs, sinkers and sliders was, like the Bird himself, "too good to be true." His performance not only restored pride to a whipped team, he made a depressed city laugh, and they loved him for it.

After his first appearance on the mound, attendance at Tiger games began to rise, first slowly, then exponentially. The 14,583 fans who saw him pitch his first game grew to 17,894 for his second outing, then swelled to 36,377 for his third start, and by midseason every seat in Tiger Stadium was filled to capacity with more than 52,000 fans. To accommodate as many fans as possible, the front office had to take the unprecedented step of limiting bleacher seats to eight per customer.

Crowds lingered after the game in a stadium resounding with thunderous applause that would not stop until Fidrych emerged or was dragged from the dugout to receive the standing ovations they never tired of lavishing upon him. They rose to cheer him whenever his name was announced, when he went to the bullpen to warm up, when he went to

ONE-SEASON WONDERS

Despite his short career, Mark Fidrych walked away as an indelible footnote in baseball history, complete with adoring fans and a secured pension. Few "one-season" wonders—in any sport—depart under such fortuitous circumstances.

Joe Charboneau
OF, Indians 1980-82
He was wacky "Super Joe"—.289 BA, 23 HR, 87 RBI, AL Rookie of the Year, but could he open beer bottles with an eye socket? You bet. Sadly, the next spring he hurt his back. He was a goner after '82, finishing with only 56 at-bats.

Bob Hamelin
OF, Royals, Tigers, Brewers 1993-98
"The Hammer" lived up to his moniker in '94—.282 BA, 24 HR, 65 RBI, Rookie of the Year. In 1995, his stats dipped to .168, 25 RBI. In 1999, he quit on the spot after making a groundout during a minor league game.

Jim Carey
Goalie, Capitals, Bruins, Blues 1994-99
At 22, he won the Vezina Trophy with a 35-24-9 record and league-high nine shutouts. But a 2-4 record in the '95 postseason and 6.19 goals-against average in the next season's playoffs landed him in Boston, where he went 8-15-1 over two seasons.

Pelle Lindbergh
Goalie, Flyers 1981-85
During the 1984-85 season, he won the Vezina (40-17-7) and became a star. But he was killed when his sports car hit a wall in November 1985. Fans voted him a starter for the All-Star game anyway.

"Ickey" Woods
RB, Bengals 1988-91
As a rookie, Elbert Woods rushed for 1,066 yards (NFL-best 5.3 per carry), created the "Ickey Shuffle" to celebrate his frequent (15) trips to the end zone, and helped his team reach the Super Bowl. He never came close to that again in his short career, which ended unceremoniously after a series of knee injuries.

Timmy Smith
RB, Redskins, Cowboys 1987-88, 1990
His '87 regular-season rushing total was a paltry 126 yards. But in Super Bowl XXII, he broke loose for a record 204 yards and two TDs. He then reported to camp overweight, and Joe Gibbs cut him after the season.

Reggie Brooks
RB, Redskins, Buccaneers 1993-96
After a 1,063-yard rookie season, he could only muster 297 the next, due to hamstring injuries. In 1997, he failed to make the Bucs' roster after averaging 1.8 yards in the preseason.

Robert Edwards
RB, Patriots 1998
He rushed for 1,115 yards and nine touchdowns before suffering a career-threatening injury in conjunction with Pro Bowl weekend. He was cut after two years of rehab in preseason, and is still trying to make his way back.

Don Majkowski
QB, Packers, Colts, Lions 1987-96
In 1989, the Packers' "Majik Man" threw for 4,318 yards, 27 TDs and completed almost 59 percent of his passes. Injuries and Brett Favre's ascension in 1992 made him expendable, and he never returned to his '89 form.

Gheorghe Muresan
C, Bullets/Wizards, Nets 1993-96, 1998-99
The NBA's Most Improved Player in 1995 with the Bullets (14.5 points, 9.6 rebounds per game) missed most of the next three seasons with injuries. Though he was never again an effective player, he became a 7-foot-7 celebrity after co-starring with Billy Crystal in *My Giant*.

Richard Dumas
G, Suns, 76ers (1992, 1994-95)
He missed his rookie season after failing the mandatory drug test. In 1992, he averaged 15.8 points and 4.6 rebounds per game. He played in only 54 more games in his career as a result of repeated suspensions and injuries.

Buster Douglas
Heavyweight boxing champion
In 1990, as a 44-1 underdog, he delivered a 10th-round KO to undefeated champ Mike Tyson, only to lose the title to Evander Holyfield in less than a year. Douglas ballooned to almost 400 pounds in 1994 and lapsed into a diabetic coma, though he recovered sufficiently to mount a brief but uninspired comeback.

the mound, and when he left it; they cheered when he won and, most tellingly, they also cheered when he lost. "He is the idol of a whole city," crowed sports columnist Falls, who was happy to eat his preseason words. "They are saying his almost childlike spontaneity, his raw enthusiasm, his joy of living, is just what the game needs."

So Mark Fidrych had become the public answer to poet Lawrence Joseph's private prayer: "Remember, at any cost, what is crucial and good." Part of what Detroit fans identified as his goodness was his poverty. The young pitcher who was credited with bringing an extra $1,000,000 to the Tigers that summer was making the minimum of $16,500. **Even at season's end, when it was time to renegotiate his contract, he continued to behave as if he were playing just for the love of it. "I don't need no agent," he said. "The people of Detroit are my agent."**

Those were radically innocent words for a baseball player to utter in 1976, the year that had begun with a spring-training lockout of players by owners who were fighting a losing last-ditch battle against the advent of free agency. Owners had inflamed the fear in fans that free agency would mean the end of baseball as we knew it. Many sports columnists, echoing the owners, had foretold the breaking of the bond between a city and its local heroes, railed against the ascendancy of money-grubbing players whose loyalty could be bought by the highest bidder.

For Detroit fans, made to feel as insecure in their players' affections as they were in their jobs, The Bird's seeming indifference to money meant a fond return of love. **As if his poverty were next to godliness, they sent him alms, stack after stack of letters filled with five- and 10-dollar bills.** In the Michigan legislature, a bill (that went nowhere) was introduced that demanded the Tigers give him an immediate raise. Babies were named after him. "In all my years in baseball, I've never seen anything like it," said Tiger manager Ralph Houk. "There's never been a love affair in our city to match it," wrote a swooning Falls.

Was The Bird "a theological concept," the good revealed to those who remained "vigilantly capable of recognizing it, and accepting it"? Were those laughing, clapping, love-bedazzled fans gathering themselves into a

How big a phenomenon was The Bird? America's No. 1 sports cartoonist—Bill Gallo of New York's Daily News—*honored him with a drawing. And Fidrych was an out-of-towner!*

cult of St. Mark, who would remain forever the boy who arrived in their hour of need, because his light, like Kinnick's, shone only for that one glorious season?

No, Fidrych did not die. The brevity of his career was born of his intense exuberance. During spring training 1977, The Bird kept leaping recklessly into the air to shag flies, despite Rusty Staub's repeated stern advice to cut out the foolishness. His last leap landed him on the disabled list with torn knee cartilage. Later in the season, he tore a rotator cuff, the result of trying to change his pitching motion to accommodate his surgically revamped knee. Mark Fidrych stayed with the Tigers for three more years, most of it spent on the bench, but he was never really The Bird again.

Though the memory of him in Detroit is as sweet today as it was that phenomenal summer of '76, nobody is likely to place him in the heroic tradition of the early Christian martyrs. If he enjoys the status of saint among his fans, it is sainthood of a different nature, one that came to be honored when The Holy Roman Empire was approaching its bicentennial year and worldly enticements posed more of a threat to Christians than martyrdom. If there is a tradition of sanctity that can shed light on Detroit's response to The Bird, it is the tradition of the holy fool.

■ Sweet Fool

From a secular perspective, of course, all saints are holy fools in their rejection of the tangible rewards of this world for the heavenly intangibles of the next world. In this sense, Christ is considered the prototype of the holy fool, and the martyrs were following in his tradition. But in the late 6th century, a separate strain of holy fools entered church hagiography.

Their foolishness resided not in an explicitly unworldly message, but in their behavior. These rare saints were comedians, and their comedy was low, slapstick, often X-rated, something like what the Three Stooges might have done without censors.

St. Symeon the Fool, whose 6th-century life was recorded by Bishop Leontius of Neapolis in the 7th century, set the standards for foolery. After an early life as a desert ascetic, Symeon decided on another approach to salvation. He headed for the city of Emesa in Syria, dragging a dead dog behind him, and proceeded for the rest of his life to breach every convention of both sanctity and civilized urban behavior.

In Leontius's account, St. Symeon walks about naked, farts and defecates in public, invades women's baths, and attempts to restore a blind man's sight by putting mustard in his eyes. He is, of course, only pretending to be mad, hiding his own virtue in an effort to improve the moral life of the city. By shocking its citizens, releasing them from convention's hold, the logic went, he jolted them into consideration of other, higher values. In 20th-century Detroit, other methods did the trick. I certainly don't mean to besmirch The Bird's reputation by associating his clean fun with Symeon's divinely inspired obscenity. But I do mean to suggest that "the

The Bird and Big Bird (above, left). The Bird and little birds (above, right).

BIRD TODAY

■ "These days I do my pitching at MotorCity Casino," says the beaming pitchman as he rolls his dice during the commercial.

Yes, it's Mark Fidrych, and he has made yet another comeback of sorts more than 25 years after he enlivened the game. Sure, you're thinking, this free spirit must have changed. Not much.

Well, he is about 20 pounds heavier than the 175 he weighed as a pitcher. His wardrobe now includes wool shirts and long underwear, not just T-shirts, jeans and sneakers. The frizzy, curly 'do? Still there, but shorter. Fidrych has his locks shorn five to six times a year now; in the '70s, it was once or twice.

Let's see . . . music. Then: Lynyrd Skynyrd, Elton John, Stevie Wonder. Now: Whatever his daughter, Jessica, who's a high school student, listens to. (No Britney Spears, he says.)

Wheels? He still has his '55 Chevy, but his ride when he's not working is a Ford F350 pickup. His promotional appearances—a paint company and a department store, among others—are more prosaic than his famed Aqua Velva ads (he still has a case).

Need any more proof? Ask him to say Boston Garden. He remains a classic case study in regional accents.

Fidrych's last comeback with the Triple-A Pawtucket (R.I.) Red Sox ended with his retirement in June 1983. He foundered a bit afterward, working jobs as diverse as building swimming pools to selling liquor. Now, he runs a trucking business out of Northboro, Mass. (pop. 14,013), where he lives with his wife, Ann, and Jessica, who has decorated their house's finished basement with her dad's memorabilia.

The Bird's ties to Detroit and the game have never been stronger. Fidrych was one of the former Tigers chosen as rotating color analyst during the 2001 season for Channel 50, and he pitched for the Tigers alumni against the Red Wings in their annual charity softball game.

When Detroit bid farewell to Tiger Stadium in September 1999, Fidrych was the first of the players from different eras to take his position on the field. He dashed to the pitcher's mound, where he kneeled to scoop dirt into a bag, reminiscent of his obsessiveness in manicuring the mound during his playing days.

He's older now—aren't we all?—but little about The Bird has changed.

frizzy-haired flaky phenom," as he was often described, provided more than 19 wins and comic relief. In his own idiosyncratic way, The Bird improved the moral life of Detroit by loosening the chokehold of a convention that was strangling the city: devotion to money. He raised the public's spirits high enough to contemplate other values: love of the game, love of their city, perhaps even love of one another, at least during those minutes when 50,000 rose to applaud a young man who had just lost a game.

He sweetened the city of Detroit and the game of baseball, both in their sour seasons of labor strife, and he did it by playing the fool, on the field and off. After hours, in the discos, he did a dance called The Fried Egg, which involved lying down on his back on the floor and rolling around. He poked his finger into the coin return slot, checking for dimes, every time he passed a coin phone. He purposefully spit tobacco juice all over the front of his shirt to look more like a baseball player. His public speaking style, the antithesis of Kinnick's Churchillian rhetoric, was described as "three parts frenzy, one part anarchy, and two parts 33 rpm record being played at 78 rpm."

To borrow a phrase used by Philadelphia sportswriter Mark Heisler that summer, **Fidrych became "an institution of gaiety" wherever he went. In Cleveland, they sprinkled birdseed on the mound before he pitched. In Milwaukee, they released a dozen doves.**

Yankee Graig Nettles told ESPN about the time he stepped to the plate and heard Fidrych talking to the ball: "So I stepped out of the box, and I started talking to my bat, and I said, 'Now don't you listen to that ball.'"

Now you know and I know, and Graig Nettles knew, that The Bird wasn't really talking to that ball. He was talking to himself, generating the concentration that stood him well. "Let them think what they want" Fidrych said when asked how he felt being called "a flake." Spoken, I imagine, like a holy fool.

Not all holy fools had the good of a city in mind. But St. Symeon, and baseball's 20th-century Mark, were improbable do-gooders, whose antics rejuvenated the souls of others.

The Tigers did not move from the bottom to the top of the charts in '76, yet it was one of the most memorable sports seasons in Detroit's history, because a young man with frizzy hair reminded them, when they most needed to be reminded, that sometimes laughing and loving is more important than winning.

Mark Fidrych was not made in the likeness of Nile Kinnick. No one would think to compare the diamond to the battlefields of Europe, or the Rookie of the Year Award to the Croix de Guerre. Kinnick, like the early martyrs, found his place in a heroic tradition. Fidrych, as befits the game called the national pastime, worked his magic through inspired comedy. He was not a man for all seasons, but he was exactly the right man for Detroit in the summer of '76.

Perfection on Four Legs

OR BOTH NILE KINNICK AND MARK FIDRYCH, IT WAS THE BREVITY of their spectacular careers that ensured the longevity of their cult. The intense love they inspired in their fans had no opportunity to dissipate, as it almost inevitably does when it is directed toward athletes whose careers are more prolonged and fluctuating. Kinnick and Fidrych exist for their fans, only and forever, at the moment of their peak. And the bond of locality, which fed the sense of intimate connection, can never be broken. Nile Kinnick is tied forever to Iowa '39, Mark Fidrych to Detroit '76.

But if brevity alone had the power to transform fleeting glory into a lasting transcendence, cults would routinely arise around racehorses. A depth of identification, often but not always based on locality, is also essential, and the feeling that an athlete is giving his all to claim victory for his fans, as well as himself. Hope often rides on horses, but only in very rare circumstances does group identification ride there, as well. Only once that I know of, and only for 45 seconds, on July 6, 1975.

The horse was Ruffian, a filly, and although only track aficionados had seen her race before that day, **almost 20 million viewers had turned to their televisions that Sunday afternoon to watch her run in a $350,000 match race for bragging rights against the winner of that year's Kentucky Derby, the colt Foolish Pleasure.** Of course, it wasn't Ruffian or Foolish Pleasure who would be doing the bragging. It would be those who chose one side or the other in what was billed "The Battle of the Sexes."

Ruffian was dark brown, nearly black, with a white diamond on her forehead, and she was large, taller and heavier than even outsized colts like the majestic Secretariat, the 1973 Triple Crown winner with whom she shared a bloodline. Her appearance fostered comparisons to every girl's first love, Black Beauty, and she was reputed to be the fastest filly that ever raced, perhaps that ever lived. In her 10 outings as a two- and three-year-old, she was not only undefeated, no horse had ever gotten anywhere near her after the opening few strides of a race. She routinely won by 9, 13, 15 lengths; her average margin of victory was just over 8 lengths. Eight of her 10 victories were in stakes races, and in all of them she set or matched record times while making it look easy.

Ruffian would take the lead at the start of a race, and seem to coast effortlessly, stretching her lead all the way to the finish line while looking as if she were simply floating above her long, beautifully reaching strides. Everyone who saw her race knew she was a great horse, but just how great remained a matter of speculation, because she had raced only against other fillies—not in the venerable Kentucky Derby, Preakness and Belmont Stakes, but in races with names like Comely, Fashion, Sorority and Mother Goose. As *Sports Illustrated* forthrightly worded it, "Racetrack tradition

The camera catches Ruffian in a most uncharacteristic pose—at rest.

TRAGIC INSPIRATIONS

Jane Schwartz is the author of Ruffian: Burning from the Start. *Originally published in 1991, it was reissued in May 2002.*

■ I first heard about Ruffian on the day she died. I was living in Boston at the time and read about the Great Match Race and its heart-wrenching aftermath in the sports pages of the *Globe*.

I cut out the article and put it in a file folder. Something about the filly—her brilliance, her perfection, the senselessness of her death—touched me in a way that was both painful and inspiring. For 10 years, the folder sat in a desk drawer. Then in 1985 my first novel was published and I began wondering what my next project would be. One night I woke up at 3 a.m. and said to myself, I'm going to write a book about Ruffian. Just like that. Although I followed sports in general, I had never paid any attention to horseracing. I had never even been to a racetrack. In fact, I knew nothing at all about that world except what I'd absorbed as a child from the books of Walter Farley and Marguerite Henry.

Writers are usually advised to write about what they know. But I've always written about what I wanted to know; what I had somehow missed out on knowing. To do that, of course, first you have to find things out. I spent almost five years uncovering Ruffian's story: reading, researching, interviewing, observing, and finally writing.

I concentrated on the people who had worked directly with the filly—her "human family," as they were called—but I also talked to broodmare managers, yearling managers, race-callers, stewards, starters, trainers and jocks who rode against her, handicappers, turf writers, breeders, vets, feed salesmen, van drivers, night watchmen. I talked to dozens of backstretch workers and racing fans who had witnessed all or part of Ruffian's career. I must have asked a million questions. I heard so many stories about so many horses, people and races that I could never write enough books to include them all.

holds that females generally are unable to compete on even terms with males."

If Ruffian had been born to another decade, that racetrack tradition, like so many off-track traditions, might have gone unchallenged. But this was 1975, and the pressure to test her against male competition was relentless. Only two years earlier, Billie Jean King had trounced Bobby Riggs in tennis volleys seen and heard round the world. But what bragging rights had been won in that contest remained a matter of dispute, because Billie Jean had not been pitted against the best of men. Her victory over Riggs brought a collective sigh of relief to champions of women's rights, but not a full-throated cry of vindication.

■ ## The Times They Are a-Changing

In 1975, the women's movement in the United States was still gathering heat, momentum—and passionate opposition. Then as now, the movement had many fronts. Three years earlier, *Ms.* magazine had been founded, and the legislation known as Title IX, prohibiting sex discrimination in schools receiving federal funds, had passed into law. In 1973, the year of the King-Riggs match, the Supreme Court upheld abortion rights in Roe v. Wade and women were integrated into the U.S. military. In 1974, the Equal Rights Amendment was making its rounds of states in a losing battle for ratification, and Little League opened its fields of play to girls.

Women were pushing for change on every front, and traditionalists were pushing back just as hard, trying to hold a line against women's rights

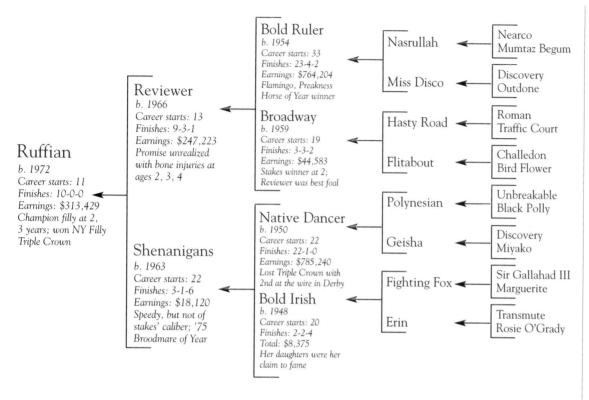

Ruffian
b. 1972
Career starts: 11
Finishes: 10-0-0
Earnings: $313,429
Champion filly at 2,
3 years; won NY Filly
Triple Crown

Reviewer
b. 1966
Career starts: 13
Finishes: 9-3-1
Earnings: $247,223
Promise unrealized
with bone injuries at
ages 2, 3, 4

Shenanigans
b. 1963
Career starts: 22
Finishes: 3-1-6
Earnings: $18,120
Speedy, but not of
stakes' caliber; '75
Broodmare of Year

Bold Ruler
b. 1954
Career starts: 33
Finishes: 23-4-2
Earnings: $764,204
Flamingo, Preakness
Horse of Year winner

Broadway
b. 1959
Career starts: 19
Finishes: 3-3-2
Earnings: $44,583
Stakes winner at 2;
Reviewer was best foal

Native Dancer
b. 1950
Career starts: 22
Finishes: 22-1-0
Earnings: $785,240
Lost Triple Crown with
2nd at the wire in Derby

Bold Irish
b. 1948
Career starts: 20
Finishes: 2-2-4
Total: $8,375
Her daughters were her
claim to fame

Nasrullah — Nearco / Mumtaz Begum
Miss Disco — Discovery / Outdone
Hasty Road — Roman / Traffic Court
Flitabout — Challedon / Bird Flower
Polynesian — Unbreakable / Black Polly
Geisha — Discovery / Miyako
Fighting Fox — Sir Gallahad III / Marguerite
Erin — Transmute / Rosie O'Grady

RUFFIAN'S FAMILY TREE

■ It's in the blood and in the bones, but, most important, in the performance. Although pedigrees are studied by prospective owners with a scrutiny usually reserved for a racing form, they are no guarantee of how well a horse will fare on the track.

"There is no way you can look at a pedigree and say, 'Oh, it's gotta be.' Even the best sires in history only produce 25 percent stakes winners," said John Sparkman, the bloodstock/sales editor of the *Thoroughbred Times*. "One in four is not great from a normal point of view, but in this business it's great."

Ruffian's bloodline is impressive. Her forebears include great thoroughbreds (Native Dancer, Bold Ruler, Nasrullah, among others) and notable broodmares (Bold Irish, Broadway, Rosie O'Grady).

The first three or four generations of a pedigree chart are examined most closely, with special attention to the sires. Much can be foretold from the racing records, distances run and how their offspring performed.

Ruffian was in Reviewer's first crop. Reviewer was a large horse, and a fast one. "If he was an athlete, you would know he was definitely a tight end or linebacker, not a running back or wide receiver," said Sparkman. "That would tell you something."

Broadway, Reviewer's dam, foaled a filly, Con Game, who later produced Seeking the Gold, a winner of the Dwyer Stakes and Super Derby who also finished in second place in the Wood Memorial and the Breeders' Cup Classic.

Broadway's sire was Hasty Road, a Preakness winner, and her dam was Flitabout, who foaled Flirtatious and Funloving, both major winners.

Reviewer's sire was Bold Ruler, who had a great stud career, siring 82 Stakes winners, including Triple Crown winner Secretariat.

Shenanigans, Ruffian's dam, was well-bred, sired by one of the 20th-century's greatest horses, Native Dancer. The general quality of the female family is often overlooked, but in the case of Ruffian, it was particularly important. Bold Irish, Shenanigans' dam, comes from a family that has been producing superior horseflesh since the 1890s.

that was, to a great extent, a line of argument, the same line that underlay track tradition—"females generally are unable to compete on even terms with males." Perhaps because the argument of inherent female inferiority was assailable on so many fronts, opponents of women's rights placed a disproportionate amount of passionate emphasis on the front where it seemed most self-evident—in sports. Female athletes made convenient poster girls for those who wanted to put a face on everything they didn't want women to be or become.

In 1973, Little League, Inc. was so upset when an 11-year-old girl was allowed to play on a Hoboken, New Jersey, baseball team that they revoked the charter of the city's Little League chapter. Defending their action in court, a Little League lawyer argued, "The charter of the Little League says it was formed for education and recreation to help boys reach manhood. And manhood includes physical strength and courage. Society does not ask for that in girls and women." Introduced as evidence that American girls were not fit to play baseball was a 1956 study, comparing adult male and female bones culled from Japanese cadavers.

The fiercest opposition to women athletes, however, was mounted by the National Collegiate Athletic Association (NCAA), which governed men's college sports. Although Title IX passed Congress in 1972, its provisions for equal opportunity in the nation's schools did not take effect until several years later, largely because of protests brought by the NCAA.

Surely, it argued, the mandate against sex discrimination didn't apply to sports. Since American colleges and universities were spending less than 2 percent of their athletic budgets on women's sports at the time, one can understand its fear of the changes equality might bring. "Two percent is enough," Walter Byers, then executive director of the NCAA was quoted as saying, as if women were milk. More, he repeatedly warned, would mean "the end of intercollegiate sports as we know it."

■ On the Frontlines of Gender Politics

The NCAA would learn the results of its lobbying in July 1975, when the long-awaited guidelines for how to implement Title IX were scheduled to be published. Walter Byers actually used the term "impending doom," summoning ghostly visions of empty gridirons throughout the land if college athletic departments were forced to provide equal opportunity to women. That, of course, is precisely what they were ordered to do in July, 1975—which coincidentally happened to be the month and year of Ruffian's scheduled race against Foolish Pleasure.

It's not that everyone who tuned in to watch the horses race had the legal intricacies of Title IX of the Education Amendment Act of 1972 on their minds. Rather that the cultural debate surrounding the status of women's rights in general, and the status of women athletes in particular, was extremely overheated at that moment in time. And so it happened that **Ruffian and Foolish Pleasure temporarily became the front-runners in a long campaign of partisan sexual politics.**

On race day, CBS, which had put up the $350,000 purse for the race, passed out "Him vs. Her" T-shirts. The televised pre-race interviews at Belmont Park emphasized the obvious. "I pick Foolish Pleasure just because he's a male," said one man who looked like Pat Boone. "Ruffian

Except for her tragic final race, when Ruffian ran (in the Coaching Club American Oaks, top left, and the Acorn Stakes, top right, both 3-year-old filly Triple Crown events), the rest of the field was lucky to make it into the finishing photo.

Classic MOMENTS **Racing** *Daily* **Form**

12 BELMONT
18 GARDEN STATE
23 PIMLICO
28 SUFFOLK

Vol. 19 No. 142   HIGHTSTOWN, NJ. SATURDAY JULY 6, 1975   PRICE $2.50

Foolish Pleasure Meets Ruffian In 'Battle of Sexes' at Belmont

because she's a female," said the woman who had been paired with him in the editing booth. "I like Foolish Pleasure because I'm a male chauvinist pig," another man proudly announced.

Who liked whom was not strictly a matter of gender. Ruffian had many male fans. Some of them knew a spectacular horse when they saw one. Perhaps others were fathers of those little girls who wanted to play baseball. Virtually all of the women, though, were rooting for Ruffian. The promise of a clear-cut symbolic victory for the female sex playing on a level field was rare enough to bring out legions of women who had never been to a racetrack before. Many of them knew nothing about "the other horse," except, of course, his sex.

■ Broken Dreams

Foolish Pleasure was not, as Ruffian was, undefeated, but he had won 11 of his 14 races, including the Kentucky Derby, and his losses had been narrow ones. Both horses were grandchildren of Bold Ruler, who had been Secretariat's sire, which made Ruffian and Foolish Pleasure cousins, a niece and nephew of Secretariat. Ruffian, weighing in at 1,125 pounds, was the larger (by 64 pounds) and taller of the two, and a front-runner. Foolish Pleasure was a come-from-behind horse, but track experts agreed that if he didn't keep up with Ruffian from the start, he would never be able to gain on her, because, as jockey Jacinto Vasquez put it, "She breaks running and finishes running. The rest of the horses don't run that way."

At 6:20 p.m., after a long afternoon of pre-race festivities, the two horses broke from the gate, and "the battle of the sexes" was on. Jacinto Vasquez, in red and white silks, was riding Ruffian. Braulio Baeza, in black and white silks, rode Foolish Pleasure. Ruffian immediately took the lead on the inside, but Baeza kept Foolish Pleasure just off her right flank, matching Ruffian stride for stride and only a neck behind. Ruffian blazed through the first quarter-mile in 22$\frac{1}{5}$ seconds and began to expand her lead, inch by inch, through the second quarter until she was a half length ahead as they approached the half-mile point. Then, the unimaginable happened. Both jockeys heard the sound—"like a baseball bat snapping in two," Vasquez said.

"Ruffian has broken down!" the track announcer screamed. "Ruffian

MATCHLESS RACES

Bravado, bucks and brawn are the essential ingredients for a compelling match race, and in the 1900s, these were the 10 most important.

1. Nashua vs. Swaps
1955, Washington Park (Chicago)
Swaps' Derby victory stopped Nashua from winning the Triple Crown, but in this $100,000 race, Eddie Arcaro's handling and a quick start propelled Nashua to a 6 1/2-length victory. Would Swaps, nursing a sore foot, have won if healthy? The debate rages on.

2. Ruffian vs. Foolish Pleasure
1975, Belmont Park (N.Y.)

3. Man o' War vs. Sir Barton
1920, Kenilworth Park (Windsor, Ontario)
Running on tender feet on a hard surface, Sir Barton, who had won what would later be called the Triple Crown, lost by 7 lengths to a younger horse, the people's champion, whom some observers believe is the best racehorse that ever lived (11 starts, 11 wins that year; only one loss—in which he finished second—in a two-season career.)

4. Seabiscuit vs. War Admiral
1938, Pimlico Race Course (Baltimore)
FDR and the nation listened as the '37 Triple Crown winner raced against Seabiscuit, winner of just 5 of 35 starts as a two-year-old. In the stretch, Seabiscuit pulled away for a 4-length victory and a course record. Shirley Temple starred in *The Story of Seabiscuit.* Laura Hillenbrand's *Seabiscuit: An American Legend* was a bestseller in 2001.

5. Alsab vs. Whirlaway
1942, Narragansett Park (R.I.)
Picked up for a bargain $700 as a yearling, Alsab, the Derby runner-up, was matched against 3-10 favorite Whirlaway, the '41 Triple Crown winner. In the stretch, Alsab lost almost all of a 2-length lead, but managed to hang on by a nose.

Man o' War vs. Sir Barton

Nashua vs. Swaps

Seabiscuit vs. War Admiral

6. Zev vs. Papyrus
1923, Belmont Park
"Zev's Victorious Grin" was the headline above Zev's photo in one newspaper, after the Kentucky Derby winner beat the English Derby winner by 5 lengths. Papyrus's handlers ignored warnings that their horse was improperly shod for the muddy track conditions.

7. Hourless vs. Omar Khayyam
1917, Laurel Park (Md.)
In a role reversal, foreign-bred Derby winner and inveterate closer Omar Khayyam went to the front immediately. Belmont winner Hourless—with a new jockey chosen 10 minutes before being saddled—pulled into the lead at the eighth pole, winning by 1 1/4 lengths.

8. Capot vs. Coaltown
1949 Pimlico Race Course
After taking the lead on the first turn, Capot coasted to a 12-length victory; Coaltown, in his final race at four and lacking his usual speed, was not pushed. The match victory confirmed the validity of Capot's $1^1/_2$-length win over Coaltown in the Sysonby Stakes, and he was named the Horse of the Year.

9. Clang vs. Myrtlewood
1935, Hawthorne (Ill.) and Coney Island (Ohio)
The three-year-olds met twice within three weeks. In the first race, the filly Myrtlewood, a heavy favorite, won by a nose. In the rematch, Clang galloped in 1:09 1/5 to establish a six-furlong record, but the margin of the victory was the same.

10. Iron Mask vs. Pan Zareta
1914, Juarez (Mexico)
Two great sprinters on a fast track equaled a sure bet for an American record (1:09 3/5) for six furlongs. Iron Mask hit his best stride early and pulled away to win by 5 lengths over Pan Zareta, a filly and future Hall of Famer. Winner's take: $400; second, $100.

has broken down!" Exclamation marks can't do justice to the shock and horror in his voice, as he repeated himself until the crowd of 50,000, still roaring, grasped what was happening, which took a few moments, because Ruffian hadn't stopped running. Her right front foreleg was broken, visibly flopping, but she continued to race on momentum and heart for another 40 strides before Vasquez was able to bring her to a standing halt. **"I tried to pull her up and stop her," he recalled. "She wouldn't let me. She wanted to keep running." She never fell.**

Dr. Manuel Gilman, the chief veterinarian for the New York Racing Association, rushed to Ruffian and put an inflatable plastic boot on her shattered leg to staunch the bleeding. "It was as bad an accident as could happen," Dr. Gilman told *Newsweek*. "She had been going so fast and was so full of herself—she was in the race of her life—that she kept running on the fracture, grinding, grinding, grinding the bones. It was an unbelievable injury. The ligaments were shattered. The bones were like pieces of glass."

Ruffian was sedated and taken to an equine clinic near the track. Meanwhile, Foolish Pleasure, who had finished the race alone, was posing for his photos in a winner's circle ceremony that gave no one pleasure. Veterinarians worked to save Ruffian, performing a 3½-hour surgery on her leg. Millions who had seen the televised race, who had known Ruffian in her glory for no more than 45 seconds, followed news dispatches on her condition through the night. They went to bed on the news that she had survived the surgery.

■ Death of a Champion

About 1 a.m., when the anesthesia wore off, Ruffian awoke and began thrashing her front legs as if she were still running. "Several men tried to hold her down," said veterinarian Dr. Alex Harthill. "But she threw us around as if we were rag dolls." She kept paddling her legs, spinning around in circles on the floor, kicking a special boot off her leg and knocking her plaster cast to pieces, reinjuring the leg they had worked so hard to repair. At 2:20 a.m. on July 7, the decision was made. Ruffian was given a lethal injection of phenobarbital and died within seconds.

She was buried that evening in the infield at Belmont Park, just beyond the finish line she had died trying to reach. *I was ____ when I heard the news.* Millions can still fill in that blank. More than a quarter-century later, people still leave flowers at her grave site. One man who saw Ruffian race that day asked that his ashes be scattered on Ruffian's grave when he died, and his request has since been honored.

"It may seem strange to mourn a horse like a human," wrote sports columnist Cyndi Meagher, who had covered the race for *The Detroit News* that day. But for Meagher, and for uncounted others, Ruffian was something besides the best filly who ever raced. "Name me another female athlete who died trying to prove she could compete with a male," Meagher wrote, with more than a touch of anger at "the trainers, the owners, and

TRACK ANNOUNCER CHIC ANDERSON'S CALL

■ Both horses are in the gate and we're ready and they're off.

Breaking very sharply, Foolish Pleasure on the outside, a head in front. Ruffian is along the inside, and both of them are now together.

Now Ruffian moves up. And Ruffian has taken about a head lead, but Foolish Pleasure is right there with her. Those two are going to go together, apparently, just what we might have expected.

No whips in sight at this point. Vasquez hand riding, Baeza on the outside hand riding. Both riders seem to have a handful of horse at this point, at least.

It's a head for Ruffian. Foolish Pleasure is outside and holding right steady with her. They are about to get to first quarter. We've gone three-eighths and some change.

Now we are coming up to the first quarter of a mile. And it will tell about this pace. It is Foolish Pleasure going by fast . . .

Ruffian has broken down! Ruffian has broken down on the backstretch! This race is over!

Ruffian has broken down indeed to the outside fence. Foolish Pleasure is on his way, and it's all over but the shouting, folks. Ruffian, the great filly, has broken down on the backstretch. I don't know the nature of the injury.

Here's Foolish Pleasure, and he'll just jog to the wire, of course . . . as Braulio Baeza, realizing what happened, very easily eased his horse back, and he's just going along at a common gallop . . . He'll come around to the wire.

But more important, at this point, I suppose, is what happened to Ruffian. I'm looking across and Vasquez has dismounted from the horse . . .

She's definitely broken down, and she's definitely broken down in her front leg. It appears to be the left front ankle or knee and, at this distance, at least, that's all I can see.

This is Foolish Pleasure and he's on his way right now. He's passing the quarter pole, and he's just going to gallop, eased up, to the finish line.

Vasquez, on the backstretch, is now beginning to take the saddle

off of Ruffian. And let's certainly hope this is not a serious injury.

We're going to have a winner in about a sixteenth of a mile now, as Foolish Pleasure will win this race by default, as Ruffian has given it up on the backstretch with an injury.

Here's Foolish Pleasure, eased up, crossing the line, an easy winner. And, of course, it was just a workout for him. They were blazing along . . . (when) this injury occurred. They had gone over a quarter, not much more than a quarter, in 22-and-1, which is very fast when horses are attempting to go a mile and a quarter.

Now they are on the backstretch, and this is the horse ambulance that has now pulled up alongside Ruffian. Ruffian is standing just behind it. And now there will be some very careful care in getting her into the horse ambulance.

And I'm certain right now this is a terrific disappointment to Jacinto Vasquez, to the Janneys, well almost to everyone, because she was a fantastically great filly, but an injury has come up at a very, very inopportune time.

Already mortally stricken, Ruffian starts to fall behind Foolish Pleasure (above), before finally limping to a halt (above right).

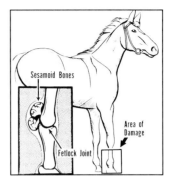

A MEDICAL CATASTROPHE

■ Vets call it a "breakdown," a catastrophic injury, usually to the bone, suffered by a thoroughbred during a race. Once, it was synonymous with death, because the extraordinarily fragile physical structure that makes a horse in motion one of nature's examples of grace also makes healing almost impossible.

According to Dr. Carl Kirker-Head of the Tufts School of Veterinary Medicine, "Racehorses sustaining catastrophic injuries these days stand a better—not a fantastic—likelihood of making it through, but probably no better than a one-in-four shot, because they are such amazingly delicate creatures in spite of their size."

For a thoroughbred to survive a catastrophic injury requires one part medicine to one part physics. A 1,000-pound thoroughbred goes from 30 mph to zero in no time after snapping a forelimb bone. (Most of the horse's bulk is carried on the front end.)

The high adrenaline level produced by racing can contribute to panic, flailing of the leg and, ultimately, the horse's destruction. If, however, the horse will stand or allow the jockey to support the injured leg until a vet can administer a sedative and immobilize the limb in a splint, there is a chance the horse can be treated. Still, the bone may pierce the skin, which could introduce infection, or damage the soft tissues surrounding the bone, and so hinder the blood supply to the injured area.

The next step is to repair the bone under anesthesia, often with metal plates and screws, like those used in human trauma victims. Speedy surgery is a necessity: a horse cannot lie down for an extended period—their weight can compress muscles and nerves, depriving tissues of blood. Toxins released from dead muscle can cause severe kidney damage and eventual renal failure.

But rehabilitation may be the most difficult step of all. In rehab, the horse must be able to walk, putting full weight on the limb, without redamaging the leg. Sometimes a sling or swimming pool can provide support for the long healing process.

Even if a major fracture—say, to the cannon or sesamoid bones—is treated successfully, a return to racing is doubtful, although a future as a broodmare or stallion may be possible.

The medical techniques available today might save a horse that in the past might have been doomed by an injury, but so much depends on the spirit of the horse. "In Ruffian's time, they didn't have that opportunity and the nice drugs we have these days," said Kirker-Head. "And Ruffian was one of those horses that panicked."

the racing press who all agreed Ruffian was great—for a filly."

Fortunately, we cannot name another female athlete who died for that cause. In fact, I can't think of any other event since Ruffian's death in which an individual female was pitted against an individual male with the presumption that anything of value or significance could be proved by such a contest. Perhaps that is Ruffian's most important legacy.

Candace Lyle Hogan, a sports journalist who in the '70s had followed every battle in the war over Title IX, said recently of Ruffian, **"We should never have made her carry that burden. No one should ever have to carry that burden."** The burden, she meant, of bearing an entire gender on your back. If Ruffian had finished that race, whether she won or lost, she would have remained forever "something besides the best filly who ever raced." But for many of us who saw her last race, it was precisely in the moment of her collapse that she stopped being a symbol, and became a horse again—an extraordinary creature whose natural splendor was enough to rejoice over and whose destruction was more than enough to grieve over.

That Ruffian broke down while carrying such a disproportionate weight of hope was, we must presume, a coincidence. She may have experienced an atmosphere of heightened, frenzied expectation that day, but she couldn't have known what she was carrying. She may have died because of our sins, but she didn't die for our sins. Ruffian was blameless,

but she was not a saint. Rather she reminded us that sainthood must be chosen, not imposed by those who seek redemption in another's victory.

We routinely ask our athletes to be more than they are, forgetting it's a rare human who is willing to shoulder the load of other people's hope. When the hope is frivolous, as it often is, no more than the wish for a quick fix of vicarious glory, the burden is light. But there are times when the hope is desperate, the burden crushing. If in those times, there arises an athlete who willingly takes on that burden, and who succeeds in restoring faith in the "possibility of victory," or the possibility of love, or the possibility of community, he is adored. And if fate suddenly wrenches that athlete from his fans, we are stunned into a keen appreciation of just how much had been asked and how much given. Idolatry becomes true reverence for an athlete who, through the improbable avenue of his sport, lofted us beyond self-aggrandizement to an apprehension of the goodness less self-regarding efforts can bring to our lives. The mighty Kinnick, the irrepressible Fidrych, the perfect Ruffian: The sudden revelation of their frailty was also the sudden revelation of their grace.

Ruffian was rare. The Bird was rare. Rarest of all was Nile Kinnick.

"What is a man's obligation to society?" he asked. He died before he could answer that question for himself. But by the way he lived and died, he ensured that those for whom he played football in 1939 would have to ask that question of themselves. Beautiful, unwitting Ruffian forced another question upon us: "At what cost do we shift the weight of our own chal-

EYEWITNESS TO A TRAGEDY

William Nack, who wrote Secretariat: The Making of a Champion, *which is being reissued this year, was the turf writer at* Newsday *and spent almost 23 years as a* Sports Illustrated *writer. He recalls his most vivid memories of Ruffian's tragic day.*

■ At the moment Ruffian broke down, I was in the clubhouse seats at Belmont Park, sitting near Ruffian's owner, Stuart Janney and his family and friends, and all I remember was this stunned silence from them as they rose from their seats, their hands clasped over their mouths. Leaping up, I dashed through the clubhouse seats and down the winding stairs and onto the tunnel that led to the track. As I reached the track, a uniformed Pinkerton guard held up his arms to block me.

"Where do you think you're going?" he asked.

"I gotta get across the track!" I yelled. "That filly's broken down on the backside."

"You can't go there!" he yelled back. At this moment, a clutch of photographers swept up about 10 feet to my right, and the beefy guard moved over to block them, too. Now unopposed, ignoring the cries of the guard, I ducked under the rail and started across the track. Just as I got to the crown of the oval, I heard the throbbing sound of hoofbeats in the distance and I stopped. It was an extraordinary moment. Looking left, I saw Foolish Pleasure racing toward me at 40 miles an hour. I heard the colt's jockey, Braulio Baeza, scream at me: "Watch out!" I froze on the crown. And felt the wind and heard the sound of hooves as he swept past me at the wire.

Here I took off from the crown, ducked under the rail fence, and ran as fast as I could across the infield grass, stopping only to catch my breath. I reached the backfield fence, 30 feet from the mare, and watched the racetrack veterinarian, Dr. Manuel Gilman, fit Ruffian with a plastic inflatable cast. Emerging from beneath her, his hands bloody, Gilman started walking toward me. He looked ashen.

"What happened, doc?" I asked him.

"She shattered her sesamoids," he said, referring to the pivotal bones in her ankle.

"Why the blood?" I asked.

"They exploded out and ruptured the blood vessels. It's terrible."

"What's the prognosis?" I recall asking him.

"Not good," he said.

Not 24 hours later, in the settling darkness at Belmont Park, a handful of people gathered around an open grave on the racetrack infield, by the finish line, waiting for her. No one said a word. The headlights from a truck glinted in the distance, slowly approaching us. It backed up to the open grave and a half dozen men scurried about the truck. Ruffian was dressed in a white bolt of canvas that had been shaped like a suit around her body. They pulled her off the truck and lowered her gently into the hollow.

Trainer Frank Whiteley was too choked to speak. He was carrying the blanket she had worn to the paddock for the Great Match Race.

He handed it to one of Ruffian's handlers, Mike Bell.

"Here, Mike, put this on her," Frank said.

Bell descended into the grave and spread it out over her. He climbed out with tears in his eyes.

No sound of rifles called her to this rest. No eulogies. No dirge of taps. The spreading of that blanket was the final, most eloquent salute to her—the fastest, gamest filly that ever lived.

lenges onto another's back?" And Mark Fidrych, in his own inimitable way, made us think for at least one rare season about what we really want when we think all we want is to win.

■ They Held Back Nothing

Kinnick, Fidrych and Ruffian endure in the imagination, because those questions endure in our lives. For those who witnessed them in their seasons, the images—of Kinnick kicking, passing, punting, of Fidrych loping, leaping, hurling, of Ruffian floating toward the finish—seem to contain a hidden wisdom. The images contain clues to the answers, answers that could be ours if we just let the power of the images expand before our mind's eye, answers we might even live by some day if ever we are ready, as they were ready.

All three put everything they had into every performance. Ironman Kinnick with his five consecutive 60-minute games; Fidrych with his back-to-back 11-inning games; Ruffian breaking fast from the gate and running full out the whole way until she had stretched her lead as far as it could be stretched, and then kept running even when she was finished. There was nothing calculated or self-preserving in their performances. They gave everything every time out. They didn't hold back, pace themselves, save something for the next game, the next season.

And in the act of giving everything, they seemed to miraculously transcend their own physical limits. The short, not very fast Kinnick

Dr. Manuel Gilman applies an inflatable splint to Ruffian's shattered leg, which, sadly, was not enough to save the great champion (left). Meanwhile, Foolish Pleasure—largely forgotten by history, despite the fact that he won the Kentucky Derby and was later inducted into racing's Hall of Fame—galloped to an empty victory (above).

became unstoppable. The kid from nowhere couldn't seem to miss the plate. The filly ran as no filly was believed to be able to run. They all inspired a "too good to be true" feeling in those who saw them. And when they fell from the sky, the too-good-to-be-true feeling seemed in retrospect a premonition, and the feeling underwent a change, a translation into "too good for this world."

Fans suddenly realized what they had witnessed. Not just the extraordinary achievements of extraordinary physical beings. **It was in their moments of death and injury that fans realized the flesh of their heroes was weak, just as theirs was, and that what they had witnessed was grace.**

Fifth-century Christians understood this about the martyrs they venerated. The martyr's ability to transcend physical limits did not arise from strength and courage beyond the ordinary, but from faith beyond the ordinary. "For the sufferings of the martyrs were miracles in themselves," Peter Brown explains in *The Cult of the Saints*. "The heroism of the martyrs had always been treated as a form of possession, strictly dissociated from normal human courage."

Links to a Heroic Past

It may seem irreverent to compare the fan's relation to an athlete, any athlete, to an early Christian's veneration of the martyrs, but that presumes a standard of decorous piety that developed over centuries of institutionalized worship. There is much to suggest that the festivals of the martyrs, when they first spread throughout the Holy Roman Empire in the 5th century, had far more in common with modern sports than we might think.

According to historian R. A. Markus, the annual cycle of martyrs' festivals served two main purposes: They linked the triumphant post-Constantinian church to its heroic past, and they promoted social cohesion among diverse populations of Christians by providing group identity through group celebrations. The festivals provided the only occasions in which the normally strict boundaries of class were spanned, where rich and poor, educated and uneducated freely mingled, and where the greatest social division in late antique society, that between the sexes, broke down.

Although social cohesion and connection to the heroic past are noble goals, many who went to the festivals, like many of those who attend sporting events, used the occasions for other purposes. Drink flowed freely and many loves were kindled, Peter Brown writes, under cover of "the unregulated sociability" of these feasts. A biographer of one holy man boasts that he remained "chaste all his life, although he had frequently attended the festivals of the martyrs as a young man."

Commercialization also undermined the more exalted possibilities of the festivals, providing early precedents for the modern big business of both mass-produced sports paraphernalia and collector's items. Images of the martyrs replaced traditional decorative themes on lamps and table-

Ruffian was not only swift and beautiful, she was a physical monster—actually larger than Foolish Pleasure, her male foe in racing's Battle of the Sexes.

RICHARD STONE REEVE

ware. Among the wealthy, relics of the martyrs, both genuine and fraudulent, became the desired objects of a lively trade. Bishops, who wanted the relics enshrined in churches, where their power would be available to all, entered into disputes with wealthy laymen, who could arrange the private purchase of holy remains in the hope that it would confer special status and benefits upon their families.

St. Augustine's concern about influential individuals depriving the public of access to relics can be heard echoing oddly across the centuries in the disputes that arose in 1998 over Sammy Sosa's bats. "The Baseball Hall of Fame says it has the bat Sammy Sosa used to hit homer No. 66, not [New York] Mayor Rudolph Giuliani," begins an AP dispatch of November 11, 1998. "Also, Gov. George Pataki thought the bat he got from Sosa was the one used to hit homer No. 59 . . . But the Hall of Fame says it has both bats."

Issues of authenticity and rightful possession did not end with the bat. Three people in Chicago claimed to be the rightful owner of Sosa's home-run ball No. 62, and the Chicago police couldn't determine which was the genuine article. Sosa personally appealed for its return, so it could go "to the American people and the Hall of Fame."

The halls of fame, like the early Christian church, try to orchestrate the unruly passions we bring to the celebration of our heroes. By controlling the canonization process, establishing a monopoly of the most coveted relics, erecting shrines that funnel the faithful to its doors, institutions install themselves as middlemen between the athlete and his fan, the saint and his devotee. But no amount of high-minded rhetoric about social cohesion or links to the heroic past can make the celebration of either an athlete or a martyr serve its ordained purpose. That requires a miracle.

At least three times in the last century, historical circumstance collided with the individual fate of an athlete to produce that miracle.

Is it wrong to mourn for an animal as we would a human? More than a quarter-century later, fans still leave flowers and mementos at the Belmont grave site of the tragic filly.

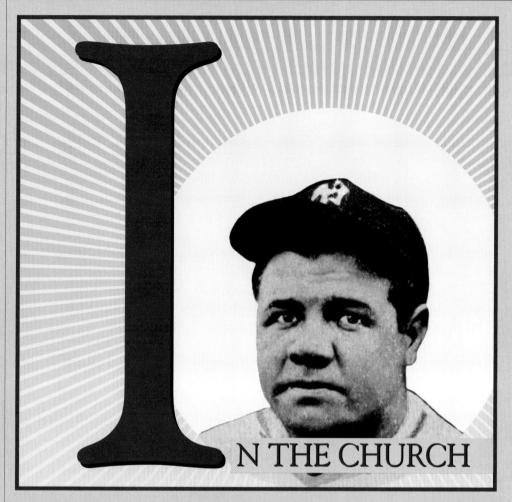

IN THE CHURCH

OF GOOD FAITH IN ALL BALL, IN THE CATHEDRAL OF CLASSIC AMERICAN SPORTS, IN MY FATHER'S HOUSE, THERE ARE MANY MANSIONS AND HIGH MUCKETY-MUCKS, BUT VERY FEW REAL SAVIORS. "SAVIOR LIKE A SHEPHERD LE-EE-AD US, MUCH WE NEED THY TENDER CARE." OH . . . YEAH . . . TOO ORNERY AND TOO FLAWED TO BE SAINTS, TOO SELF-CENTERED AND SINGLE-MINDED TO BE PROPHETS; OH . . . YEAH . . . OFTEN, THEY WERE NOT LIKE GODS. MORE LIKE SONS-OF- . . . WELL, LIKE UN-GODS, LET'S JUST SAY, TO KEEP FROM USING THOSE SAME PROFANITIES THEY OFTEN USED, AND IN SOME WAYS APPROPRIATELY, ON THOSE RARE OCCASIONS WHEN THEY DIDN'T PERFORM ANOTHER MIRACLE.

SAVIORS

by Ralph Wiley

They made it possible for a new kind of religion. They gave us something else to believe in . . . *oh . . . yeah.*

The Saviors literally "saved" their sports from the sweaty margins of American society, and maybe even from extinction. They did it by force of will, talent, dint of personality and a transcendent ability to change the game. Not just play, but *change* the game. To change ball, and also to make us like it, *love* it—feel it in our bones, in our hearts and minds, in our eternal and evolving souls.

"He can't do that . . . Hey! *Nobody* else can do that! Nobody else would've even *thought* of doing that! . . . Jeez-sus! . . . Only *he* coulda done that! Yes! *That's* how that game can be played! Hey! Can he do it *again?!*" *Oh . . . yeah.*

Our collective "WOW!" is like the congregation saying "Amen." For what they did was also somehow the right thing to do, proper—sometimes, almost coincidentally right in a moral sense . . . but always right in the sense of the games themselves. Go ahead on then, sisters and brothers. Testify. Bigger than we ever thought. Better than we ever dreamed.

■ Our Mythmakers

So. Here be Saviors: George Herman "Babe" Ruth, Jack Roosevelt "Jackie" Robinson, Larry Joe Bird, Earvin "Magic" Johnson, Alvin Ray "Pete" Rozelle, Eldrick "Tiger" Woods. The names were part of it—simple, easy, unforgettable. The names made them human, more accessible, and also more than human. Familiar, yet otherworldly. Their skills and missions, and our possibilities and flaws, all defined at once.

Big-league baseball, NFL football, NBA basketball and PGA golf would not be the preeminent, ascendant spectator sports they are in this new 21st-century world without these performers. Our culture wouldn't be what it is without them. **All we are or might become, good, bad, sad and magnificent, we have the Saviors to thank for revealing it.** They are immortal, as long as we say so. For all we might become, for all we do, no matter who comes along to become "The Babe Ruth of . . . " whatever, whoever is "Quicker'n you can say Jack Robinson . . . "

They are Our Myth. And really, there can never be anyone else like them. For if there were, that would be . . . sacrilegious.

The Saviors didn't just save their games, they transfigured them (right, the "Transfiguration," by Raphael)—and themselves in the process. As American League president Will Harridge said, "To say 'Babe Ruth' is to say 'Baseball.' "

George Herman 'Babe' Ruth
(born February 6, 1895—died August 16, 1948)

ABE RUTH. HOME RUN. SAME DIFFERENCE. NOW BABE RUTH was a great baseball player, even without the Home Run. But it was the Home Run, that quintessential American blow, that made him an encompassing sports Savior.

He came to the big leagues at the age of 19, out of dingy rooms and a smoky, shadowy upbringing, mostly over a Conway Street bar and a home for incorrigible boys in his native Baltimore. He was raw, unlettered, without any social grace or skill; he was unused to discipline, even to clean drawers. Just let him go, his parents George Ruth and the former Kate Schamberger seemed to be saying. We have seven other children, living and dead, and can do nothing with this one. And so he ran the streets and went unschooled and had none to rein him in.

Until baseball saved him. Gave him a Why.

It wasn't big 6-foot-5 Brother Matthias at the reformatory, St. Mary's Industrial School for Boys, that saved him. No, it was big Brother Matthias hitting one-handed fungoes a country mile high and 10-year-old George sitting there, cross-legged and open-mouthed, looking at the big man swinging the bat, that saved him. He was later called a natural, uninhibited Tarzan, a man who "just did things." But is human behavior ever that simple? Surely baseball, as practiced by a big man swinging a bat, was more impressive than petty larceny.

George Herman Ruth was not saved or even overly impressed by his bartending old man, who died breaking up a dumb fight before Ruth was 22; nor even saved by his mother, who died August 23, 1910, when George was 15. He was out of the reformatory when she died. Within the year, he was back in St. Mary's. Pinching produce had become knocking back hard liquor to a most alarming degree. George was an old 16.

■ ## Just What the Doctor Ordered

He broke into pro baseball as a waif and naif, as Jack Dunn's bonus baby, Dunn being owner-manager of the Baltimore Orioles of the International League. "Dunn's Babe," a 19-year-old fish (but a *big* fish) with a left arm good enough for the big leagues, yet not needing to shave. **He was pure baseball player. Naive? He had not so much as been on an elevator.** "Just what the doctor ordered, Keed," he liked to say in later years.

The doctor, as it turned out a few years later, was a judge, Kenesaw Mountain Landis; no Savior he, but an oddly nicknamed reed of a man brought in to be "commissioner" by baseball owners to resuscitate integrity in baseball, after the 1919 Chicago White Sox threw a World Series to the Cincinnati Reds at the behest of one Arnold Rothstein, whose front man got to the players by reminding them of the unfair wage that cheap

Even the Babe was once a real babe (left, in undated photo), though he grew into the kind of hero who not only hit homers but predicted them (right, painting by Robert Thom). His famous—and disputed—"called shot" in Game 3 of the 1932 World Series against the Chicago Cubs is considered by many to be the game's greatest moment. According to legend, he let two called strikes go by, pointed toward the center-field fence, then blasted the very next pitch out of the park for the longest home run in the history of Wrigley Field.

THE NO-HITTER THAT WASN'T

■ If anyone were to ask whether Babe Ruth had ever pitched a no-hitter, you could provide this simple answer: yes and no.

In 1917, he was on his way to compiling a 24-13 record with a 2.01 ERA for the Red Sox, when he came up against the Senators. Instead of loosening up during warm-ups, Ruth chatted it up with fans, though he did take the customary throws off the mound before the first batter stepped up.

Ray Morgan led off for the Senators, taking the first pitch for a ball. The Babe grimaced at umpire Brick Owens' call, and when the next pitch was also deemed to be just off the plate, he started yelling his critique of Owens' skills.

The third ball was clearly too high. The fourth pitch was grooved down the middle but was still called ball four. Ruth began barking at Owens; the umpire said something to get under Babe's skin, and he came barreling off the mound with fists flying.

His catcher, manager and even policemen in the grandstands tried to intervene, but Ruth threw down his catcher and landed a punch to Owens' mask-protected face.

When order was restored, Ruth was ejected. Reliever Ernie Shore came in to retire the next 26 batters—and Morgan was thrown out trying to steal second to complete the 4-0 no-hitter that Ruth had started.

bastard who owned the White Sox, Charles Comiskey, paid them in the first place.

As a pitcher in Boston from 1914 through 1919, Ruth had already been part of World Series–winning teams with the Red Sox, which is enough to make you a religious icon in New England to this day. This was in the era of Little Ball—pitching ruled, and a hit, a bunt, a hit batter, the hit-and-run was the game. A line drive in the gap was awe-inspiring. This was just before the Roaring '20s, and the Home Run, but not before Babe Ruth. **"Jidge" had already pitched 29²/₃ straight scoreless innings in the World Series, a record that stood for almost a half century.** In 1916 alone, Ruth outpitched Walter Johnson—often considered the best righty pitcher who ever lived—four straight times. That year, Ruth shut out nine teams and finished 23-12 with a 1.75 ERA.

Introducing Homerology

And yet, by the end of 1919, the scandal of the so-called Black Sox had eclipsed not just Babe Ruth, but baseball itself. Turned it into jai alai. But then, by accident or design, Ruth was sold to the Yankees for 100 large. Col. Jacob Ruppert, brewery magnate, bought Ruth—and, as it turns out, the rest of the 20th century—for the New York Yankees. Up till then, Ruth had only been clearing his throat. He didn't become the Bambino until he stopped pitching and started hitting, and the Italian immigrants got ahold of his name.

He'd hit 11 home runs as a pitcher with the Red Sox in 1918 to lead

From an early age (left, at 15—he's the one in the middle, and his father is at right in the photo), Ruth lived hard and played hard. In 1920, the Boston Red Sox, for whom he was a Hall of Fame quality pitcher (near right, above), sold him to the New York Yankees (right, the transfer agreement), for whom he became the game's premier slugger. That first year with the Yankees (far right, above), he hit 54 homers, shattering his own major league record by 25. How'd he do it? "All I can tell them is pick a good one and sock it," he explained. "I get back to the dugout, and they ask me what it was I hit, and I tell them I don't know, except it looked good."

(ll agreements, whether for the immediate or prospective release of a player, to which a M
orwarded to the Secretary of the Commission for record and promulgation within five days af
7, National Agreement, on back of this Agreement.)

UNIFORM AGREEMENT

R TRANSFER OF A PLAY

TO OR BY A

Major League Club

blish uniformity in ac-
player, released by a
a minor league club,
club to a major league
t to and contract with
he is transferred, the
he club securing him to
to the deal from re-
lary during his insub-
ly suspending him.
r in whole, of the con-
ase of such player will
he is reinstated and
actually enters the service of the purchasing
club.

WARNING TO CL
tions that arise over t
are directly due to the
parties to promptly
Agreement. The Comn
countenance dilatory t
appeals to it to inv
claims which, if made
required by the laws of
would not require adju
of this character, the c
establish that it is not
neglect to sign and file
which its claim is precale.
sentence of Rule 10.)

This Agreement, made and entered into this 26th day of December 191 9

by and between................Boston American League Baseball Club..

(Party of the First Part)

and................American League Base Ball Club of New York..

(Party of the Second Part)

Witnesseth: The party of the first part does hereby release to the party of the second

part the services of Player................George H. Ruth........................under the following conditions:

(Here recite fully and clearly every condition of deal, including date of delivery; if for a money consideration, designate time and method of payment; if an exchange of players, name each; if option to recall is retained or privilege of choosing one or more players in lieu of one released is retained, specify all terms. No transfer will be held valid unless the consideration, receipt of which is acknowledged therein, passes at time of execution of Agreement.)

By herewith assigning to the party of the second part the

contract of said player George H. Ruth for the seasons of 1919,

1920 and 1921, in consideration of the sum of Twenty-five Thous-

and ($25,000.) Dollars *Cash* and other good and valuable considerations

paid by the party of the second part, receipt whereof is hereby

acknowledged.

STILL THE SULTAN OF SALES

Patrick A. Trimble is an instructor of Integrative Arts at Penn State and the author of Persistence of Vision: Babe Ruth and the Media of the 1920s *which will be published this year.*

■ The Babe made an estimated $500,000—a fortune during his lifetime—selling everything from sporting goods and men's fashion apparel to candy bars. His name is still synonymous with merchandising—not to mention up for sale, along with his likeness and voice, all of which advertisers are eager to make use of.

More than 200 firms sell products ranging from ceramic beer steins to ice tea that generate $50 million in annual sales, according to the Curtis Management Group, a licensing firm which represents celebrities and the families and estates of deceased ones.

When Ruth died in 1948, his estate and the rights to the name and famous face belonged to his heirs, notably his two daughters, Dorothy and Julia. The Babe Ruth Foundation was established to manage that business and to aid charitable causes. It foundered, however, in the 1970s, when investments and endorsements for the Ruth name were at an all-time low. The foundation turned to professional licensing representation in 1981, and changed its name to the Babe Ruth League, Inc.

By the early 1990s, an NBC television movie and a theatrical film, *The Babe*, starring John Goodman—along with the 1995 centennial of Ruth's birthday—rekindled merchandising interest.

The Babe has been linked to A&W Root Beer, Bell Telephone, Citibank (investment portfolios), Brown & Williamson (cigars), Seagram's and Anheuser-Busch. Ruth's popularity translates lucratively in foreign countries as well. Conduit Street Restaurants of London opened Babe Ruth's Restaurant in 1996, and Ruth has appeared for firms such as Ford Canada, Remy Japan, and even the Saskatchewan Department of Health.

The 1998 Claymation commercial for Brisk Ice Tea that showed a hungover Babe belting the long ball was selected as one of the five most popular commercials to air during a Super Bowl.

So even in death, the Babe has proven to be a legend in an entirely different arena.

the American League. Before that, a man named Frank "Home Run" Baker was considered to have had a monstrously good year if he hit, say, 10. But then Ruth had hit 29 home runs in 1919, the major league record by far, and after he moved on to the Yankees, "right off the bat," he hit an astounding, incredible, head-slapping, totally sick 54 home runs.

It is nearly impossible from our vantage point in history to grasp the full magnitude of this feat. **It would be like a Barry Bonds or Mark McGwire hitting, say, 135 homers in a single season.** Except what Ruth did caused even *more* of a stir, because people were then unused to home runs, and also to how he hit them, which is to say majestically.

Babe Ruth introduced what might be called "homerology" into the American lexicon. If you wish someone big success, you want them to "hit a home run," "hit it out of the park." His body of work remains one of life's true inspirations. How else to explain that Home Run in the guise of brilliant sports biography, a genre that didn't really exist before Robert W.

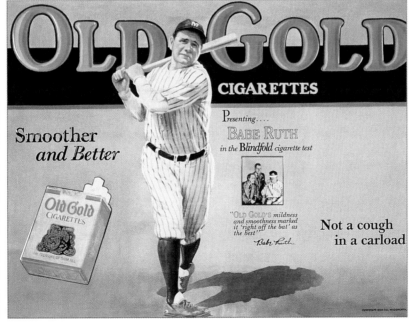

The kids of America loved the Babe (left, showing off one of his bats, which weighed as much as 52 ounces, compared to the 32-ounce toothpicks today's sluggers favor) as they had loved no other before him—and the marketeers of the '20s and '30s were quick to take advantage (right). Said teammate Waite Hoyt, "Every big leaguer and his wife should teach their children to pray, 'God bless Mommy, God bless Daddy, and God bless Babe Ruth.'"

BIG MAN, BIG APPETITE

■ What Babe Ruth remembered most from his first pro season was the team dinner.

He was told, "Order whatever you want, kid, the club pays our feed bill." Clearly, they had little appreciation of the Babe's voracious appetites, gastronomic and sexual.

"It wasn't unusual for Babe to have two ham steaks, some fried eggs, a stack of toast and a pot of coffee for breakfast, then have a snack before the game," said Jimmie Reese, Ruth's roommate.

Team trainer Doc Woods would bring him his pregame bicarbonate of soda, which Ruth would gulp down and, as Jim Cahn would say, "would let out a belch, and all the loose water in the showers would fall down."

These meals were similar in scope and frequency to his carousing around town, where Babe would seek more of everything. One night Babe and a woman "friend" were keeping his roommate Ernie Shore up all night. Ernie finally was able to fall asleep and awoke the next morning to find Babe alone, five cigar butts next to the bed. When Ernie asked about the cigars, Ruth exclaimed, "Oh that! I like a cigar for every time I'm finished." Shore later went to management and told them he would leave the club if he didn't get another room.

Teammate Waite Hoyt said Ruth always would feel a little guilty about his frolicking. "After a rousing Saturday night on the town, the Babe would drag us to Mass with him on Sunday morning. When the collection plate came around, he'd peel off 50 bucks, figuring, I guess, that he'd paid for his sins for the week."

Creamer wrote *Babe: The Legend Comes To Life* in 1974? That book is "the Babe Ruth of sports biographies."

So what manner of man could so inspire? Ruth used a 43-ounce bat, a 46-ouncer and even a 52-ounce wagon tongue. By comparison, today's big leaguers, attempting to achieve the bat speed that helped Ruth launch 714 home runs, use bats as light as 30 ounces, with the standard being 32. Everything he did was outsized, humongous, larger than life. "Ruthian."

He was married twice and had innumerable lovers. His sexual appetites were voracious. He once told a wild party of revelers, after the Yankees had won another World Series, in 1929, "Any woman who doesn't want to fuck can leave now!" One old Yankee who remembered the scene for Bob Creamer also remembered this: "Not that many left."

Yet he was kind—if not very loyal—to his first wife, Helen Woodford Ruth, and gave himself and his business matters totally over to his second wife, divorcee Claire Hodgson Ruth. He loved to wrestle and fool around, was often a big blowhard, but was never known to hurt a fly on purpose. Lou Gehrig once recalled a night Ruth spent with two damsels. In the wee hours of the morning, one of them called in Gehrig, Ruth's roommate on the road at the time, saying, "You'd better come see about your friend." Gehrig found Ruth sitting on the side of the bed, buck naked, alternately chuckling and weeping ruefully. It seems he was too far gone to service both ladies.

The Comfort of True Excellence

Whether baseball fans or not, we understand, desire and are often comforted by true excellence, especially as it is represented by the dynastic New York Yankees professional baseball club, winners of 25 World Series titles in the 20th century. Now, also understand this: The Yankees had not won *a single World Series* before Ruth arrived.

Ruth saved baseball by giving it a bigger, more emblematic blow than betting on it. In 1921, a year after he'd hit 54 homers in one season, obliterating his old Olympian standard of 29 homers, and just two seasons after the so-called Black Sox threatened to kill baseball, Ruth put together the greatest season any hitter ever had, before or since—a .378 batting average, 59 home runs, 171 runs batted in, 145 walks, 177 runs scored, a .512 on-base percentage, a .846 slugging percentage . . . in 152 games. These are indecipherable hieroglyphics to many Americans who are not baseball-minded, but even they know what it means when Pavarotti is called the

SCIENTIFIC MARVEL

■ There was the Babe, in full uniform and attached to wires, looking as though he were submitting to a lie detector test for murdering yet another baseball.

But New York's Finest were not conducting this 1921 test. It was an experiment by *Popular Science Monthly* and two Columbia University scientists, who were trying to ascertain what no pitcher could: why Ruth was the greatest hitter of his time.

Whisked to the university laboratory following an afternoon game in which he had hit another homer, Babe was put through a string of tests while hooked to medieval-looking machines. The scientists examined his brain, eyes, ears and muscles, and, not surprisingly, found that he was above average in every category.

Ruth's body was 90 percent efficient compared to the average of 60 percent. His eyes moved 12 percent faster than average, and his attentiveness and quickness rated 150 percent better than average. American League pitchers must have noted that his favorite pitch was low, outside and right above the knees.

Perhaps the most surprising revelation was that this ballplayer had a powerful and quick brain. His intelligence, as demonstrated by quickness and accuracy of understanding, was 10 percent above normal.

The scientists came away from their tests with one hypothesis: that Babe Ruth would have been as successful in any profession he pursued with such eagerness and dedication as he did baseball.

Babe Ruth of tenors, or Michael Jordan is called the Babe Ruth of hoop.

Take the home run stats alone: He blasted 54 in 1920, 59 in 1921, 60 in 1927. Records? Mythic. Ruthian. The 54 bombs in 1920 were more than every other American League team's total. The 60 bombs in 151 games in 1927 were a single-season standard for 34 years, until Roger Maris hit 61 in 161 games for the Yankees in 1961 . . . and Maris was not applauded for the feat; in fact, he was tortured by fans and press for daring to be Ruthian.

Ruth's record 714 homers in a career lasted from his retirement in 1934, past his death from throat cancer in 1948, far into the future, until 1974, when Henry Louis Aaron hit number 715, and, as with Maris, only much worse, withstood death threats and gnawing, bitter resentment for daring as a mere mortal to surpass Babe Ruth.

■ Baseball's Ideal Expression

The last words should be Bob Creamer's, who called Ruth, "[an] indefinable standard of superiority called Babe Ruth . . . Have you seen that old film clip of Ruth taking batting practice? If you like baseball, you remember the pretty things about the game—the individual moments of craftsmanship and, sometimes, artistry within the mathematical precision of three strikes, three outs, four balls, four bases, nine innings, nine men. Ruth, easing along at three-quarter speed in batting practice, stepping into the pitch, flicking the bat around, meeting the ball cleanly, cocking the bat back for the next pitch, is for me . . . the epitome of baseball, its ideal expression . . . "

Ruth and Lou Gehrig (far left, fishing together in 1933) combined to give the Yankees the best one-two punch in baseball history. For that, the Babe expected to be well rewarded. In 1930, he demanded—and got—a raise to $80,000, which was $5,000 more than President Herbert Hoover was making. When an indignant reporter pointed this out, Ruth said, "I know, but I had a better year than Hoover." He was also an insanely popular entertainer (above), of whom long-time Detroit Tigers broadcaster Ernie Harwell said, "He wasn't a baseball player. He was a worldwide celebrity, an international star."

Jack Roosevelt 'Jackie' Robinson
(born January 31, 1919—died October 24, 1972)

"N IGGER THIS, NIGGER THAT . . . ALL THE VITUPERATIVE CHANGES on the theme that Jackie Robinson was to endure thirty years later," Bob Creamer wrote, not of Jackie, but of Babe Ruth. "Ruth was called nigger so often that many people assumed he was indeed partly black. Even players in the Negro baseball leagues believed this and generally wished the Babe, whom they considered a secret brother, well in his conquest of white baseball."

African-American critic Stanley Crouch once said conspiratorially that he'd never seen any white man who looked like Babe Ruth. Creamer had already written that although there were people who resembled actor William Bendix (who portrayed Ruth in the movie purported to be about his life), no one had ever seen any man who looked like Babe Ruth. Thus was Ruth's legend more entrenched. Many of the enduring works of art have an aura of mystery. Is the Great Sphinx of Giza man or woman, lion or griffin? Is *Adventures of Huckleberry Finn* racist or anti-racist? And what's Mona Lisa smiling about, anyway?

There was no such ambiguity in the face and story and legacy of Jackie Robinson. Neither Jesus nor Moses had it so clear-cut. And he knew what he was fighting and playing for. "We ask only to be permitted to live as you live, as our nation's Constitution provides," he said. The *Pittsburgh Courier* sportswriter Wendell Smith wrote that "the hopes, aspirations and ambitions of 13 million black Americans were heaped upon his broad, sturdy shoulders."

What better place? None better.

Jackie Robinson himself? Total hard core. A real piece of work. Something burning, burning deep inside him, fueling him, firing his resolve, consuming him in the end. His autobiography, written with Art Rust Jr., was appropriately titled, *I Never Had It Made*. But *you* had it made, if you came with him. Jackie Robinson never let down anybody in his life. **Until the very end, if you were with him, you knew he'd cut off an arm—his, or yours—to win. (If you were against him . . . then you were really in trouble.)** Even if the odds were a million to one. To integrate big league baseball, to make America live up to its creed. Fat chance, Jackie was given. He was the one in a million, charged with remaking baseball into a thrilling game again, giving a full currency and legitimacy to the game's claim as the national pastime, giving it a resonant truth, and dragging to a mirror the country that defeated the Nazis, so that it could see and recognize the warts on its own face.

Branch Rickey: "Jackie, we've got no Army, virtually no one on our side. No owners, no umpires, very few (white) newspapermen. And I'm afraid that many fans may be hostile. We'll be in a tough position. We can

One of the scariest sights in baseball in the late '40s and early '50s was Robinson on third (left), threatening to steal home (right). In 1949, he successfully accomplished that rare feat five times. Roger Kahn, author of The Boys of Summer, *wrote: "Robinson . . . had intimidation skills, and he burned with a dark fire. He wanted passionately to win. He bore the burden of a pioneer and the weight made him more strong. If one can be certain of anything in baseball, it is that we shall not look upon his like again."*

win only if we can convince the world that I am doing this because you're a great ballplayer, and a fine gentleman."

"Mr. Rickey, are you looking for a Negro who's afraid to fight back?"

"Robinson, I'm looking for a player with guts enough *not* to fight back!"

This was the famous and likely true Q&A in which Rickey and Robinson engaged before Robinson signed a contract with the Dodgers organization in 1945. The quote foreshadowed the nonviolent Civil Rights movement in America, and Gandhi himself, freeing India. Maybe—maybe?—that was why they all called Branch "The Mahatma." Oh, he was one shrewd cat, Rickey.

■ 'Buked and Scorned, Spurned and Banished

How had it all come to pass? Well, first off, Jackie Robinson was no day at the beach. How could he be? Born in rural Georgia to a sharecropper who abandoned his family, he was black, original black, and therefore, by definition, 'buked and scorned, spurned and banished. *If you're white, you're all right, if you're brown, stick around, if you're black, get back.* Get back? When you are smart, intuitive, fast, supple, agile, determined and indefatigable? All the things Jack Armstrong was supposed to be . . . except one.

In *Champion: Joe Louis, Black Hero in White America,* Chris Mead relates a story about Jackie and his earned temper, told by Truman Gibson, a lawyer, U.S. government aide, acquaintance of Robinson and confidant

All Robinson asked for was justice—for his team (right, arguing a call with an umpire), for his people (above left, with Branch Rickey, signing the historic document that would make him the major league's first black player), for himself, for all of us. In 1984, 12 years after Robinson's death at the age of 53, President Ronald Reagan presented Robinson's family with the Presidential Medal of Freedom and said, "He struck a mighty blow for equality, freedom and the American way of life. Jackie Robinson was a good citizen, a great man, and a true American champion."

PAYBACK

■ One afternoon in 1954, the New York Giants bore witness to what happens when you face a man who doesn't turn the other cheek.

Playing at Ebbets Field, the Dodgers were being rudely held in check by Giants pitcher Sal "The Barber" Maglie, who brushed back Jackie Robinson time after time, including one frightening pitch that sailed behind Robinson's head.

Before Robinson's next at-bat, team captain Pee Wee Reese took him aside and told Robinson that there had to be a payback. A bunt up the first base line would draw Maglie to first and into the hard-charging Robinson.

Baseball historian Roger Kahn noted that the Dodgers' adult batboy overheard the whispered conversation and pleaded with Robinson to "let one of the others do it. You do enough."

Robinson put the ball where it needed to be, but Maglie didn't cover first. Second baseman Davey Williams took the first baseman's toss and Robinson, looking like the star running back he was at UCLA, slammed into Williams, knocking him out of the game and onto a stretcher.

Later in the game, Giants' short-stop Alvin Dark—a man not known for his racial tolerance—tried to stretch a double into a triple, heading full speed toward Robinson at third. Robinson, aware that Dark would be looking for revenge, stepped away and, with the ball in his bare hand, tagged Dark between the eyes. The ball popped loose, and Dark was called safe, heightening Robinson's fury.

Robinson growled, "This isn't the end. There'll be another day."

Dark, through a reporter, sent a message to the Dodgers' club-house after the game, "Tell him we're even. Tell him I don't want another day."

to Joe Louis. "Toward the end of [Jackie Robinson's officer training], he was on a drill field and a white officer referred to a black soldier as a 'stupid nigger son of a bitch.' Jackie went to him and said, 'You shouldn't address a soldier in those terms.' [The white officer] says, 'Oh, fuck you: that goes for you, too.' "

Interruption: This was an error, to underestimate Jack's regard for his mother, Mallie, who raised him and Mack, his brother, and other siblings on love, discipline and no money in Pasadena, California, where they escaped from the red clay dust of Cairo, Georgia. Jack looked the officer over briefly. And, as Gibson put it, **"That was the last that guy knew. Jackie had an explosive, terrible temper. He almost killed the guy."**

Joe Louis helped Jackie get off with the commanding general. That time. "Then," as Gibson tells it, "Jackie went to Camp Swift in Texas and was getting on the bus going to camp, when the bus driver, who along with most of the white bus drivers in the South was deputized and carried a pistol, and whose resolve was to see that Negro soldiers would get to the back of the bus, said, 'All right, nigger, get to the back of the bus.' Jackie said, 'I'm getting to the back. Take it easy.' The bus driver said, 'You can't talk to me like that.' Jackie said, 'I can talk to anybody, any way I want' . . . So the bus driver pulled his pistol, and Jackie said, 'That's a mistake. You're going to eat that son of a bitch.' " So, according to Gibson, Jackie took the pistol from the bus driver and "broke every tooth in his mouth," in the

LOST STARS

Jackie Robinson was the first, and Satchel Paige the next-best known,
but most Negro Baseball Leagues players never got the chance to show their stuff in the majors.
However, it was a haven for some of the best baseball around, black or white, and its teams
routinely won exhibition games against white major league teams.
One can only wonder how these players—all later elected to the Baseball Hall of Fame—
would have performed in the majors if given a chance.

Cool Papa Bell (1922-46): Reportedly the fastest man ever to play the game, he once was clocked rounding the bases in 12 seconds. Stories of his speed are legendary, but the most popular is that Bell could switch off the lights and get into bed before the room went dark. One year, he stole 175 bases in just under 200 games, and he had a lifetime .341 batting average.

Ray Dandridge (1933-49): Often called the best third baseman never to make the major leagues, Dandridge was a cog in the "Million Dollar Infield" of the late-'30s Newark Eagles, along with Willie Wells, Dick Seay and Mule Suttles. After years in the Negro Leagues and Mexico, he was signed by the New York Giants in 1949. He was assigned to their Minneapolis farm club, where he led the team to an American Association championship and was the league MVP. But the Giants wouldn't promote him to the majors nor sell his contract to another team. There was a "quota rule" in effect in the majors, limiting each team to two black players. (The Giants already had Willie Mays and

Monte Irvin on their major league roster.) Dandridge finished with a career batting average of .355 in the Negro Leagues.

Leon Day (1934-49): Known as the best pitcher of his time, Day had a 13-0 record in 1937; he also played every position except catcher. He was among the Allied troops in France that landed on Utah Beach. Returning to the Newark Eagles in 1946, he pitched a season-opening no-hitter against the Philadelphia Stars.

Martin Dihigo (1923-45): Dihigo played all nine positions and is the only player elected into four different Halls of Fame, including Cuba's, Mexico's and Venezuela's. Dihigo never got a shot at the majors, because he was "too dark-skinned," according to the Negro Leagues Baseball Museum. Historically, the only player with similar versatility was Pete Rose, but he played only five positions.

Josh Gibson (1930-46): Paige's battery mate, Gibson hit more than 800 home runs against all levels of competition, includ-

ing 84 in one season. Historians call him "the Babe Ruth of the Negro Leagues." Witnesses at one of his games against the Black Yankees in Yankee Stadium claim Gibson hit a home run over the left-field roof, which, if true, makes him the only player ever to hit a fair ball out of Yankee Stadium.

Buck Leonard (1933-50): He and Gibson were the leagues' best power combo, helping the Homestead Grays win nine consecutive Negro National League championships (1937-45). The first baseman batted .341 over his career. Historians compare the two to Ruth and Gehrig of the 1927 New York Yankees' Murderers' Row.

Hilton Smith (1932-48): During a 12-year run with the Kansas City Monarchs, Hilton never failed to win at least 20 games per season. From 1939 to 1942, he went 25-2, 21-3, 25-1, and 22-5. When the Negro Leagues broke up in 1948, his career record was 161-22. He was 36 years old with arm troubles when the color barrier was finally breached.

Cool Papa Bell

Buck Leonard

Ray Dandridge

Hilton Smith

Leon Day

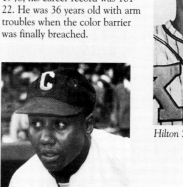

Martin Dihigo

Josh Gibson

process. "They discharged Jackie for the good of the service."

It was probably a good thing that Jackie Robinson married a nurse—Rachel Robinson, a beautiful coed at UCLA, who fell in love with him despite the disgruntled reaction from some members of her own family. She was a nice brown-skinned girl and Robinson was black. Original black. But she and Jack persevered. It was good practice for them, persevering.

No problem. He fought with UCLA football backfield mate Kenny Washington; another teammate, Woody Strode, said he was not the easiest guy in the world to like. "Jackie was not friendly," said the stoic Strode. Robinson's style was combative. But in the end, it was not anger or aggressiveness he brought to big-league baseball. For anger and aggressiveness were already there. What Jackie Robinson brought long before and after anger was the ballet, the *fast* ballet.

Changing America Forever

He'd been honorably discharged November 28, 1944, from the Army. In 1945, barnstorming with the Kansas City Monarchs and not liking it very much, he hit .387 in 47 games there. Baseball commissioner A. B. "Happy" Chandler, a Kentucky politician, was more progressive than Judge Landis (hey, a sponge was more progressive than Judge Landis). So Robinson was signed by the Dodgers, and America was forever changed. Turned out being white or another flesh-bearing color is actually about the least important thing about a ballplayer, when it comes time to actually play. It is both historical fact and flourish that in the 2001 season, Japanese out-

Robinson (upending Yankee Phil Rizzuto, above) turned the world of baseball upside down with his ability and his courage. "I don't know any other ballplayer who could have done what he did," said teammate and fellow Hall of Famer Pee Wee Reese. "To be able to hit with everybody yelling at him. He had to block all that out, block out everything but this ball that is coming at a hundred miles an hour . . . to do what he did has got to be the most tremendous thing I've ever seen in sports." "Every time I look at my pocketbook, I see Jackie Robinson," Willie Mays said.

fielder Ichiro Suzuki of the 116-win Seattle Mariners won the 2001 Jackie Robinson Award as the undisputed American League Rookie of the Year. Ichiro was the first man to lead a big league in batting average and stolen bases since, well . . . Jackie Robinson, in 1949.

Of course, in the beginning, there were a few . . . bumps. **Minor league manager Clay Hopper, a Mississippian who managed Jackie for one season in Montreal, asked Rickey, "Do you really think he's human?"**

Branch Rickey's thought balloon: "Clay, I know it's crazy, but sometimes, in my weaker moments, I even think that *you* are."

Hopper asked no more such questions after Jackie's play won Montreal the Little World Series in 1946. The New York sportswriter Jimmy Cannon then asked that Jackie "be judged by the scorer's ledger and not by the prejudices of indecent men . . . " Still, there was an aborted players' strike from the St. Louis Cardinals, Chicago Cubs, even a couple members of the Dodgers. There was unmerciful heckling, insults hurled by Ben Chapman and the rest of the Philadelphia Phillies, and once, in Baltimore, Rachel thought Jackie might even get lynched.

Not Just Wrong, but Evil

But Dodger shortstop Pee Wee Reese, a Kentuckian, gained praise merely for treating Jackie like a teammate, and the other Dodgers, the ones Rickey kept, followed suit. Robinson's teams won six pennants in the 10 years he played for Brooklyn, and in 1955, they finally beat the hated Yankees for Brooklyn's first and only World Series title. Robinson was unleashed by Rickey after his second year in the National League and had his share of confrontations with the likes of Sal Maglie and Alvin Dark, but confrontation is the nature of baseball. What happened to him off the diamond was of nearly equal import.

Unlike Ruth, he was young enough to star in the movie about his life, *The Jackie Robinson Story*. This film was important in that it actively taught that racism, bigotry and overt discrimination were wrong, and not just wrong. Whenever a bigoted incident was recreated in the film, the musical score took a downturn, implying villainy. It seems small, but before then, many didn't believe you could be inhumane to a *thing* that wasn't human. The movie positioned bigotry as inexcusable. Continue to practice it after its ignorance was exposed, and you become not ignorant but evil.

As Robinson's career wound down, a story had it that Dodgers owner Walter O'Malley saw Robinson leave a hotel room one night and confronted him about what he was doing therein. Robinson said, as was

THE GREATEST GAME NOBODY REMEMBERS

Jules Tygiel is a professor of history at San Francisco State University and the author of Baseball's Great Experiment: Jackie Robinson and His Legacy.

■ Jackie Robinson's greatest day in baseball occurred on Sept. 30, 1951. The Brooklyn Dodgers and the New York Giants entered the final day of the season tied for first place. The Giants quickly finished off the Boston Braves, 3-2. A loss would mean the end of the Dodgers' season and, in Philadelphia, they had fallen behind 6-1 after three innings. Then the Dodgers, and Robinson in particular, began to fight back.

In the fifth inning, the team put two runners on in front of Robinson. Jackie slashed a triple to drive in two runs and then scored on a single, making the score 6-5.

The Phillies scored two more runs, but in the top of the eighth, the Dodgers tallied three to tie the score at 8-8. The game remained deadlocked into the 12th when, with the bases loaded, Phillies slugger Eddie Waitkus hit a low line drive to the right of second base, seemingly destined for center field. Robinson launched himself at the ball, stretching the full length of his body. The impact as he hit the ground left him shaken and groggy. But somehow he had speared the ball inches above the ground to record the final out.

Robinson had to be helped off the field. Pee Wee Reese had to push the still-aching Robinson onto the field for the 13th inning. In the 14th, Robinson came to the plate with two outs and stroked a fastball into the left-field seats. The Dodgers had tied the Giants for first place, sending the two teams into the fateful three-game playoff. *New York Post* sportswriter Arch Murray dubbed Robinson's home run, "the shot heard 'round the baseball world."

Three days later, that appellation would be usurped when the Giants' Bobby Thomson hit a three-run homer to defeat the Dodgers in the playoffs (below). But if not for Robinson's heroics, the Thomson home run, baseball's most famous moment, would not have come to pass.

Robinson's wont, he'd do and be with whomever he pleased. It was not long after this that Robinson was traded to the Giants.

He swore he'd never play for the Giants and promptly retired, but he likely would have continued to play just to stick it in O'Malley's ear, if his incredible skills had not already been mostly all but consumed by his competitive fire. He stayed in the public limelight in one fashion or another until his induction into the Baseball Hall of Fame in 1962, where Bob Feller lost all kinds of brownie points by saying he'd rather not be inducted with Jack. He must not have seen *The Jackie Robinson Story*.

"His Was a Victory Over Absurdity"

By 1972, he was all done—his son, Jackie Robinson Jr., had gone to Vietnam and developed a heroin habit, and died in a traffic accident the year before. Howard Cosell said it tore Jackie apart that he hadn't been able to stop it. He blamed himself, starting with the fact that he'd been proud beyond reason to name his son Jackie Robinson Jr.

Rachel bore up gracefully and well; she gave Jackie years of good counsel, love, daughter Sharon, and Jackie Jr. She had her career, positions at Albert Einstein College of Medicine, Yale School of Nursing and the Connecticut Mental Health Center from 1965 until Jack died of complications of diabetes, hypertension and a broken heart. "I was neither little nor behind him," Rachel said. "I felt powerful by his side, as his partner, essential, challenged, greatly loved."

Years later, essayist/journalist Roger Rosenblatt, speaking for Jackie Robinson aficionados from Tom Brokaw to Spike Lee, wrote: "His was a victory over absurdity . . . over the ludicrous. The ridiculous. What we're celebrating 50 years later . . . is that when Jackie Robinson played, he turned an upside-down nation right-side up. Life created by white Americans for black Americans is nuts . . . "

So much more than a mere ballplayer, Robinson met and moved some of our country's most important and powerful citizens (above, far left, with First Lady Eleanor Roosevelt). In 1997, on the 50th anniversary of Robinson's arrival in the major leagues, AL president Gene Budig said, "He led America by example. He reminded our people of what was right and he reminded them of what was wrong. I think it can be safely said today that Jackie Robinson made the United States a better nation." Robinson would have liked that thought, because he once said, "Life is not a spectator sport . . . If you're going to spend your whole life in the grandstand just watching . . . in my opinion, you're wasting your life."

Larry Joe Bird
(born December 7, 1956)

Earvin 'Magic' Johnson Jr.
(born August 14, 1959)

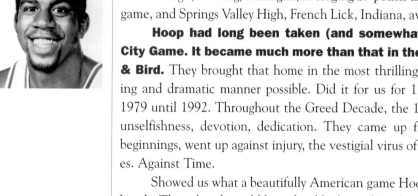

THEIR STORY IS ONE STORY. NO WAY TO TEAR THEM APART. They are twins, joined at the hip, not just when grinding down low for a rebound. On a mission. At times they seemed unalike, so opposite as they struggled. But in the end, theirs was like the struggle between corn flakes and milk. No struggle at all. A slice of Hoop Heaven, really. They filled us up. Know how old folks go to church and get "filled up"? Like that.

Bird & Magic, authors of the renaissance of a sports league, in this case, the National Basketball Association, that jazzy jumping boogie NBA, whose rep as family entertainment in American society Magic & Bird saved. But maybe they saved more.

This much is dead-on true: Before Bird & Magic came along, the NBA Finals, if they were nationally televised at all, were not necessarily in prime time, but sometimes shown via tape delay at 2 a.m. on a slow week-night. The league had come to be seen as not appealing to a national audience. Today that seems almost inconceivable, as central to the whole culture as basketball and video have become—Hoop via the rituals of high schools, which were always there, then the NCAA national tournament, which became Itself after it got the Bird & Magic treatment. Then the NBA, which now has worldwide interest.

Now it is the Game of Basketball that, in its season, is the great American game. Basketball, unappealing to a national audience? What planet are *you* from? The planet that was here before Magic & Bird, Earv & Lar, eventually Buck & The Total Menace, came respectively out of Everett High, Lansing, Michigan, averaging 29 points and 17 rebounds per game, and Springs Valley High, French Lick, Indiana, averaging 31 and 21.

Hoop had long been taken (and somewhat dissed) as the City Game. It became much more than that in the hands of Magic & Bird. They brought that home in the most thrilling, engaging, appealing and dramatic manner possible. Did it for us for 12 solid years, from 1979 until 1992. Throughout the Greed Decade, the 1980s, they gave us unselfishness, devotion, dedication. They came up from the humblest beginnings, went up against injury, the vestigial virus of race, other illnesses. Against Time.

Showed us what a beautifully American game Hoop was, in the right hands. Those hands could be either black or white, but the game was best served in black *and* white, just to help the audience identify.

In a way, Bird & Magic made the league theatrical, took it Hollywood. They set the stage and made possible the game's ultimate

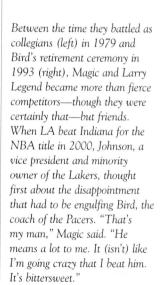

Between the time they battled as collegians (left) in 1979 and Bird's retirement ceremony in 1993 (right), Magic and Larry Legend became more than fierce competitors—though they were certainly that—but friends. When LA beat Indiana for the NBA title in 2000, Johnson, a vice president and minority owner of the Lakers, thought first about the disappointment that had to be engulfing Bird, the coach of the Pacers. "That's my man," Magic said. "He means a lot to me. It (isn't) like I'm going crazy that I beat him. It's bittersweet."

expression of greatness, whose name is Michael Jordan, of course. They saved the game so that he—Jordan, that is—might live, and be fundamentally sound too.

In general, successful men have oversized egos; feeding these egos requires some nourishment by statistic. That's what the merely good pro athlete feeds off—that and mass adulation. Magic and Bird fed off the game itself. **"We weren't about stats," Magic said. Except one. In the 1980s, of 10 possible championships, Magic's Los Angeles Lakers won five, Bird's Boston Celtics won three.** In basketball, it's all about the teams, how they fit together. It is the great player's responsibility to manage this, do the math, not score a set amount of points or rebounds.

Eight of 10 in the 1980s they won between them! Magic's Lakers scored the first repeat championship in 19 years in 1987-88, first since the historic days of Bird's predecessors, the '60s Celtics of William Felton Russell, who was also no stat freak except when it came to winning. To illustrate the flaws and reality of mere statistics, in Game 7 against Detroit in the 1988 Finals, a Laker win, Magic had "only" 19 points, five rebounds and 14 assists.

Of course, since Jordan came along in the mid-'80s, we've let go all holds on the past, all comparisons. Jordan's Chicago Bulls won six titles in the '90s—three in a row twice. Consider this, though—if one is without the other, how many of the other's titles in the '80s would Bird or Magic have won then? What we do know is they had eight combined, which at last count was more than the six or seven they might've had alone. Each time the other won, the one who didn't was just as validated, validated by the relief and joy on the other's face. They had issued and met the highest challenge of Hoop. Only then did they go to work on saving a league, and some of us. In some ways, them saving the league was just a happy coincidence.

It turned out to be such drama watching them, in some cases for reasons that have nothing to do with Hoop. But everything has something to do with Hoop. That's what makes it a great game.

Hoop Is in the Eye of the Beholder

Basketball is not merely anonymous asphalt single combat on outdoor courts in North Philly, Harlem, Brooklyn or Chicago. It is our hearts and minds. It is a rim over a garage door in a driveway with cement cracked open from the pounding on the other side of the tracks in a college town in Michigan. A milk crate nailed to a tree so you can shoot over the clothes drying on a line in a yard with a tire for a swing and a broken-down pickup, somewhere in rural Indiana.

Hoop is this dirt-poor country boy born Bird in West Baden, then schooled in French Lick, Indiana, but schooled before that by poverty; the Bird boy was tall, though, had good length of bone, and he could see. He had the Second Sight, in a spiritual Hoop sense—he could flat shoot the

TESTAMENT

Michael Cooper is a former All-Star guard with the Los Angeles Lakers, and most recently coached the Los Angeles Sparks to the 2001 WNBA championship. Larry Bird has called him, "the best defender I ever faced."

■ In the 1984 Finals, Larry and I had both been giving each other problems offensively. On this particular play, I had just scored and I was pumped up going back on defense. Now Larry sees this, looks at me and quietly says, "I'm gonna wear you out on this one, Coop." So I'm thinking that this guy's getting ready to score.

I get in my defensive stance as they run a simple pick-and-roll. Larry turns the corner and goes up for the shot, and I'm thinking that I'm gonna be able to block this. Kareem comes over to help, and we've got him covered . . . when he somehow—I still don't know how he did this—dumps the ball down to Robert Parish for a dunk. Larry was just shaking his head and had a little smirk on his face as he ran back upcourt.

But this was how he would get you. Most players would talk and then try to do something individual, but Larry was happy getting two points anyway possible to help the team win.

Bird, who won three straight MVP awards with the Celtics (left) in 1984, 1985 and 1986, is basically a loner, unlike the almost compulsively social Johnson. "I stay home and enjoy it," Bird said. "I'm not the type of guy who wants a lot of people following me around and watching me and saying, 'Larry Bird uses soap, too.' I have all my fun in the summer back home" (right).

eyes out of it, from anywhere. From downtown. Downtown Indianapolis, seemed like sometimes.

Hoop is one of 10 children of a General Motors assembly line worker and a devout Christian woman named Christine in Lansing, Michigan. **Christine believed it blasphemous for a sportswriter to call Junior "Magic." Nothing more right to call him, though, since he was 6-9, wanting to play point guard, and doing it.** Doing it better and from a different, higher plane than it had ever been done before. A 6-9 man in the middle of a 3-on-2 fast break, showing handle, full-speed wraparound dribble, then behind-the-back . . . no, check that, a *fake* behind-the-back pass, and a no-look dish to a finisher on a wing, then peeling off, not charging, holding up a finger, looking for a steal on the in-bounds, washed in an explosion of the curious and universal roar of the sound children make when happy.

Larry Bird was born and raised hardscrabble, with hardscrabble expectations. He went to Indiana University, but Bloomington had too much of the hurly-burly for him at the time. The only thing he could count on was that the hoop was 10 feet high. He went to play for Bobby Knight but was back home in less than a month, resigned to life on the back of a garbage truck. But to be 6-9 and to have the Second Sight is to hoop in the state of Indiana—and your state, too, and everywhere else.

Bird was coaxed to Indiana State in nearby Terre Haute in 1975. Wasn't hard to coax him. Joe Bird, Larry's father, had gone and committed suicide with a shotgun on February 3, 1975. So it wasn't hard for Larry to go away. All he thought he'd do is go up there, shoot hoop, maybe "get a little bit of education, and then come back and be the boss of you guys," as Bird said later, meaning only the guys on the garbage truck, then.

■ First Meeting of the Titans

Two years and a couple of quick state lines away, Earvin Jr. was in the process of leading Lansing Everett to a state title and a 27-1 record in 1977. Michigan State offered him the comforts of home. Indiana State was less than unheralded when Bird arrived, but by his senior year, 1978-79, Bird's 29 points and 15 rebounds a game led the Sycamores to the number that really counts, an undefeated regular season and the No. 1 ranking in the country. As a junior, in 1978, he'd already been selected in the first round of the NBA draft by Arnold "Red" Auerbach, the famed general manager and former coach of the legendary Boston Celtics. And, as the result of a trade with the then-New Orleans Jazz, the Lakers already had the first pick of the 1979 draft. They would take Magic. The NBA had it already lined up.

But the first meeting of the titans came March 26, 1979, in the NCAA championship game at Salt Lake City. What was mere setup for the salvation of the NBA was also a pivotal drama that set up the NCAA Tournament from then on. There was no aspect of Hoop they did not

Johnson's impact on the Lakers (left) was obvious from the beginning, when he started at center for injured superstar Kareem Abdul-Jabbar in Game 6 of the 1980 NBA Finals against the 76ers and led LA to the title, becoming the first rookie ever to be named MVP of the Finals. At the end of his career, during his retirement ceremony in 1992 (right), he cried—and the world cried with him. "It is not a very happy moment in any of our lives," said Abdul-Jabbar about Johnson's forced retirement from the game he loved after he contracted HIV.

touch. The 1979 NCAA title game between Indiana State and Michigan State, between Bird & Magic, is probably the one game, college or pro, that everyone old enough remembers not only knowing about but watching.

The brackets served us, giving us a mythic final, won by—well, Michigan State won the game 75-64, but that was a matter of surrounding casts and fate, as much as anything. They both won. They had given the game new standards of drama, excellence and achievement.

And they had only begun to reveal us to ourselves.

As they lifted the NBA from minor category to the upper echelon of spectator sports, people argued to death which was the superior player, rather than reveling in the fact there were two of them—and, ironically, that they were basically *the same player*!

Vessels of True Genius

It was us who drew a line of demarcation between them. Bird, the "fundamental, solid player, great shooter, work ethic, great game intelligence." Magic, "flashy" point guard who ran "Showtime." One "played white." One "played black." Bird would have been a great Laker. Would Magic have been a poor Celtic? Magic smiled too much. Sometimes, the game was too easy. Bird was too stoic . . . should have more fun.

This according to our perceptions, needs, not them. They were the same. They had or did develop the ability to do all things relative to winning at basketball. They had the dual identity of total game. In the parlance of the game they helped revise, Bird was a forward-point-forward, both a "small" or shooting forward, a "3," and also a "big" or rebounding forward, a "4," who had the ability to play up top like a "point" guard if he had to . . . in other words, a "total menace." Magic was a guard-center, both a "point," a "1" and a "5," a center, the hub around which an offense can rotate, and a "2," a "3" and a "4." He could "play all five."

And remember: Bird & Magic were 6-9. Nice edge to have in basketball. (Some say God had a hand in this, and since God did not want anarchy, He made Dr. J and Michael Jordan "only" 6-6.) Both had good athletic ability, though not the extreme athletic ability of a Jordan, a Dr. J, a David Thompson. Bird & Magic were vessels of true genius when it came to the peculiar but irreducible mathematics that make a basketball player into . . . Bird & Magic.

Hoop is a game, and also a function in which genius can show itself. Hoop is both scientific and intuitive, science and art. There are certain constants—five players on each side, the hoop is 10 feet high, the court 94 feet long; in the NBA, a shot must be taken within 24 seconds of possessing the ball, six fouls disqualify you from the game, etc. Then there are the variables—height, skills and weaknesses of the four teammates on court with you at any given moment, the same traits among your five opponents, the score, time remaining, number of fouls a player has left to give, the general tendencies of players, their rough percentages of success and skill

TOP 10 AMERICAN SPORTS RIVALRIES OF ALL TIME

1. Muhammad Ali vs. Joe Frazier. They fought three times, with two of the bouts considered among the greatest fights in boxing history. Ali's taunting of Frazier—he called him, among other things "ugly" and "an Uncle Tom"—turned mutual respect into hatred, and turned a mere sports rivalry into a racial-political morality play.

2. Brooklyn/LA Dodgers vs. NY/SF Giants. Most important: Their move to the West Coast truly made baseball the "national pastime." On the field? Alvin Dark and Sal Maglie against Jackie Robinson in 1947. Bobby Thomson's shot in '51. The '62 playoff. Roseboro and Marichal and the bat in '65. Joe Morgan knocking the Dodgers out of the '82 pennant race. Mike Piazza returning the favor in '93. Bonds setting the HR record last season against—who else?—the Dodgers.

3. Magic Johnson vs. Larry Bird. Magic's Showtime Lakers vs. Bird's blue-collar Boston in the '80s saved pro basketball at a time when it was in danger of being lost to ennui-ridden "stars" and drugs.

4. Duke vs. North Carolina (men's basketball). Two of the four winningest teams in history—located only 11 miles apart in the same state—going at it at least twice a year, often for the national championship.

5. Alabama vs. Auburn (football). More than just two prominent college programs slugging it out each season, this is intrastate, blood-on-the-floor, family-splitting hatred. In other words, the football equivalent of Duke-North Carolina hoops.

6. Ohio State vs. Michigan (football). From 1970 through '75, Michigan came into this regular season-ending game without a loss. The Wolverines won just once. Ohio State was 9-0-1 in '93, 11-0 in '95 and 10-0 in '96. The Buckeyes lost each time. As has been said many times, both teams would rather beat the other and lose all the rest of their games than win all the rest of their games and lose to the other—and their fans feel the same way.

7. Wilt Chamberlain vs. Bill Russell. Russell's Celtics always won, which helped create Russell's rep as the ultimate team player and Wilt's as the selfish Goliath.

8. UConn vs. Tennessee (women's basketball). The most compelling rivalry in women's sports, these teams have won nine of the last 16 NCAA championships, with the Huskies twice beating the Lady Vols in championship games.

9. Chris Evert vs. Martina Navratilova. They played 80 times—often in the finals of major tournaments—with Martina holding a 43-37 edge.

10. Arnold Palmer vs. Jack Nicklaus. Arnie and the Golden Bear brought golf to the masses in the 1960s, during which they captured 13 of 40 majors.

at each ball function—handling (and with which hand best), shooting (and from what distance), rebounding (and how robustly), etc. There must be a constant calculation and re-evaluation of this data, a total orchestration of humanity, if one is to achieve ball genius.

Magic & Bird possessed this genius as perhaps no two players ever possessed it before while competing. And they were black and white together. So they had everything.

In 1980, a spring removed from helping Michigan State win the NCAAs, Magic replaced injured Kareem Abdul-Jabbar and played center in Game 6 of the NBA Finals against the Sixers at Philly and dropped 42 points with 15 rebounds and seven assists. He was Finals MVP. Magic had played no position. He simply played the game. His teams had won a state high school basketball championship, the NCAA Tournament title and the NBA title in four years' time. Hard to match that.

"Oh, yeah?" That was Bird thinking. "Oh, yeah?"

◼ Tragic Johnson . . . Not

Bird was Rookie of the Year in the 1980 regular season. In 1981, Bird's Celtics won the NBA title. Magic's Lakers won in '82. Bird's Celtics won again in '84, this time beating the Lakers, as Johnson found himself losing to Bird head-to-head for the first time. He was called "Tragic Johnson" for a while after that. And Bird became the best player God ever drove breath into.

"Not for long." That was Magic thinking. "Not for long."

Magic's Lakers won in '85. Bird's Celtics won in '86; in Game 7, June 8 against the Rockets, Bird had 29 points, 11 boards, 12 assists. All these facts don't do justice to the anticipation that preceded them. Back and forth they went. Eventually Magic's Lakers won five NBA titles, while Bird's Celtics won three. Magic was symbolic here, due to a legacy of the

For both stars, their court battles were all about respect. As Bird wrote in Bird Watching: On Playing and Coaching the Game I Love: *"Magic and I are like Joe Frazier and Muhammad Ali. That's just the way it is. I knew it was going to be like that forever after I played him in college for the national championship. I never came up against anyone, other than Magic, who could challenge me mentally. Magic always took me to the limit . . . Magic Johnson was the only player that could really get to me. He knew it too."*

PROFILE IN COURAGE

Dred Scott decision by the Supreme Court, which had said blacks were three-fifths human and had no rights a white man was bound to respect. So even 100 years later, maybe Magic had to win five NBA titles and Bird "only" three for them to be seen as equals in America.

Must everything be black and white? Good question. Bird as the Answer (apologies to 21st-century prodigy Allen Iverson) shows up large here once again.

The Detroit Pistons had been frustrated by the Celtics' and Bird's excellence in the NBA's Eastern Conference throughout the 1980s, though they had been good competition in the East for the Celtics. The Pistons wanted more. In 1987, Bird made a play in Game 5 of the Eastern Conference finals. The Pistons had a one-point lead and had the ball out-of-bounds on their end of the court, and were five seconds from taking a 3-2 lead in games at the Boston Garden. Then Bird seemed to materialize out of thin air to intercept Thomas' in-bounds pass, flipping it to Dennis Johnson, who laid in a game-winning basket.

After the game, a frustrated Dennis Rodman, no diplomat, said if Bird were black he'd be just another good player. Thomas, when asked to

Though he has been criticized for not devoting enough time and energy to the battle against AIDS, Johnson, probably the most famous HIV victim, has done his share. In 1993, he and Milwaukee Bucks coach Mike Dunleavy (above right, with Milwaukee mayor John Norquist) served as co-chairs of the fourth annual Wisconsin AIDS Walk. More important, he has served as an inspiration to millions (above left). As Warren Moon, then the quarterback of the Houston Oilers and a longtime friend of Johnson, said after learning that Johnson had HIV, "So many young kids look up to him. If he goes on a crusade against the AIDS virus and he can reach kids, something good can come of this."

comment on (that is, to refute) Rodman's remark, laughed in frustration. He said it was funny, people acted like he came dribbling out of his mother's womb, didn't give him credit for all the hard work he'd put in, and he kind of understood what Rodman was saying.

This was taken straight to Bird. Bird could have whined, complained he couldn't get a break in a league that had become overwhelmingly black in its player ranks, said that they saw him in the pantheon of great players as some affirmative action hire, saw him without seeing him. If he had said that, Isiah Thomas, a great ballplayer, would've been ostracized.

▪ A Simple Display of Common Sense

So this was a Savior moment for Bird. Before he arrived, the NBA was said to be "too black" in the media, "too black" to ever become anything but a minor sport embraced by a certain class, but never to become anything like the national pastime. Bird brushed it off like the lint it was, saying, while understanding the mentality of competition, "They lost." It explained everything. He said it with a lip-curling smirk that said, "Here I am. Beat me, if you can. But don't talk about how hard it is to put up with me. Because it's been plenty hard for me, too. I'm here to hoop. What are you here to do?"

With that simple display of common sense, Bird transcended "race," as did his play. His comment led author and sportswriter Mitch Albom to later say, "It was like (Bird said), 'Come on, come back to earth.' I admired him for that. I thought it was one of the few times that an athlete had a better perspective than we did."

Sports Illustrated's Frank Deford later said to *The Boston Globe,* "Bird's race was crucial at the time. I don't think it's crucial anymore. He made it so that you'll never need another white guy to be important. That's what's most interesting of all. It's not an issue anymore . . . I also think that what was so important about Bird was not that he was white, but it was easy to identify with him. He is an everyman character."

November 7, 1991. The U.S. Olympic Dream Team was coming, in 1992 in Barcelona, the first U.S. Olympic basketball team to feature NBA players. Magic & Bird looked forward to it. Due to injury and time, their

skills were eroding, but still, put them in rocking chairs and on the same court and the same squad and the same five with young Michael Jordan and . . . put it this way. Count it.

Going One-on-One with HIV

November 7, 1991. All of a sudden, couldn't count it. At a press conference, Magic announced he had "attained" HIV, the virus that leads to AIDS, Acquired Immune Deficiency Syndrome, then seen as a death sentence. **People have said Magic was wrong to say he "attained" it. But they are wrong. He "attained" it the way a Savior attains the cross he must bear. He had to bear it, didn't he? He's got HIV and we're correcting his grammar?** So, no use in him not facing both of these nightmares. He "attained" it, then *overcame* it.

Magic said later, "I've heard that Larry cried a little about it. But I know he knew I was going to battle it."

At the press conference, Magic said he was going to try to spread awareness about the HIV virus. Just by contracting it, he did that. Six former pro athletes had died of AIDS by then—baseball players Glenn Burke and Alan Wiggins, boxer Esteban DeJesus, Olympic decathlete Tom Waddell, race driver Tim Richmond and ex-NFL football player Jerry Smith. The effect on the public conscience or on the behavior of pro athletes (and, to be fair, Hollywood actors and actresses, rock 'n roll stars and female porn filler) had been, at best, minimal. But everybody felt it when Magic got HIV. Yet there he was, smiling, saying even the worst can be handled, saying, "I plan to go on living a long time."

NBA Commissioner David Stern came to Los Angeles for the press conference, and said of both Magic and Bird, "I'd hate to think where we would be without them." Bird later said, "If I had an idol, it would be

MUTUAL ADMIRATION SOCIETY

■ As Larry Bird and Magic Johnson were beginning to build their legacies, you would have thought they detested each other just from the oft-asked question about who was the better player.

Their rivalry had started in the 1979 NCAA Tournament final and was magnified in the NBA by the intensity of the Celtics-Lakers matchup and the "Hollywood" vs. "the Hick-from-French Lick" comparisons.

Since they played against each other infrequently during the regular season, the media— through their questions—served as intermediaries. After all, the two rivals on the court had spent little time together off of it.

The setting was awkward then after the 1984 Finals when Magic traveled to Bird's home in Indiana for a day to shoot a Converse commercial with him, since the Celtics had recently beaten the Lakers for the eighth time in eight championship series.

They had time to kill during the shoot. Magic met Bird's mom. Magic and Bird drove around in Bird's truck, and they discussed family and, of course, basketball. Bird said they had a great day.

Suddenly, a bond was formed.

"For the first time, I saw him in a different way—a young guy from the Midwest who loves his family," Bird said in *Bird Watching,* an autobiography. "When you took away all the glamour, that's what was there."

In *My Life,* Magic said, "It didn't take us long to realize that all of the supposed hostility between us had no real substance. It was a creation of the press, and nothing more. It had been going on for five years, but it took us only an hour to see that there was nothing to it."

The two became friendly, if not close friends. Magic wrote the foreword to Bird's 1989 autobiography. While nursing a bad back, Bird flew cross-country to attend Magic's retirement ceremony in 1992. They buddied up at the Barcelona Olympics as members of the Dream Team. In 1993 at Bird's farewell party, Magic's testimonial was the longest and they embraced.

They left as they had arrived, Magic and Bird, but with MVP awards, fan adulation and credit for revitalizing the game.

Those earlier comparisons about their relative abilities seemed frivolous now, except that Magic's Lakers had won five titles to three by Bird's Celtics.

Magic." Bird (with our parenthetics): "Magic played the game the way I want to (and did) play it. He's been an enemy and a friend, a competitor (and teammate) . . . God works in mysterious ways sometimes (and since I know Magic knows that, something good will happen; something always has)."

Magic, to Laker trainer Gary Vitti (our parenthetics), "God gave this to the right person (I'm a leader) when He gave it to me (I'm not bitter). I can handle it (I have hope). I'm gonna take care of this for Him."

Whatever lifestyle choices Magic made are between him and God. Let he who is without sin—lust being one—cast the first stone. Wherever he is, let him do that. Most of us can't—even though we do. Didn't matter that Magic had raised $5 million for the United Negro College Fund with his Midsummer Night's Magic, held at the Forum every year. Magic had committed a turnover. This one involved sex.

As it turned out, he had many possessions left in life after November 7, 1991, and made the most of them. With diet, treatment and exercise, he proved that HIV could be lived with, beaten, that one could grow in spirit, age, even muscle with what was a death sentence. Some of the former fellows in the NBA objected when Magic announced a comeback in 1992. So he aborted it. He did come back briefly in 1995.

But the game he and Bird saved had moved on. Jordan had studied them, cubed them, taken their scientific and intuitive brilliance and made it three-dimensional, took it above the rim, incorporated Dr. J., and Walter Davis, and . . . too many to name here. The next evolutionary step after Bird & Magic was the best player ever.

And this is as it should be.

After the cheering stops, life goes on. Bird tried coaching for three years, that phase of his career culminating in a stint as the coach of the NBA East All-Star team in 1998 (above left, with Michael Jordan and Dikembe Mutombo). But despite his success, he really didn't like it and retired. "Right now, I prefer to be by myself and with my family and go on about my life," he said. Not so his one-time co-savior. These days, Magic (right, with son, Andre, now 19) is a heavy-weight businessman who still dreams of getting his hoop fix as a GM somewhere.

Alvin Ray 'Pete' Rozelle
(born March 1, 1926—died December 6, 1996)

ETE ROZELLE, LIKE ANY GOOD WORKAHOLIC, VISIONARY, CHAIN-smoking, simple salesman, took advantage of the customers' greed. We, as Americans, were his customers. We didn't even know we needed his wares until he showed us just how good they looked on us, showed us how perfect a fit it was. Now we can't do without them. The Super Bowl? Pete's Pagan Rites? The greatest man-made spectacle in the history of all civilization? Looks good on us, eh? Is that legacy enough?

Pete Rozelle used the facts of John Unitas, telegenic QBs, running backs like the old knights of the Round Table, their powerful legs like new-age steeds, their uniforms their armor, their helmets and forearms their battle-axes and swords, great coaches like Lombardi, Ewbank, Shula . . . hell, even Hank Stram . . . as the great Kings; violent collisions, jousts; the regional rivalries between the great, teeming, burgeoning city-states of the nation—oh, it all played so perfectly.

Pete read us, all right, read us like so many comic books, played us like so many secondhand violins. We're tribal in the end, feudal. He put it all on television, made us believe. "On Any Given Sunday," his mantra went, any one team in the National Football League, be it from Green Bay, Pittsburgh, Cleveland, could beat any other team in the National Football League, be it from New York, Chicago or Los Angeles. Everybody had an even break, a real shot. The American way. He captured our civilization heart, mind, soul and body, made Baptist, Methodist, Presbyterian and Pentecostal ministers and Catholic priests all alike, in that they shortened their sermons on the days the hometown teams had a big game. **Pete Rozelle went with the flow of established organized religion, not up against it. "On Any Given Sunday," any good Christian, or Muslim, or Jew was still a big pro football fan.**

Yeah, it was *such* a beautiful con Pete ran. "The best since P. T. Barnum," pretty much says it all. Rozelle was such a cool, deal-making, smooth operator he made Don King look like an idiot savant. Pete made WWF carnival barker Vince McMahon resemble a lame deaf-mute, as McMahon found out in early 2001, when Vince tried to run a new pro football league like a wrestling federation, and went belly-up even *with* network TV backing.

In 1984, *The New York Times* called Pete Rozelle "the architect of the greatest success story in the modern American entertainment industry." He was so successful as a pro sports commissioner, there really is no other sports commissioner to compare him with.

In a nutshell, Pete's world was an old world. He didn't just hear about the Depression. He lived through it. In a big way. His old man never really made it off the mat, or so it seemed to Pete. He had a small business that

Young (right) and old (left), Pete Rozelle seemed like a genial fellow with the comforting smile of a used-car salesman. But the one-time junior college sports information director grew up to be the most effective commissioner in the history of sports in this country. When he took over as the head of the NFL in 1960, the combined revenues of the league and all its franchises were less than $20 million. Last year, combined revenues were close to $4.5 billion.

"WHO THE HELL IS PETE ROZELLE?"

*Wellington Mara was a co-owner of the New York Giants in 1960,
the year Pete Rozelle was voted in as commissioner. Mara, at 86
still the president and co-CEO of the Giants, recalls the meetings
in Florida more than 40 years ago when it took 23 votes to pick a successor
to commissioner Bert Bell, who had died 3 1/2 months earlier.*

■ Pete Rozelle was the last straw, because we had been in Florida for 11 days, and we hadn't been able to agree on anybody. So a bunch of us got together and came up with a group of second-echelon people. It's hard to believe that Paul Brown and Vince Lombardi would have been thought of as second echelon, but we considered them along with Rozelle.

Neither Lombardi nor Brown was available, and I remember I turned to Dan Reeves, who was the owner of the Los Angeles Rams and Rozelle's employer at the time. Reeves said he would hate to lose Rozelle, but knew he would do a good job as commissioner.

We hoped for the best, and we got the best. I didn't know him very well at all. But I was very close to Reeves, and he thought very highly of Rozelle. So my endorsement was really based in some minor part on my own observations, but mostly by my confidence in Reeves's judgment. Reeves' recommendation countermanded any concern we had with Rozelle's age.

We were pretty sharply divided. There were 23 ballots, and we were getting tired of being in Florida. We wanted to get back home. So he certainly was a compromise candidate. I was kind of the spokesman for our group (of owners) at that time, and Art Rooney (of the Steelers) was the spokesman for the other group. I went to Rooney and said we think it should be Rozelle. One of the people in Rooney's group asked, "Who the hell is Pete Rozelle?" Rooney said he didn't know who Rozelle was, but "if he is okay with Wellington, he's okay with me." And that's how complicated it was. We didn't really go into the meetings with any great degree of confidence in Pete. There was just a general knowledge that he was young, progressive and reliable.

went belly-up, then he went to work handling bills of lading for an Alcoa aluminum plant, did it until he retired, and was happy to get a living wage.

Pete was born in South Gate, California, was a yeoman 2nd class in the Navy in WWII, got out in '46, then went to Compton JC and hung out at the Rams' camp because he loved football—not playing, just hanging around. Went to the University of San Francisco, where he damn near invented the job description of college sports PR guy. Nobody ever heard of USF. But Pete sat with Grantland Rice when USF played Fordham and told him that Ollie Matson, Gino Marchetti and Bob St. Clair could play. Saw what he could do with a willing journalist if he only had something to work with, something to sell. He went back to the Rams. Tex Schramm hired him. Only 12 teams in the entire NFL. A "renegade" league was in the offing, the AFL, whose owners had just bought in for 25 large—as in thousands, not millions. Then Pete saw the 1958 NFL championship game. Unitas. New York Football Giants. Overtime.

Hmm.

"Made a real impact on sports. TV discovered the game," he said.

■ 23 Ballots Over Nine Days

Not two years later, the NFL discovered Pete on the 23rd ballot of trying to find a commissioner in 1960. Pete had not exactly lobbied for the job. Sure, he'd told Carroll Rosenbloom and Donnie Klosterman and Tex Schramm, who had hired him in '52 as PR director of the Rams, maybe a few others, that he could do the job better than anybody else, but that was just talk. He knew Clint Murchison of the Dallas Cowboys never really

More than almost anyone else in a similar position of power (Walt Disney is one exception that springs to mind), Rozelle could not get enough spectacle, parade floats, marching bands, huge groups of singers and dancers in flamboyant costumes, patriotic displays. It has been said that his idea of beauty was a balloon drop. In other words, he was the perfect person to have invented the Super Bowl—though not the term itself—a kind of jock paean to kitschy decadence. The first "Super Bowl" in 1967 (above left) was a tough sell, but by 1996 (above right) Pete's game had become America's No. 1 entertainment spectacular, almost an excuse for a national holiday.

"got" him, said he had "milquetoast all over his high hand," but once Pete got rolling . . . if he got the chance . . . he figured Clint wouldn't send back the checks Pete got from the TV networks for him and the rest of the owners.

See, the thing about Pete was, he never took it personally. Certainly not at first. **He understood off the top that these NFL owners were men who could agree on nothing except that greed was not necessarily a bad thing.** Now, here came this threat to them from a renegade league. But in America, competition is considered healthy, the lifeblood of our free market. It is written into law. The NFL was not like baseball. It had no antitrust exemptions, not even limited ones.

Not until Pete Rozelle.

He'd been serving as GM of the Rams for $25,000 a year, right up until the moment he was told by Rams' owner Carroll Rosenbloom that he had been elected NFL commissioner. Took him 23 ballots over nine days. The owners offered Paul Brown the job. He said he'd take it—if the league office was moved from Philadelphia to San Francisco. No dice. Take another ballot, boys. Pete was asked to recuse himself. So he went to the men's room. When Rosenbloom came in and told him he'd been elected, Pete didn't react. Just kept on washing his hands. No problemo. Just get all these big hats to agree, and then talk the TV networks into giving up their Sundays and big bucks to televise the games, and only then go to work on Congress, the real stumbling block between the NFL owners and their formal, state-approved football monopoly.

And trying to convince Congress to give up *anything*, let alone anything like *that*, without giving them something in return, while staying completely legal at the same time, makes digging ditches, pulling teeth and hunting down Osama bin Laden seem like napping on a divan.

But Pete was smooth. Oh, man, was he. Presto, change-o. No less than JFK, John Fitzgerald Kennedy, Hancocked the bill. Then all Pete had to do was convince the owners that all of them were created equal, that the Green Bay market was no different from the LA or New York markets, and each team should share equally in the TV distribution. The first distribution was $320,000 per team. Unaware of this windfall, one owner wanted to know why the whole check for the TV contract was sent to him. He didn't feel like cutting it up for the rest. He had administrative costs. Yada-yada. Pete waited and then said, "No. That's your end." Silence on the line. You the man, Pete.

The rest was history, and good jockeying. This NFL was a cash cow, handled right. It could be milked, or it could be killed for steaks. Pete knew which way was smarter. He suspended Alex Karras and Paul Hornung in 1963 for gambling on games, even though they'd never bet against their own teams or thrown a game.

He Knew It When He Heard It

In 1966, he pulled off the masterstroke. The TV contract with CBS that year was child's play. Pete knew he had the comforting tones of Ray Scott doing the play-by-play of the comforting Green Bay Packers and their icon, Vince Lombardi. "Starr . . . Dowler . . . touchdown." And he had a perfect foil for the Pack, Clint Murchison's wild and woolly Cowboys, with their automaton coach, Tom Landry, their outsized defensive tackle, Bob Lilly, their World's Fastest Human, Bullet Bob Hayes, their dandy quarterback, Don Meredith. Worked out perfect.

And Pete also got the next sitting president, LBJ, Lyndon Baines Johnson, to sign into law a bill protecting the merger of the NFL with the so-called upstart AFL, and allowing Pete's Big Game, the "Super Bowl," to be contested without constructing a monopoly—which, of course, is what he was doing. The Big Game wasn't even called the Super Bowl that first year, when the Green Bay Packers beat the Kansas City Chiefs. But some lost wag came up with it, one of a small crowd of journalists who came to "cover the Super Bowl" and wound up as Pete's personal army of flacks.

Pete didn't name it the Super Bowl, but he knew it when he heard it. The AFL had been the rival league, based in the smaller markets, the relative hinterlands at the time, your basic Kansas Cities, Houstons, Oaklands, San Diegos, Buffalos . . . and . . . it was led strategically by a man named Al Davis, who signed several NFL quarterbacks to controversial "futures" contracts, meaning that when their NFL contracts ran out, they would play for the upstart "renegade" league. A good gambler knows when to fold 'em. Pete told the owners they'd have to bring part of this group in. Just charge 'em up the wazoo, is all.

ROZELLE'S BLOOD FEUD WITH AL DAVIS

■ Pete Rozelle may have had only one genuine enemy during his 29-year tenure as NFL commissioner, but what an enemy. Al Davis, the Machiavellian Oakland Raider managing general partner, was Rozelle's nemesis from the time of the AFL-NFL merger until Rozelle's retirement in 1989.

The seeds of the Rozelle-Davis conflict were planted in 1966, when AFL owners kept Davis, then the AFL president, out of the picture while negotiating the merger of the two leagues. When Davis was not chosen to run the expanded NFL, he returned to Oakland to oversee the Raiders. Although Davis would deny it, many have long insisted that he never got over the snub or the merger.

Davis eventually exacted some historic revenge. In 1980, when the NFL refused him permission to move the Raiders from Oakland to Los Angeles, he joined the LA Coliseum Commission in an antitrust suit against the league.

During the trial, Davis was the star witness for the plaintiffs and Rozelle the principal witness for the league. After the suit was filed, they could barely speak to each other. "There is a real hatred there," an NFL insider said at the time. "It's absolutely awful. Davis almost reaches apoplexy about Rozelle. He goes berserk. Rozelle contains himself, but the venom is just as stringent."

In May 1982, a Federal District Court jury in LA ruled against the league, clearing the way for the Raiders' move south. The jury's decision also cost the league $35 million and set a precedent for the subsequent unilateral moves of the Baltimore Colts to Indianapolis and the St. Louis Cardinals to Phoenix. Davis also benefited when he moved the Raiders back to Oakland (with the league's blessing) in 1995.

In 1983, their second season in LA, the Raiders defeated Washington in Super Bowl XVIII. Afterward, Rozelle presented the Vince Lombardi Trophy to Davis with his congratulations in the customary locker-room ceremony. "That was Pete's finest moment," Ed Sabol, the founder of NFL Films, told The New York Times in 1996. "He never flinched, while Al never looked him back in the eyes."

When he'd gone to get the antitrust exemption from Congress in 1966, Hale Boggs, the congressman from Louisiana, had aligned with him. Why? Maybe it had something to do with the fact that Pete had intimated that the next NFL expansion team just might go to New Orleans . . . if Hale Boggs came through with the House.

Hale said, "Well, Pete, it looks great."

Pete said, "Great, Hale. That's great."

Hale said, "Just for the record, I assume we can say the franchise for New Orleans looks firm?"

Pete said, "Well, it looks good, of course, Hale, but you know I can't make any promises. It's up to the owners."

Hale said nothing for a minute. Then he said, "Well, Pete, why don't you just go back and check with the owners? I'll hold things up here until you get back."

Pete's turn to say nothing for a minute. Then Pete said, "That's all right, Hale. You can count on their approval."

Within the hour, the House passed the NFL/AFL merger exemption. Any problems the other owners might have had with expansion into New Orleans were relieved when Rozelle told them that Texas oilman John Mecom Jr., in order to join The Club, would have to pony up some $8.5 million for them to split.

In 1969, ABC, having no choice, bought in. Super Bowl III and Broadway Joe Willie Namath saying, "I guarantee we'll win," probably did the trick. So Pete went back into another boardroom and emerged with another nicotine-stained, capped-tooth smile (Pete seemed unduly proud that Duke Snider had knocked out his two front teeth in a ball game when they were both in high school). "ABC has acquired the rights to 13 of what

One of the qualities that almost all great sports commissioners share is the ability to negotiate advantageous agreements with the media, with the government, and with other sports entities. Rozelle's gifts in this area were almost legendary, beginning with his facilitation of the AFL-NFL merger (above left, from left, Tex Schramm of the Dallas Cowboys, Rozelle and AFL founder Lamar Hunt of the Kansas City Chiefs, at a press conference to announce the merger). He also convinced President John F. Kennedy to sign a bill that granted the NFL a limited antitrust exemption, convinced the players' union to accept a stringent drug-testing policy, helped the NFL fight off a $1.7 billion suit filed by the USFL and negotiated the most lucrative contracts in the history of televised sports. Sadly, everyone has their limitations, and Rozelle's had a name: Al Davis.

will be called 'Monday Night Football' games, starting in 1970," Pete said.

In 1970, Pete did a four-year deal with all three major networks. But in this monopolistic heaven, problems were sure to occur. Other big-hat millionaires who thought greed wasn't necessarily bad would want into The Club. But Pete knew how to shmooze Congress. And **there was something in 1975 called the Rozelle Rule, with which Pete set the compensation for any team signing a player whose contract with another team had expired. So Pete was God.** Or damn near.

In 1985, Pete Rozelle was elected to the Hall of Fame in Canton, Ohio. "Pete got to Valhalla first," said Al Davis, whose seemingly never-ending legal battles with Rozelle over his right to move the Raiders whenever and wherever he wanted were one of the few strains of Pete's reign.

Monolith on Cruise Control

After that, any good lawyer and reputable accounting firm could've guided the ship. Pete Rozelle negotiated one more TV contract for the NFL and its team owners, in 1987, a three-year deal for $1.428 billion, which included rights for ESPN, a cable network operation, just as Pete had predicted 15 years earlier. The goose was laying pure gold. This payout wasn't counting the paid gate, face-value tickets, concessions, parking, the local re-broadcast rights, the coaches' TV shows, the radio rights and the ancillary shows, the product merchandising and marketing tie-ins with the shoe and apparel manufacturers, the income from NFL Properties, NFL Films . . .

In 1988, Rozelle suspended 25 players under the NFL's substance

ANTI-SAVIORS

Who can doom a team or kill off fan interest even before the game begins? Only owners, GMs and an occasional crooked agent. Draft picks are squandered. Deals go bad. Superstars are sent packing. Spending sprees yield nothing in return. Players are cheated. Many execs have had the opportunity to sink a franchise, but only a select handful have done it this well.

NBA

■ *Ted Stepien, Cavaliers:* The league had to approve all Cavs deals, because he had traded four first-round picks. And the NBA wrested control of the 1981 All-Star game in Cleveland, fearing embarrassment. He sold the team three years after buying it in '80.

■ *Donald Sterling/Elgin Baylor, Clippers:* This franchise is considered the league's all-time worst, with only one winning season since Sterling bought it in 1981. Baylor has been the GM since 1986. You'd need another book to list all the terrible draft picks, and all the potential stars that have been allowed to walk.

■ *Wes Unseld, Bullets:* As GM, he traded Chris Webber for Mitch Richmond and Rasheed Wallace for Rod Strickland, and signed Juwan Howard to a seven-year, $105 million deal. Webber is a bonafide MVP candidate, and Wallace is an All-Star.

NFL

■ *Mike Lynn, Vikings:* Hoping Herschel Walker would help the Vikings win a title, the GM gave up in 1989 to Dallas what amounted to seven high draft picks and five quality players. The Cowboys built a dynasty with all that talent . . . and the Vikings have yet to win a Super Bowl.

■ *Art Modell, Ravens:* Modell relocated the Browns, who had been in Cleveland since 1946, to Baltimore in 1996, and renamed them the Ravens. Worse for Cleveland fans, Baltimore won the Super Bowl in 2001.

■ *Dan Snyder, Redskins:* He bought the Redskins in 1999 for a record $800 million, the most ever paid for a sports franchise. He signed over-the-hill players to high-priced contracts and charged fans to watch training camp. Snyder is already working on his fourth head coach (Steve Spurrier, who Snyder made the highest-paid coach in NFL history, despite the fact that he's never coached in the NFL).

MLB

■ *Peter Angelos, Orioles:* Fiscal responsibility? Nah. Angelos signed high-priced players who failed to produce a title: Brady Anderson, Albert Belle, Will Clark, Charles Johnson. In the process, he has destroyed the image and competitive quality of one of baseball's class franchises.

■ *Charles Comiskey, White Sox:* His penurious treatment of players led to the Black Sox scandal of 1919. He was so cheap that he refused to pay to have uniforms cleaned. Players wore the same uniforms for weeks on end, which is how the nickname "Black Sox" was coined.

■ *Harry Frazee, Red Sox:* The Red Sox owner sold Babe Ruth in 1919 for a paltry $100,000 and a $300,000 loan. Ruth went on to torment the Red Sox and hit 659 of 714 home runs in pinstripes. The Red Sox haven't won a World Series since, while the Yankees have won 26.

■ *Kevin Malone, Dodgers:* Never has a GM put his foot in his mouth more. He told reporters that it was good the Yankees got Roger Clemens so he could face Kevin Brown in the World Series. Brown was the first baseball player to break the $100 million mark. Malone doubled the team's payroll from 1998 to 2000, won fewer games than his predecessor, and was fired in 2001.

NHL

■ *Alan Eagleson, president NHLPA:* An agent, lawyer and friend of NHL owners, he served six months in jail for defrauding the NHLPA, stealing the pensions from the players he represented from 1967 to 1991.

■ *Doug Risebrough, Flames:* The GM was fleeced in 1992 by his predecessor, Cliff Fletcher (now in Phoenix), in a 10-player trade in which Risebrough gave up Doug Gilmour and four other quality players. The deal is considered one of the most one-sided in league history.

abuse policy. It was not unlike what he'd done to Hornung and Karras some 25 years earlier. Life was beginning to repeat itself. The '80s and Al Davis and chain-smoking had taken their toll.

And besides, what was left for Pete Rozelle to do, besides try to make his wife Carrie a little bit happier? So, in the end, Pete was not so different from his old man. Counting bills of lading. Shmoozing. Remembering people by their first names. Working the job for 30 years, until he retired. Not having much life left after. Feeling unappreciated outside his own house. But looking at the American entertainment landscape at the dawning of the new millennium, one would have to say . . . not bad, not for a guy with "milquetoast all over his high hand." No, not bad at all.

◼ Pete's Golden Legacy

In 1989, Alvin Ray "Pete" Rozelle retired. He died of brain cancer at home in Rancho Sante Fe, California, at the age of 70, on December 6, 1996.

The next TV contract to be negotiated by Rozelle's successor, a tall Georgetown lawyer named Paul Tagliabue, will be the richest in the history of all television entertainment. Each of 30-odd teams stands to make upward of $100 million a year from it, once the blood is on the floor, once the deal is signed.

And on that day, someplace dry and warm, a widow named Carrie Rozelle, who once judged the decadent festivities of Super Bowl week to be "like the Mad Hatter's ball," will sip a beverage poolside, adjust the nose plate of her sunglasses, look from under a wide-brimmed designer straw hat and her thought balloon just might be: "Oh, Pete, my Pete . . . he would've gotten more."

And who dares disagree?

At a 1997 memorial service in Beverly Hills (above), Rozelle was remembered for his loyalty, professionalism, honesty, cool negotiating style and love of tchotchkes. His daughter recalled how, as a single father, he had hunted for the talking Barbie that she passionately desired for Christmas. "Dad went to every black-market source he could," Anne Marie Bratton told the crowd. "And there it was at Christmas. When I pulled the string for her to talk, she said, 'Buenos diás. Dónde está Ken?' She also told of a meeting at Rozelle's apartment, which took place when she was eight, between her father and Joe Namath, whom she desperately wanted to meet. Rozelle told her to stay in her room, but that was asking too much. "As Joe was about to leave," Bratton recalled, "I bolted from my room, leaped into his arms and said, 'Joe, I love you, even if my father hates you.'"

Eldrick T. 'Tiger' Woods
(born December 30, 1975)

YGER, TYGER, BURNING BRIGHT . . .

Tiger, Tiger . . . what a life.

He was born to it, for it, with it, in it. To the manner born. That's why he always acts like it's no surprise, not to him, this walking on water hazards that he does. "I expect to win every time out," he said upon arrival.

He'd learn, we thought.

No. *We* learned.

The Chosen One who always leaves us with this pleasant feeling that The Best Is Yet to Come. By the time he's through, he'll be the best anybody ever saw, if for no other reason than all those who think they saw somebody better will be dead and gone. If Jack Nicklaus says he never saw a better golfer than Tiger Woods, what kick do the rest of us have, for God's sake? "He's better than the other players by a greater margin than I was," the clinical and sometimes sardonic Nicklaus has said. "He can go on a run and win three or four of these things (golf's four major titles, of which Nicklaus won a record-by-far 18—and finished second 19 other times) in a row, and all of a sudden that majors record isn't that far away." Nicklaus said this before Woods's "Tiger Slam," when Woods won four majors in a row in 2000-2001.

In some ways, Nicklaus speaks a language only he and Tiger among the living can understand. After Tiger won his second Masters in 2001 (Nicklaus won six; basically Tiger uses Jack as his measuring stick, tries and so far succeeds at doing everything a little better and a little faster than Jack) to complete the "Tiger Slam," he came to Nicklaus's Memorial Tournament in Ohio, which, upon Jack's prompting of "You ready?", he proceeded to win for the third straight year.

Jack: "How many tournaments have you played this year?"

Tiger: (pause) "Five."

Jack: "How many have you *won?*"

Tiger: "Four."

Jack: "Which one *didn't* you win?"

Tiger: (pause) "The Byron Nelson."

Then they laughed. They *laughed!* Others might have whistled, shaken their heads in awe, even if they'd managed to do such things. Jack Nicklaus and Tiger Woods *laughed*. Now that is high-level and healthy competition. As for the rest of us, golfers or not, we might as well come along quietly. We've all been converted to Tiger's mission. Those who haven't are bitter agnostics of a lunatic fringe.

Tiger Woods, world's No. 1 golfer, author of miracle shots. How far is it from there to Tiger Woods, world's No. 1 citizen, as recognized as kings, popes, authors of miracles of intervention? Tiger's father Earl thinks

Tiger was always a good kid (left), according to his father— no drugs, no alcohol, never needed to be spanked. "I never even admonished him," Earl Woods said in an interview with Golf Digest. "He totally understood my tone. You know how you can stop a dog on a dead run? It's all in the voice. And this was without fear—he didn't fear me. He just knew when he was supposed to stop."

PRAYING TIGER, HIDDEN DRAGON

■ Every year on his birthday, Tiger Woods visits a Buddhist temple with his mother, Kultida, bearing gifts of rice, sugar and salt.

Around his neck he wears a Buddha on a chain, a family heirloom. "I like Buddhism, because it's a whole way of being and living," says Woods. "It's based on discipline and respect and personal responsibility." And it involves meditation, which may account for his incredible power of concentration on the golf course.

Though he was born and raised in California, Woods followed the faith of his mother, who comes from Thailand. When he was a boy, Tiger visited Thailand and Buddhist monks with his mother. A monk told her he was special.

"Buddhism helps him balance his life and not get too absorbed in illusory fame and monetary success," Kultida says. "When he was young, he had to pray before going to bed."

While Woods is not what you would call devoutly religious, he takes what he needs from his religion. "I believe in Buddhism," he says. "Not every aspect, but most of it. So I take bits and pieces. But I don't believe that human beings can achieve ultimate enlightenment, because humans have flaws."

Though some have fewer flaws than others.

it's not that far. He's thinking that might even be a letdown.

Let that just hang there for a while.

For thinking like this, totally out of the box, Earl is considered by many to be a charming eccentric (loony, maybe?). He also was considered some of that when he said his little multiracial-but-when-all-else-fails-African-American boy would become "the first intuitive African-American golfer," who'd not only win the Masters but win it repeatedly one day.

Tiger has been asked, if he could play one round with one person, living or dead, who would it be? He always answers: "My dad." Quite an uplift from back when Senator Daniel Patrick Moynihan called the African-American family "a tangle of pathology." Senator Moynihan didn't have a full grasp of the hows of why that might be. But whatever the whys, in the case or Earl and Tiger Woods, they were overcome, and to great effect.

Tiger was born right place/right time, under Capricorn, December 30, 1975, after the Vietnam War ended. His father had fought in it. December 30, 1975, close enough to Christmas to have a warm feeling from it, far enough from conflict to form a sense of self, close enough to New Year's Day, with its promise of better days, new resolutions. Promise is important to religion, promise of a reward in a better place—maybe a place inhabited, if not run outright, by Tiger Woods. Wouldn't be so bad. At least we'd know that in *those* Green Pastures nobody would beat our side in golf.

Our last and final Savior, until The Next One comes along, was

By the time he was 3, Tiger already had a swing to make a touring professional envious.

raised by a shy yet determined Thai lady named Kultida and her husband, Earl, a relentless yet thoughtful former Green Beret lieutenant colonel, who has many strains of ancestral blood coursing through his powerful body— Native American, African American, Scotch, Irish, Chinese . . . mostly Midwestern Protestant. Work ethic rules. Earl Woods was in his 40s by the time the boy Eldrick was born. He would be the only child of Earl's second family. Earl had learned things from his successes and his mistakes, but mostly he had slowed down enough to be with his son most of the time. And most of the time, Earl was out somewhere "hitting it."

He was guilty of golf.

When he saw his baby watching him drive balls into a mat, he didn't think much of it. But when the two-year-old did it himself without prompting . . .

Tiger was built from the ground up to do what he does now, golf at an ethereal level. He plays like the Angel Gabriel might play horn. He has a built-in combination of pride, passion, poise, intuition, skill and sonar on the greens. A near-perfect swing, power and distance off the tee that takes the breath not just of galleries but of other pros. *They* could watch him all day. That's some but not all of what made him the Savior of golf. You may ask, "Did golf *need* saving? A game played by the richest, most powerful men on earth, men of leisure, on the finest swatches of real estate in the world? Are you trying to say that *Pebble Beach* needed saving?"

Though his parents live apart, Woods has remained close to both. At the Western Open in 1997 (above right), he celebrated with his mother, Kultida, after becoming the second-youngest person in golf history to win six PGA events—at 21, he was less than a year older than Horton Smith, who won seven tourneys in the '20s before he turned 21. At the 1999 Tour Championship, he received a hug from his father, Earl, after winning the $900,000 first prize, which raised his winnings for the year to a then-record $5.6 million.

Well, there are all kinds of ghettos. Golf was exclusive, conducted in exclusive surroundings, with covenants so restrictive that even a man like Arnold Palmer, just because he wasn't born with a silver spoon in his mouth, was seen at first as an outsider, different, and in the end that helped give him his

cachet (but also had him smoking like a chimney).

Before Tiger, a man of color like Lee Trevino was considered an aberration, someone to look down on, with his gauche Band-Aid covering his crude forearm tattoo. The rest of us, after all, were born with our tattoos, so secretly most of us thought Lee was pretty cool. **Restrictive covenants in real estate to keep brown and black people out also keep the full humanity of those inside those restrictive covenants boxed in, on a lower frequency. Goddamned right golf needed saving.**

If golf was to become all it could become, it needed Tiger Woods. He in turn did the impossible for it, opened up the eyes of the rest of the world to the promise and the rewards of golf, such as they are. What golf does best is teach humility. But it took Tiger Woods to bring that humility to bear. Boy, did he. He took a niche sport—the coziest niche of all, but still only a niche—and made it universal. His game was so good that even as it was driving up PGA purses and PGA TV contracts, because so many people wanted to see him, it also forced PGA Tour golfers, who'd been for the most part motoring along on restrictive-covenant-cruise-control, to get better. The PGA Tour pros, since the retirement of Jack Nicklaus, had been engaged in rather leisurely competition. Tiger's game forced them to see themselves differently, to know they could improve, because they'd have to improve if they wanted to compete.

A Swing That Takes the Pain Away

We can talk about Tiger's golfing accomplishments—and we will in just a minute—but his golfing accomplishments so far are hardly anything when compared with what his future accomplishments might be. Tiger Woods, for all he's done already, is actually just getting started on his mission. He's not even halfway home. But, because of him, *we* are. A Tiger Woods makes it all worth it—all of man's past inhumanity to man, all the bloody and nonsensical racial history of not just the United States but the world.

His swing takes the pain away. The United States in particular became the greatest country in the world precisely because of the diversity once seen as at best a nuisance and which now Tiger Woods so ably represents. That is part of the good timing of Tiger Woods. He gets to live out the promise of the nation's creed.

To make litany of Tiger's accomplishments is to talk all day, until they seem to become mundane. To Tiger, they *are* mundane—he had goals and he has achieved some of them.

Still, in 2001, he won five of the 19 Tour events he entered, including the Masters, clinching what has come to be called the Tiger Slam—golf's four major titles won consecutively. He also won the NEC Invitational, in a thrilling seven-hole playoff over Jim Furyk, drawing the second-highest prime-time television audience of that August week. He won the Vardon Trophy for lowest adjusted scoring average for the third

WARNING: TIGER'S FANS CAN BE DANGEROUS TO YOUR GAME

■ Before Tiger Woods arrived on the scene, professional golfers had few distractions. Galleries would offer up polite applause or a controlled cheer after someone sank a tricky putt or ripped a long drive—all befitting the genteel manner of the sport.

Now when Tiger putts out first on a green, the gallery leaves, even if the other players in his group have yet to finish. Sometimes, fans are nearly trampled as they rush to Tiger's next hole. There were five streakers at the 2000 British Open, and fans were knocked into Swilken Burn when too many tried to jump the small creek to watch Woods finish his record-breaking day at the 18th hole at St. Andrews.

To Notah Begay, a former college teammate of Woods at Stanford and a fellow PGA Tour player, playing with Woods in a group tests a golfer's ability to concentrate. "It's like magic playing with Tiger, because once you are in Tiger's group, you are invisible. People start moving after he hits. That's why you see the younger players really struggle when they are paired with him, because it's a circus. You have to be prepared for all the people walking around, cheering. I feel different because we're friends.

"Two things really stick out about playing with him. The first was when I was a senior at Stanford in the 1995 NCAA championship. I was supposed to play the No. 1 position, but because I knew what was going to happen (with the galleries), coach put me in the No. 2 spot so I could play in front of Tiger's group. I knew people would be crazy. He brought a new energy to the game, and new fans . . . not just golf fans, but sports fans.

"The second is at the 2000 U.S. Open at Pebble Beach (which Woods won). You know the Raiders' fans who paint their faces? Well, this one guy wore a Tony the Tiger suit and painted his face. I'm talking from head-to-toe, following Tiger around the entire course. It was the funniest thing I have ever seen."

straight year, made more money—$5.7 million—than anyone on the Tour for the third straight year, and was elected Player of the Year for the fourth time in five seasons. And yet, Tiger's 2001 was seen by some as an *off-year*!

The year before, in 2000, Tiger had . . . well, let's work our way up to it. Tiger first started winning when he hit that ball into that makeshift netting in back of the house in Cypress at the age of 2. After his mother called LA sportscaster Jim Hill and invited him out to watch her son hit some balls, Tiger was on *The Mike Douglas Show* hitting balls, charming the host, Bob Hope—everybody on the set, basically. He was in *Golf Digest* by age 4, probably because the year before he'd shot 48 over nine holes at the Navy Golf Course in Cypress, California. Earl said he drove from the red tees, though, and all his shots from out of the fairway had been teed up for him. Nothing special.

Earl took him to a par-3 course and introduced him to instructor Rudy Duran, who said, "He was like a shrunken-down Nicklaus." At nine, Tiger was taken by Earl to John Anselmo, an aficionado of Hogan and Sam Snead and a teaching pro at Los Alamitos, a muni one mile from the Woodses' home. It was on these vicious greens—"slopy, grainy and funky,"

Early in his career, Woods often complained about living life under a microscope, about too many people trying to get too close to him (above). Butch Harmon, his swing coach, told him he had two choices, "Retire and count your money, or deal with your life, have fun with it." Woods listened—and learned. Now, said Harmon, "he's comfortable being Tiger Woods."

according to Earl—that Tiger learned to read breaks. Anselmo told *Sports Illustrated*, "I'll never forget the day he . . . said, 'How do you get rid of backspin?' I said, 'Tiger, 99 percent of golfers are dying to get backspin, not get rid of it. Why don't you keep the spin and play the ball past the hole and bring it back?' He nodded his head. I could tell he filed it away . . . "

Tiger won the 1991, 1992 and 1993 U.S. Junior Amateur Championships. No one had won more than one before. No one has since, either. He won the 1994 U.S. Amateur at the TPC at Sawgrass at 18, becoming the youngest man to ever win that event. Then he became the second-youngest man to win it the next year. In 1996, he became the first man to win the U.S. Amateur three straight times. He'd won six consecutive national amateur championships.

Golf is not a game to be treated like this. You do not beat it, it beats you, like a drum. But Tiger was on his way to the Promised Land, the Land Where We'll Never Grow Old, the Land of Do What's Not Been Done Before.

He was just getting started.

Soon enough, Tiger began to make golf matter to just about everybody. How? Like so. He joined the PGA Tour in 1996, leaving Stanford, which had first sent him a scholarship letter when he was 13. On the Tour, his first event was the Greater Milwaukee Open. His first pro shot was a 336-yard drive down the middle, and he finished the first day with a four-under 67. He finished on Sunday with a 68, seven-under 277, tied for 60th. Even then, there was something about him. Veteran Bruce Lietzke played with him that day and later said, "A lot of 20-year-olds would get frustrated, or angry. He never lost his temper. If he's going to be the game's next great ambassador, then the game is in good hands."

He began the final round of the Las Vegas Invitational four strokes back, closed with a 64 to force a playoff with Davis Love III, then parred the first extra hole for his first PGA Tour win.

Reinventing His Game

In 1997, he shot 70-66-65-69=270 to win the Masters by 12 shots. The sight of what could be called a "black" man blowing away the field at the Masters did not merely boggle the mind—it *changed* the mind. *Opened* the mind. Spectators didn't grow unruly. They seemed charmed by it. **And when he came off the 18th green and hugged his father, buried his face in his old man's shoulder and held on, you knew this was more than just golf.** Among other things, it was the fifth-greatest margin of victory in the history of the PGA, and a Masters record, and an Augusta National course record at the same time, all this after shooting 40 on the front nine the first day.

In 1998, Tiger Woods went alone to the wilderness, to improve his game, tailor it so it would fit the more exacting course setup that characterized his next goal—the U.S. Open. The Open, where fairways seem as narrow as telescope barrels, where the rough is high and thick enough to hide dead bodies, and where greens are as hard and fast as glass. His prodigious length off the tee would not help him here as much as it had at Augusta (architects were already setting about changing that course).

Tiger made his trip to the woodshed with swing guru Butch Harmon, learning to drive the ball low and straight, learning to stop his irons, soften and sweeten them, hit what he calls "high sweepers," and other such golf-swing exotica. In the meantime, he tied for eighth at the Masters, tied for 18th at the U.S. Open, was third at the British Open and tied for 10th at the PGA. He also won the BellSouth Classic. He played 20 events and finished in the top 10 13 times. His scoring average was a truly absurd 69.21. And for the first time, he didn't miss a single cut—and he hasn't missed one since.

Even as he was woodshedding, he competed. "He's fascinated by the process (of improving)," said golf writer Jaime Diaz. "He loves to break down where his flaws are, isn't afraid to tear down the house to build a better one." And so, in 1999, Woods won $6.6 million in prize money on the PGA Tour—nearly $3 million more than the No. 2 money winner, David Duval, and a record by far. By now he was a force of nature. The PGA prize

THE GOLDEN BEAR VS. EL TIGRE

A comparison of Jack Nicklaus and Tiger Woods from the players' first six years on the PGA Tour. (Note: Tiger only played eight events his first year on the tour.)

Jack Nicklaus: 1962-67	**Tiger Woods: 1996-2001**
Events Played: 134	*Events Played:* 109
Cuts Made: 132	*Cuts Made:* 107
Missed Cuts: 2	*Missed Cuts:* 2
Placed 1st: 24	*Placed 1st:* 29
Placed 2nd: 20	*Placed 2nd:* 8
Placed 3rd: 16	*Placed 3rd:* 9
Top 10: 92	*Top 10:* 69
Earnings: $716,363	*Earnings:* $26,191,227
Yearly Ranking:	*Yearly Ranking:*
1962: 3	1996: 24
1963: 2	1997: 1
1964: 1	1998: 4
1965: 1	1999: 1
1966: 2	2000: 1
1967: 1	2001: 1
Major Tournament Wins:	*Major Tournament Wins:*
1962 U.S. Open	1997 Masters
1963 Masters	1999 PGA Championship
1963 PGA Championship	2000 U.S. Open
1965 Masters	2000 British Open
1966 Masters	2000 PGA Championship
1966 British Open	2001 Masters
1967 U.S. Open	*Total:* 6 majors
Total: 7 majors	
When Jack Nicklaus won his first major, the 1962 U.S. Open, he earned $15,000.	Tiger Woods earned $486,000 for his first major win at the 1997 Masters.

money was going up, because there was more general public interest in the tour, and there was more interest because of Tiger Woods. He was a self-sustaining, self-contained unit now, like the sun, warming orbiting worlds, not the other way around, as was previously believed.

He won the 1999 PGA to become the youngest player since Seve Ballesteros to win two majors. He became the first since Nick Price in '94 to win five PGA Tour events by winning the NEC Invitational. Won his next start at the National Car Rental Classic at Walt Disney World in Orlando. Became the first since Tom Watson in 1980 to win six PGA Tour events. The next week, he won his third straight start at The Tour Championship. The following week he won the World Golf-American Express Championship and became the first since Johnny Miller in 1974 to win eight times in a year, and the first since Hogan in 1953 to win four straight starts. Everything he did became historic.

He was only 23.

■ ## Supernatural Season

And all that was before his *good* year, 2000.

He shot 75 in the first round of the 2000 Masters, recovered to finish fifth behind champion Vijay Singh. After that, he truly set sail, embarking on a run through the major championships that now seems incredible, beyond belief, even by his own otherworldly standards. First came the 2000 U.S. Open held at Pebble Beach—the tournament he'd gone back to the woodshed in 1998 to prepare to win. He won that U.S. Open by an astounding 15 shots! He finished at 65-69-71-67=272, 12-under, becoming the first man in the 106-year history of the U.S. Open to finish 72 holes at double-digits under par. **His 15-stroke victory sets the standard for all the majors. The previous widest margin of victory in a U.S. Open—11—had been set in 1899.**

"His level of play at the 2000 U.S. Open was the highest ever attained," said Diaz. "Even he may never reach that level again. But, in a way, I was more impressed by his eight-shot victory a month later at the British Open at St. Andrews. He wasn't as possessed or inspired, didn't do as many spectacular things. It was clinical, so calm, so matter of fact, it might have sent an even more chilling message—'I can do this over, and over, and over.' "

That August, Woods and a pro named Bob May tied the 72-hole record of 18-under at the PGA Championship, then played a gripping three-hole playoff that Woods won. While doing so he also set up a new, telegenic format we will call "Tiger Golf." At the end of 72 holes, preferably at a major, one or two golfers' games rise to take the challenge of meeting Tiger at the summit in a playoff. Riveting television for that or any week; the other golfer becomes Everyman's Champion. Bob May was a hero just for giving Tiger competition, not by cattily sniping and bitching, but by testing him, making him raise his game.

Woods is not only one of five golfers to have won a "career" Grand Slam (clockwise, from top left, the British Open, the U.S. Open, the PGA Championship and the Masters), he is the only one to hold all four titles at the same time—the 2000 U.S. Open, British Open and PGA, plus the 2001 Masters. (He also holds the scoring records in relation to par for all four majors.) Technically, Woods's amazing feat is not considered a Grand Slam, which would require winning all four tournaments in the same calendar year. Some have called it the Tiger Slam, though Jack Nicklaus said that "the Fiscal Slam" would be more fitting.

IS GOLF A SPORT?

■ Tiger Woods's ascension to golf greatness was calculated. But his turning golfers into athletes was purely coincidental.

Since emerging as a pro in 1996, Woods has been as relentless in his workouts as he is on the driving range. He committed to a strength and training program that helped him add 20 pounds of muscle to his once spindly frame. When he was troubled by back pain in '98, Woods included more flexibility training in order to reduce the likelihood of injury.

He worked for a year and a half with Vegas personal trainer Keith Kleven, who operates an orthopedic sports institute. Woods lifts weights three times a week and, it is said, once took a helicopter to private workouts during the 1999 British Open at St. Andrews.

Gary Player, who was known as the fittest man on tour in his day, has said, "Isn't it something to see Tiger Woods pumping iron and eating right? His work ethic is his greatest attribute."

Woods's fitness gives him an edge, and his competitors are taking notice. David Duval works out 13 of every 14 days. Justin Leonard hired a personal trainer and runs up to four miles daily. Ernie Els, Greg Norman, Vijay Singh and Colin Montgomerie are also emphasizing fitness.

Oddly enough, just after Tiger's arrival on the scene, a health-care company began providing training and treatment vans for the PGA, Senior and LPGA Tours. Pros can lift weights, undergo cardiovascular trainings, and receive nutritional advice and a biomechanics evaluation of their swing. Even Senior Tour players like Hale Irwin and Tom Watson can be found in the fitness van up to four times a week.

Some, like Hal Sutton, have beaten Tiger. Others will. Tiger Woods has been and will be beaten. He takes it graciously. He accepts it, just doesn't necessarily believe in it. Gary Player said it was a man's demeanor when he lost that impressed him most. In many ways, that is a good indicator of character. But it is the drama of competition, head-to-head, mano-a-mano, that impresses the TV audiences and the booming galleries most. We can look forward to more of this for, oh . . . the next decade. Or two.

So he *was* a Mozart. Comparisons are easy to throw about, as this essay—if nothing else—has proved. Perhaps the hardest thing to be is your own best self. So he was Tiger Woods. He changed the face, reach and scope of golf, made it more than it was, and healed its afflictions. With that written, said and done, think about this:

He just turned 26!

The latest contract between the PGA Tour and the TV networks— ABC, CBS, NBC, ESPN, USA and the Golf Channel—for 2003-2006, is worth upwards of $850 million, nearly double the last contract. Tiger TV. Tiger Slam. Tiger Golf. Anybody who says his dominance isn't good for golf can't count very well.

■ We Need Saving, Every Now and Then

Tiger won't be the last one. As a group, the American flock tends to need saving, every now and then. So the Book of Eldrick, while an age-old story, is also but a beginning, the first chapter of the New Testament of 21st-Century American Sports. Where (and with whom) our story will take us from here, we don't know. We can only know it'll be a ride, as it was with Babe, Jackie, Bird & Magic, or Pete's Super Bowl. We can only follow whoever comes along next.

For it is already written in our Scriptures: *We screw up, then a Savior comes along and makes things right.*

We are nothing if not consistent.

Is Woods a genuine prodigy, destined to be a star of lasting brilliance? Sports psychologist Joel Fish told writer Dave Kindred: "There's talent, personality, mental toughness and timing. All that must come together to create the prodigy. If it's not all there, you've got something pretty good, but it's not a prodigy. With the prodigy, there's no debate. Everybody accepts the fact that this is a one-in-a-million person. And Tiger has the whole prodigy package. What Mozart is to music, Tiger is to golf. Of course," Dr. Fish added, "people are trying to defeat Tiger on the field of battle. No one did that with Mozart."

HEN I WAS

10 MY FATHER TOOK ME TO THE POLO GROUNDS TO WATCH A WORLD SERIES GAME BETWEEN THE YANKEES AND THE GIANTS. I REMEMBER COMING THROUGH A PORTAL AND BEING TAKEN ABACK BY THAT FIRST SIGHT OF A MAJOR LEAGUE BALLPARK, BY WHAT THOMAS WOLFE DESCRIBES AS THE "VELVET AND UNALTERABLE GEOMETRY OF THE PLAYING FIELD." WHAT I REMEMBER MOST WAS THE GIANT PITCHER, A TALL LEFTHANDER NAMED CLIFF MELTON. I HAD AN EXCELLENT VIEW OF SOMETHING I'D NEVER SEEN BEFORE, AN ADULT THROWING THE BALL AT UNBELIEVABLE SPEEDS. THERE WAS NO PREPARATION FOR THE SIGHT, THIS BEING LONG BEFORE THE DAYS OF TELEVISION. THIS WAS SOMETHING BEYOND THE REALM OF MY KNOWLEDGE. AT SCHOOL WE WERE STUDYING MYTHOLOGY —THAT IS, WE WERE READING ABOUT THE GREEK GODS AND THEIR ABILITY TO THROW THUNDERBOLTS AND SUCH THINGS, AND MR. MELTON, THOUGH EARTH-BOUND, SEEMED IN MY MIND SURELY TO BELONG IN THEIR GALAXY. TO PUT IT SIMPLY, HE WAS GOD IN MY EYES, A SMALL-G GOD.

GODS

by George Plimpton

As I think about it, hero worship, this process of giving mortal man a higher god-like status, tends to diminish somewhat as time goes on. As one grows older, and more sophisticated, other heroes from the worlds of culture, politics and international affairs move in and tend to push the sports people to the sidelines, because what the latter are doing—throwing baseballs, hitting a golf ball into a cup—seems rather inconsequential by comparison. As Red Smith put it: "I've always tried to remember—and this is an old line—that sports isn't Armageddon. These are just little games that little boys can play, and it isn't important to the future of civilization whether the Athletics or the Browns win."

Nonetheless, sports remains so surely a secular religion inhabiting the minds of most Americans (with its saints and sinners, its popes, its bishops, and so on) that it bears inspection; to that end, I've put together a conversation with myself . . . one part of me the inquisitor, occasionally offering a comment or two, and the other a long-winded respondent who may or may not know what he is talking about.

■ Why don't you start from a lofty position, a discussion about God in sports—that is, God with a big G?

Sports and God. Well, God with a big G is invariably invoked before a game, often during, and is invariably given credit for a victory. Some teams actually think of Him as their own. The Dallas Cowboys often said that when the roof of their indoor stadium was opened, it was because they wanted God to have a better view of His team. The San Francisco Giants had a pitcher, Bob Knepper, who attributed a game-winning home run against him to God's Will. My old friend Roy Blount Jr. once semi-facetiously suggested that there were so many Christians in big-time sport that when he put his mind to picking an All-Religious Team and an All-Heathen team in his imaginary "Christians vs. Lions Bowl," he couldn't find enough heathens to field a team!

■ It would be fair to say that a version of this sort of thing is the country singer Bobby Bare's "Drop Kick Me, Jesus, Through the Goal Posts of Life."

I hadn't thought of that. I'm glad you brought it up. Certainly, the pre-game prayer in NFL football is almost universal. Night Train Lane of the Detroit Lions once told me that there wasn't much point in praying for victory, because the people in the locker room across the way were doing the same thing, and surely God was not the kind who would count the votes and hand the victory over to the team that had the most prayerful players. Beau Jack, the lightweight fighter, a onetime shoeshine boy at the Augusta National who was discovered by Bobby Jones, expressed the same conclusion as follows:

For what did you pray?

"I pray nobody get hurt. Then I pray it be a good fight."

Good to be king, better to be a god, best to be God Himself (from a watercolor by William Blake).

Don't you pray to win?

"No, I would never do that."

Why not?

"Suppose I pray to win. The other boy, he pray to win too. Then what God gonna do?"

■ Knute Rockne said it about as well as anyone: "Prayers work best when players are big."

Here's a rather vivid example of pre-game ritual, half in fun, but then perhaps not—an invocation delivered by Father Edward Rupp before the 1976 World Hockey Association All-Star game: "Heavenly Father, Divine Goalie, we come before You this evening to seek Your blessing . . . we are, thanks to you, All-Stars. We pray tonight for Your guidance. **Keep us from action that would put us in the Sin Box of Hell. Inspire us to avoid the pitfalls of our profession, help us to stay within the Blue Line of Your commandments and the Red Line of Your grace. Prohibit us from being injured by the Puck of pride.** May we be ever delivered from the High Stick of anger. May the wings of Your angels play at the Right and Left Wing of our teammates. May You always be the Divine Center of our team, and when our summons comes for eternal retirement to the heavenly Grandstand, may we find You ready to give us the everlasting bonus of a permanent seat in Your Coliseum. Finally, grant us the courage to skate without Tripping, to run without Icing, and to score the Goal that really counts—the one that makes each of us a winner, a champion, an All-Star in the hectic Hockey Game of Life."

Then we have a story about a former head coach at Florida State, Bill Peterson, great record there, great college coach, who gathered his team around him for a pre-game prayer, bowed his head and, doubtless thinking about who he was going to start at offensive tackle, began as follows: "Now I lay me down to sleep, I pray the Lord my soul . . ." and then realizing what he was saying, caught sight of a player he knew was thinking of joining the ministry and called out to him, "Take it away, Bobby . . ."

■ Wow!

I have in my notes a description of the kind of trouble one can get into with too much of this sort of thing. It was the habit of a goalkeeper named Isidore Irandir with the Brazilian soccer club Rio Petro to kneel in the goalmouth before a game and pray for the Lord to keep anything from getting by him into the net. Aware of Irandir's ritual, the celebrated Roberto Rivelino of Corinthians, noted for the power of his leg, blasted the ball toward the Rio Petro goal, where it sailed past Irandir, still on his knees concluding his prayer. According to the account (in a delightful book entitled *Great Sporting Eccentrics*), while the Corinthians were celebrating, Irandir's brother ran onto the field brandishing a revolver and pumped six shots . . . not into his brother, or Roberto Rivelino, but into the ball!

Washington Redskins QB Sammy Baugh once said of a very religious linebacker, "He knocks the hell out of people, but in a Christian way."

NOT NAMED IN VAIN

■ *Long before athletes started thanking "the man upstairs" for taking time out of his busy schedule to personally lift their team to victory, religion was playing an intricate role in sports.*

In the 19th century, Billy Sunday, an evangelical preacher and former baseball player, started a religious movement called "Muscular Christianity," the idea being to change the notion that Christian men are spineless and effeminate. Sunday fed his flock a "hard-muscled, pick-axed religion, a religion from the gut, tough and resilient."

Obviously, things have changed over the years. But what hasn't is the ever-present link between sports and religion when it comes to terminology. Whether it's as simple as the Anaheim Angels, or as clever as "The Immaculate Reception," somehow sports and religion always seem to find one another.

GOD'S CHILDREN I

Hockey

St. Patrick: PATRICK ROY. Colorado Avalanche goalie is NHL's all-time leader in victories.

Golf

The Devil: BRUCE DEVLIN. Won eight PGA events in the '60s and '70s; now plays on the Senior Tour.

Basketball

Black Jesus: EARL MONROE. Star guard for the great Knicks teams of the '70s.

Jewish Jordan: TAMIR GOODMAN. Orthodox Jew is a guard for Towson.

Allah the Rim God: ALONZA ALLEN. Swingman for SW Louisiana in the 1980s.

The Sun God: PAUL WESTPHAL. Averaged 15.6 ppg during his NBA career (1972-84); now head coach at Pepperdine.

Missionary Impossible or The Mormon Tabernacle Crier: SHAWN BRADLEY. 7-foot-6 Dallas Mavericks center, starred at BYU.

Miracle Mike: MIKE WOODSON. Played for the Knicks, Kansas City and Sacramento Kings, Clippers, Rockets and Cavs during his NBA career (1980-91).

The Spirit: MICKEY DAVIS. Bucks reserve swingman, 1972-77.

■ A sight to delight the imagination!

Incidentally, where pre-performance praying is most evident is among the bullfighting fraternity. Granted what they do is hardly a sport (after all, there is only one possible winner), but those who do it invariably carry with them a portable altar, along with a Madonna figure, which is set up in the hotel room where they dress in the "suit of lights" and before which they pray—a solemn ritual indeed. Not meaning to be fatuous, but here, of course, all the prayers come from one side of the issue: No one prays on behalf of the bull. Oddly, the Catholic Church has always been against bullfighting, considering it a pagan ritual—which, indeed, it is—but by the same token there are no agnostics among bullfighters. In Triana, near Seville, the tradition at the famous bullfighters' cafe Anselma's is for everyone after the last drinks of the evening to rise and, facing the Madonna over the bar, sing the Benedictine holy hymn, "Salve Regina."

■ How do the rituals of sport compare to those of religion?

Gertrude Stein, upon seeing a football game, was very much taken by the religious aspects—the prayerful attitude of the players grouped in a huddle. Then immediately following, they march to the line of scrimmage and crouch down in obeisance to the ball. Indeed, one speaks of the "hallowed" ground on which great athletic deeds have been enacted, the "sacred" turf of such-and-such a cricket pitch or ballpark, suggesting that a near-religious activity goes on there.

The sociologist Harry Edwards points out that **sports has its rules, which are accepted very much as a liturgy is in church, though indeed ministers of the faith blow whistles only metaphorically.** As we know, sports has its saints, its fallen angels, its patriarchs (owners, managers, coaches), even its shrines—the many halls of fame with their trophy rooms, the silver cups and, in the Baseball Hall of Fame at Cooperstown, true reliquaries in the form of Babe Ruth's 52-ounce bat, as well as Ty Cobb's teeth.

■ Ty Cobb's teeth?

I have gazed upon the thing—in fact, his bridgework—interesting in that only some of his back teeth had to be replaced; his two front teeth survived the baseball wars.

■ What about the gods with small g's?

Well, we must go back to the Greeks with their pantheistic system, the notion that there are many gods looking on. Their presence is overwhelming. Homer attributes all the accidents in sports events to the gods taking a hand. In a chariot race, Diomedes, just as he is about to pass Eumelus, drops his whip—which is Apollo's doing—upon which Athena not only returns the whip to his hand but, in revenge, breaks the shaft of

SACRED KEEPSAKES

Sacred splinters and shreds have captivated worshippers for centuries.
Faithful sports fans, too, venerate the hallowed keepsakes of their favorite athletes. Private collectors would pay top
prices for a lock of Babe Ruth's hair, while Ty Cobb's dentures fascinate visitors to Cooperstown.
Although most sports relics are less exotic than the polished tibia of a martyr, they are no less cherished.

SS Lou Gehrig's christening bottle   Pop Warner's death mask   Didrikson's harmonica

Baseball

■ The Baseball Hall of Fame's collection includes a bible used by legendary New York Giants pitcher Christy Mathewson and his Sunday school teacher in Mathewson's hometown of Factoryville, Pa. He dominated hitters in the first two decades of the 20th century, but they could rest easy on Sundays, when he would not pitch.

■ The bottle used in the early 1940s to christen the SS *Lou Gehrig* resides in Cooperstown. It was donated to the Hall in 1955 by Gehrig's mother, Christine, upon her death. The *Gehrig* was a Liberty ship, a common cargo vessel commissioned during WWII.

■ Jackie Robinson sent a telegram to President Lyndon Johnson after demonstrators were injured during a Selma, Ala., march. It reads, in part, "One more day of savage treatment by legalized hatchet men could lead to open warfare by aroused Negroes. America cannot afford this in 1965." The telegram is filed at Johnson's presidential library.

Football

■ It's no surprise to find a death mask for a Pope or king in a museum, but a football coach? Pop Warner's death mask resides at the College Football Hall of Fame in South Bend, Ind. Who made it and how it got there are mysteries. Warner was an early football legend who won 319 games, coached Jim Thorpe, and invented the single-wing formation and the three-point stance.

■ Notre Dame QB Joe Montana was suffering from hypothermia when Houston and the Irish played in the 1979 Cotton Bowl in a freezing rain. To help his condition, he was fed chicken soup—to which some describe sacred healing power—and his bowl and spoon are on display in South Bend. Montana rallied the Fighting Irish for 23 points in the fourth quarter to win the game, 35-34.

■ Vince Lombardi was a staunch Catholic who lived his faith fully. The Green Bay Packers Hall of Fame has his membership papers in the Franciscan Mission Association in Trenton, N.J., a group with which he had a life-long affiliation. Wide receiver Cris Carter, who is also deeply religious, inscribed "God Bless" on the football he caught in 1994 to break the record at that time for most receptions (122) in a season.

Basketball

■ James Naismith, as a devout Presbyterian minister, wanted missionaries to have a simple game they could take with them on their missions. Thus, basketball was born. The Basketball Hall of Fame in Springfield, Mass., has Naismith's bible from when he graduated the Presbyterian College in Montreal in 1890, the year before he invented basketball. In inventing basketball, Naismith was inspired by a children's game he played, "Duck on a Rock," that combined tag with throwing rocks.

Golf

■ Babe Didrikson Zaharias, the great all-round athlete who helped found the LGPA, played the harmonica and, as the legend goes, performed in a vaudeville act. The World Golf Hall of Fame in St. Augustine, Fla., has the harmonica, along with the lunchbox Sam Snead toted to his childhood golf lessons and Nancy Lopez's Barbie Doll, which her father said he would buy more clothes for if Nancy won her tournaments.

Hockey

■ The moment selected the greatest in NHL history is of Bobby Orr flying through the air to score the Stanley Cup-winning goal in OT against the Blues in 1970. It brought Boston its first Cup in 29 years. The knee brace he was wearing at the time is on display at The Hockey Hall of Fame in Toronto.

Boxing

■ Hometown fans of "Boston Strong Boy" John L. Sullivan, the world heavyweight champion (1882-92), got together $10,000 for a gold-plated prize belt studded with 350 diamonds and a portrait of the fighter. It was presented to the last of the bare-knuckle champs in 1887. The diamonds are now lost, but the belt is part of the Smithsonian's sports history collection.

Horse racing

■ Kelso, the outstanding distance runner and the 1960-64 Horse of the Year, received tons of fan mail and was given his own mailbox at Maryland's Woodstock Farm. The horse even had his own fan club, the Kelsolanders, and was nicknamed King Kelly. The Horse Racing Hall of Fame in Saratoga, N.Y., has some of the fan mail, the mailbox and his fur collar.

Eumelus' chariot, spilling him to the ground and out of the race. That was one of the problems of playing on those ancient fields—that the athletes had more than one god to deal with, gods who were often squabbling among themselves to the detriment of humankind. Both Homer's *Iliad* and the first books of Virgil's *Aeneid* give us the account of the Golden Apple with its inscription To the Fairest rolling out onto the ballroom floor at the wedding feast of Thetis in front of a multitude of gods and goddesses. Three of them—Athena, Aphrodite and Hera—felt it was theirs. Paris, a shepherd, was selected as a referee because he was considered honest, a reputation he'd picked up judging oxen at the local fair. **The goddesses bribed him—Athena with martial glory, Hera with power, and Aphrodite, of course, offered him Helen of Troy. She was married to Menelaus, but that didn't seem to bother Paris, who left his wife Oenone for her**—a very unfortunate trade, as it turned out, because it was the cause of the Trojan War, a catastrophe (from the point of view of Boston Red Sox fans like myself) not unlike the trade of Babe Ruth to New York, which led to the ruination of the Red Sox and the dominance of the Yankees.

What was the Greek attitude about winning?

Not very different from Vince Lombardi's—that it is the "only thing." Pindar, the great lyric poet of the 5th century, wrote a number of odes that were often sung by choirs of boys when a hero came home to his native town (very much the sort of parade and honors that greeted Sarah Hughes on her return to Great Neck after her gold medal in the 2002 Olympics). The highest prize in ancient Olympics was the wreath of wild olive—far more prized by athletes than an ox, or a bowl, or a tripod, or a cup, or even a woman skilled in some handicraft. On the other hand, another matter for the losers. The winners never shook the hands of the losers. **The chivalry we are supposed to display toward the loser is not something that the Greeks understood. Defeat was felt to be a disgrace.** In fact, the Spartans forbade their citizens to take part in athletic events for fear they might lose. Those who did compete and lost got little sympathy from their fellows. No "tough luck," no sympathetic touch on the shoulder. The hometowns were outraged to hear the news of a favorite son's defeat, and often a statue, previously put up to honor him, was torn down, so that what he'd see when he got home was just a pedestal. "By back ways they slink away sore smitten by misfortune. No sweet smile greets their return."

Errors were not forgiven.

Hardly. The Greeks had a game of catch called *ephedrismos* that included a weird penalty for dropping the ball, namely that the one who committed the error had to assume the position of a donkey and carry the other fel-

Athena (from an engraving of a statue), like the other goddesses of her time, was not too proud to resort to bribery every now and then.

low around on his back, to symbolically make an ass of himself—and I've often wondered if that isn't the source of that expression.

Very sensitive, the fans of those times. If a good hometown athlete competed for another city, he could start a riot. A fleet-footed athlete named Astylus from Crotona, who had won races in two successive Olympiads (488 and 484 B.C.), shifted his allegiance to Syracuse. His fellow citizens not only destroyed a statue erected in his honor, but also took over his house and turned it into a prison.

Is it true that the athletes competed naked?

That is so. Vase painting and art from the time prove that absolute nudity was the norm. There was a time at the end of the 6th century when white loincloths turned up on their bodies (as one can tell by the vases of the time), but only temporarily. It was obviously an incentive for Greek youths to keep themselves in good physical condition, because if you weren't, derision was invariably to follow. There are designs on vases of fat boys being chided by their thinner peers. The Greek ideal, the duty of the citizen, was to develop his beauty and his strength to the utmost. Pindar refers to the

A simple wreath of wild olive (in a 1788 painting by Marie-Louise-Elisabeth Vigée-Lebrun), the symbol of victory, was more precious to the Greeks than riches, art, even beautiful women willing to work hard for next to nothing.

true ideal of the athlete in his 11th Olympian ode, which honors a young boxer named Agesidemus: "If one be born with excellent gifts then may another who sharpeneth his natural glory, speed him, God helping, to an exceeding weight of glory. Without toil there have triumphed a very few." Coaches in contemporary times find many ways of echoing that last sentence.

■ ## Did the athletes pray to the gods?

Almost surely they did, offering their vows at the altars of their various patron gods or heroes. Sport was definitely placed under the patronage of the gods, and the victorious athlete felt he owed his success to them—just as today so often the winning athlete, puffing slightly, starts off his TV interview by saying, "I want to thank God who made it all possible . . ." or variations thereof.

On the other hand, the former baseball commissioner, A. Bartlett Giamatti, believed that the gods have always been absent—that human beings played games from the earliest times not to please or appease the gods, but rather "we have played games and watched games to imitate the gods, and to become godlike in our worship of each other, and, through these moments of transmutations, to know for an instant what the gods knew, whether celebrated by Pindar or Roger Angell . . ."

He mentions a scholar named Allen Guttmann, who points out: **"Once the Gods have vanished from Mount Olympus or from Dante's Paradise, we can no longer run to appease them or to save our souls, but we can set a record. It is a uniquely modern form of immortality."**

I think I understand that. We have the need to re-create the instant of immortality by talking about it (locker-room chat about the brilliant birdie scored on the 10th), reading about it (10 pages of a sports section or a sports magazine), hoping to see it (one of tens of thousands attending the Olympics or a World Series) or watching it via some representative form such as movies, television, tapes. Indeed, we are either the happy few who can do great feats beyond our own gifts, or surely we are among the vast number of grateful (and indeed somehow immortalized ourselves by being on hand) to witness what they do. Thus many of us carry "visions" around in our minds—Bobby Thomson's "shot heard 'round the world," Secretariat winning the Belmont by 31 lengths, Jesse Owens' 100-meter dash in Berlin, John Havlicek stealing the ball, Henry Aaron beating the Babe's home run record—imperishable moments of immortality. Of course, a vision of delight is at the same time a nightmare for someone else—a Dodger fan in the case of the Thomson pennant-winning home run in the Polo Grounds, a horse called Sham beaten by 45 lengths in the Belmont, Adolf Hitler at the Berlin Olympics, the Philadelphia 76ers when Havlicek swiped the ball with a few seconds left to preserve one of the Boston Celtics many championships.

Not Named in Vain (continued)
GOD'S CHILDREN II
Baseball

The Heavenly Twins: HUGH DUFFY AND TOMMY MCCARTHY. Boston Braves outfielders of the 1890s.

Rabbi of Swat: MOSE SOLOMON. Played two games with the Yankees in 1923.

The Mahatma: BRANCH RICKEY. President of the Dodgers, 1943-50.

The Mad Monk: RUSS MEYER. Pitcher from 1946 to 1959 known for his explosive temper. Career record is 94-73.

Deacon: VERNON LAW. Pitched for the Pirates, 1950-67.

God: DOUG HARVEY. National League umpire for 31 years, retired in 1992. Sepulchral voice of MLB's "You Make the Call."

The Exorcist: RICH GOSSAGE. One of the most feared relief pitchers of his time (1972-94).

The Jewish Lou Gehrig: PHIL WEINTRAUB. Played for the Giants, Reds and Phils in the '30s and '40s.

Miracle Worker: GIL HODGES. Dodgers slugger hit .304 with 42 homers and 130 RBI in 1954, including many big "miracle" hits.

The Yiddish Curver: BARNEY PELTY. Pitcher for the Browns, 1903-12.

The Yiddish Yankee: RON BLOMBERG. Yankee outfielder, 1969-76.

Superjew: MIKE EPSTEIN. Played from 1966 to 1974. Epstein was dubbed Superjew by rival manager Rocky Bridges after he led the California League in batting and home runs in 1965.

Moses: JOE SHIPLEY. Giants pitcher, 1958-60.

The Pope: DONN PALL. Pitcher, 1988-98. Spent first six years with White Sox.

Jonah: GEORGE DERBY. Pitcher, 1881-83.

King Solomon: EDDIE SOLOMON. NL pitcher, 1973-82.

■ Do you have a hero supreme among the ancient Greeks?

Certainly. We all indulge the familiar daydream of being taunted and then coming back and showing up the taunter. So I would choose Odysseus from the wonderful episode described in the *Odyssey*, when he reaches the land of the Phaeacians and is entertained there by King Alcinous at a kind of sports gymkhana—wrestling, racing, boxing, throwing the discus, and so on. As the two watch these impromptu games, the king's son steps up and suggests that Odysseus join in. Odysseus, who is worn out, barely having survived a shipwreck, aching to get some rest, declines . . . upon which a rather unmannerly young courtier begins to taunt Odysseus, chiding him that he isn't worthy of being called an athlete. He keeps this up until Odysseus has had enough: He steps down off the viewing stand and grabs a preposterously heavy discus, which he then hurls into the distance, far surpassing the longest throw of the afternoon. And that is not all. He offers

Fat Boys Need Not Apply was Rule No. 1 in the code of the Greek athlete, who was expected to perform his best in the nude (painting from a Greek vase, c. 5th century B.C.).

to box, wrestle—one can see him hopping around in fury at the indignity of not being recognized as an athlete—and none of the Phaeacians, quite chastened, will take him up on it. In fact, King Alcinous not only apologizes for the upstart's rudeness but goes on to say that none of his people are really athletes: "Dear to us is the banquet and the harp and the dance, and changes of raiment, and the warm bath and love and sleep."

So Odysseus for sure. There are others who come to mind. Milo of Croton, whose training methods were memorable: His daily exercise included lifting a young bull calf until it was full-grown. Milo, according to legend, carried a 4-year-old heifer around the Altis at Olympia and then ate it the same day. I'd rather like to have met him. Babe Ruth was famous for eating all those hot dogs, but he's a bit of a piker compared to Milo of Croton.

What about more contemporary heroes?

Well, Babe Ruth. I remember a story about him when he was long out of baseball and very much neglected. Out on Long Island's Jones Beach on a weekend, he was asked to perform in one of the promotions of the day—

Nobody ever asked heifer-hoisting Milo of Croton (in an engraving by Minardi Tommaso): "Where's the beef?"

namely, to hit fungo flies into the bay. What happened was that after the first three balls had hardly splashed into the bay, the fourth still in the air on the way, a thousand youngsters, girls as well as boys, suddenly took to the water, thrashing out toward those baseballs. The fact that Ruth had hit those balls had imbued them with a kind of magic, a god's touch, enough to get a whole mass of people into the water.

■ Have you ever been in the company of anyone you would consider a sports god?

A small number. I met Jack Dempsey once, was invited to sit at his table at a rather fancy restaurant in Southampton, Long Island. He never said a word, and I don't know that anyone even talked to him. I had no wish to do so. The others at the table, including his wife, doubtless knew him as someone who preferred not to talk and to let the conversation swirl around without having to bother about it. He was rather god-like, sitting there above it all, large and impervious.

Jack Dempsey was one of the rare boxers who knew when to get out. In his later years, he rode a bicycle around Central Park to stay in shape. One night, according to author Roger Kahn, as Dempsey was getting out of a cab, a couple of thugs tried to mug him: "There he was, now white-haired, expensive topcoat, so they jumped him for his wallet. Dempsey gave them a couple of body punches, and these guys wouldn't get up until the police came to protect them."

The conversation turned to boxing, gossip about this fighter and that, and somebody mentioned a fighter (whose name, alas, I have forgotten) who was particularly known for his rabbit punch, the illegal blow to the back of the opponent's neck. Someone else mentioned another boxer who was expert at such things, upon which Dempsey's wife piped up and asked what a rabbit punch was.

At this, Dempsey, who had been as immobile as a statue, raised an arm to about head level and brought it down with a frightening crash on the tabletop. The silverware jumped, as did all of us, and many rose from their seats at the adjoining tables. People stood up in the far reaches of the restaurant. Heads craned. I don't remember that as much as a smile crossed Dempsey's face. It remained as composed as it had been all evening, quite appropriate for one who had made such a Zeus-like gesture in reply to his wife's question.

■ **I don't suppose there was much talk about punches after that. The sucker punch, for example.**

Quite right. Very gentle conversation. Nothing else said elicited a similar response.

■ **And who is another god?**

I would think Vince Lombardi. I met him as well in a restaurant. I remember the glint of his spectacles in the candlelight. He had heard of my book *Paper Lion*, but he said without any hint of apology that he hadn't read it. His players had told him it was all right. He was telling me in so many words that he wasn't ever going to read it; there were more important things. **I asked him if he would ever have let a reporter into a training camp to learn some plays, the sort of thing the Detroit Lions had let me do, and he was adamant. Absolutely not, he said, without a glint of humor, no more than he'd have let a fox into a chicken coop.**

My old friend Bill Curry, who had played his rookie year with the Green Bay Packers, told me a fine story about Lombardi—a time the players rose up against his authoritarian methods. It's in a book we did together called *One More July*, which is a phrase players use who are coming back for one last try when the training season starts in July. "I'll give it one more July."

The Packers had lost a game they should have won in Los Angeles against the Rams; there had been some singing on the plane on the way back to Green Bay, which had riled Lombardi. He let the players know his feelings at the next team meeting:

"When the coaches were out and the doors were shut, Lombardi really went at it. The meeting seemed to go on for an hour and a half, with Lombardi screaming, shouting, 'Goddamit, you guys don't care if you win

---

Not Named in Vain (continued)
GOD'S CHILDREN III

Boxing

The Praying Puncher: JERSEY JOE WALCOTT. Former heavyweight champ famous for being KO'd by Rocky Marciano.

The Preacher: GEORGE FOREMAN. The oldest man (45) to win the heavyweight title.

King Solomon: EMILIO SOLOMON. Pro boxer of the '20s and '30s.

Action Sports

Miracle Man: DAVE MIRRA. Most successful BMX'er in the sport's history.

Hell: KELLY SLATER. Pro surfer won six Association of Surfing Professionals titles in the '90s.

The Hell Fighter: SETH KIMBROUGH. Ultra-religious BMX'er. Avid follower of Christ, church-going and God-fearing.

Football

Reverend Ike: ISAAC BRUCE. All-Pro receiver for the Rams.

St. Vincent: VINCE LOMBARDI. Legendary Packers coach.

Minister of Defense: REGGIE WHITE. All-time NFL sack leader and ordained minister.

John One-Dozen—as in John 1:12: CRAIG BAYNHAM. Running back who often quoted this biblical passage.

The Pounding Pontiff: MARQUEZ POPE. Hard-hitting safety for the Raiders.

Deacon: DAN TOWLER. Bruising All-Pro fullback for Rams of the '50s.

The Pope: CHUCK NOLL. Coached Steelers to four Super Bowl titles—IX, X, XIII, XIV.

Heavenly: HAVEN MOSES. Wide receiver, 1968-81.

Billiards

King James: JIM REMPE. World Champion 8-ball and 9-ball player in '70s and '80s.

or lose. I'm the only one who cares. I'm the only one that puts his blood and guts and his heart into the game. You guys show up, you listen a little bit, you concentrate . . . you've got the concentration of 3-year-olds. You're nothing! I'm the only guy who gives a damn if we win or lose!'

"Suddenly, there was a stirring in the back of the room, a rustle of chairs. I turned around and there was Forrest Gregg, on his feet, bright red, a player on either side, holding him back by the arms, and he was straining forward. Gregg was another real gentlemanly kind of guy, very quiet. Lombardi looked at him and stopped. Forrest said, 'Goddamit, Coach . . . excuse the profanity . . . but it makes me sick to hear you say something like that. We lay it on the line for you every Sunday. We live and die the same way you do, and it hurts.' **Then he began straining forward again, trying to get up there to punch Lombardi out. Players were holding him back.** Then Bob Skoronski stood up, very articulate. He was the captain of the team. 'That's right,' he said. 'Don't you tell us that we don't care about winning. That makes me sick. Makes me want to puke. We care about it every bit as much as you do. It's our knees and our bodies out there that we're throwing around.'

"So there it was. The coach had been confronted, the captain of a

A joke (at least we think it is): Vince Lombardi and his wife Marie were in bed one cold Green Bay winter night, when Marie exclaimed, "Oh, God, it's cold in here." "Dear," Lombardi replied, "when we're alone like this, you can call me 'Vince.' "

HOLY PLACES

*"It's no accident that of all the monuments left of the Greco-Roman culture the biggest
is the ballpark, the Colosseum, the Yankee Stadium of ancient times,"
wrote legendary sports columnist Red Smith. If sports is this country's religion and
the athletes its saints and icons, then our stadia and arenas must be its temples
and shrines. In the religion of sport, every game day is the Sabbath.*

Multi-Sport Outdoor Shrine

■ *L.A. Memorial Coliseum:* A national historic landmark, as well as an athletic icon. It's the only stadium to host a World Series (White Sox-Dodgers, '59), two Summer Olympic Games ('32, '84), and two Super Bowls (I, VII). Billy Graham once packed in 134,000 faithful.

Multi-Sport Indoor Shrine

■ *Madison Square Garden:* New York is the capital of many things, including hype. But to call the Garden "the world's most famous arena" is no overstatement. It has hosted more events than one can imagine, including the Rev. Sung Myung Moon's first mass wedding (2,075 couples in 1982).

Baseball Stadiums

■ *Yankee Stadium, Bronx, N.Y.:* Most historic baseball deal: the Yanks stealing Ruth from Boston in '20. Most historic deal No. 2: Jake Ruppert's and Tillinghast l'Hommedieu's acquiring 10 acres of West Bronx land for a new ballpark from John Astor's estate in 1921. What rose from that land would come to be known as the Cathedral of Baseball.

■ *Fenway Park, Boston:* Williams. Yaz, Rice. The 38-foot-high Green Monster, baseball's Wailing Wall. Beyond the Monster, the Jimmy Fund sign. Fisk's '75 Series homer. Dent's '78 playoff dinger. When pondering Fenway's sacred status in the minds of New Englanders, just look to left field.

■ *Wrigley Field, Chicago:* As befits a shrine, in 1914 Wrigley was built on ground once occupied by a seminary. It's the second-oldest ballpark in the majors behind Fenway (1912) and the last to install lights (1988).

L.A. Memorial Coliseum

Fenway Park

Pauley Pavilion

Basketball Arenas

■ *Pauley Pavilion, Westwood, Calif.:* The House that Wooden Built is a sanctuary for college basketball; its rafters are ringed with 12 national championship banners—11 NCAAs and one NIT.

■ *The Palestra, Philadelphia:* The oldest active major college arena, it houses the Philly Big 5 (LaSalle, Penn, Saint Joseph's, Temple and Villanova), one of college hoops' most sanctified institutions.

■ *Cameron Indoor Stadium, Durham, N.C.:* It was conceived in 1935 on the back of a matchbook, so they say, and renovated (along with a struggling program) in the early '80s. With the help of the infamous Crazies, Cameron has been Golgotha for 550 Blue Devil opponents.

Boxing Venue

■ *The Blue Horizon, Philadelphia:* At one time, the stately row house on North Broad Street was as renowned for its chandeliers and rich woodworking as it was for its fight cards. But in recent years, the 137-year-old venue has suffered financial and structural problems. Said Marvis Frazier, Joe's son, an ordained minister who was himself a heavyweight, "If there's any chance it might close . . . all I can say is that we have to pray. It's time to pray, brother. Pray for the Blue."

Football Stadiums

■ *Notre Dame Stadium, South Bend, Ind.:* The most storied college football stadium in the country was based on a blueprint devised by Knute Rockne himself. Enduring images: the brilliant gold helmets raised high after every Fighting Irish victory; at the stadium's north end, the massive mosaic of Christ, arms upraised, surrounded by the world's great saints and scholars, which has come to be known as "Touchdown Jesus."

■ *Lambeau Field, Green Bay, Wis.:* Home of the fabled "Frozen Tundra," and St. Vincent Lombardi. A $295 million renovation will transform Lambeau Field into a year-round mecca for Packer fans and tourists by 2003.

■ *Rose Bowl, Pasadena, Calif.:* While it has hosted five Super Bowls, the men's soccer World Cup in 1994 and the '99 women's World Cup, it's best known as the site of the most hallowed of all college football postseason games.

Golf Course

■ *The Course, Augusta National Golf Club:* The course oozes history. "Amen Corner" (holes 11, 12 and 13), named for an old jazz recording. Rae's Creek, named for the 19th-century man whose home kept residents safe from Indian attacks. The Eisenhower tree at 17, a loblolly pine named for the former president who hit into it so often that he asked to have it cut down in 1956. The bridges, honoring three giants of the Masters—Hogan, Sarazen and Nelson.

Hockey Arenas

■ *Le Forum de Montreal:* Forgive Canadien fans if they felt blessed by a Higher Power. The Forum, where the Habs won 22 Stanley Cup titles from 1926 to 1996, sits at the foot of a mountain dominated by St. Joseph's Oratory and its basilica on one side and an illuminated cross on another. Now an entertainment complex, but hockey tradition lives on in the memories of players and fans.

■ *Maple Leaf Gardens:* The Beatles played there. Muhammad Ali fought there. The NBA played its first game there. But as a relic of the NHL's Original Six, it will always be about Leafs' hockey, as 13 Stanley Cup titles (11 in the Gardens) and 43 consecutive years of sellouts will attest.

Thoroughbred Tracks

■ *Churchill Downs, Louisville, Ky.:* Nothing is more symbolic of Churchill Downs and the Kentucky Derby than its elegant twin spires that tower above the racecourse. Joseph Baldez, architect of other structures in

Notre Dame Stadium

Churchill Downs

Indianapolis Motor Speedway

Louisville, built the spires in 1895, and former Churchill Downs president Matt J. Winn told him: "Joe, when you die, there's one monument that will never be taken down, the Twin Spires."

■ *Santa Anita Park, Arcadia, Calif.:* Its Art Deco facade and view of the San Gabriel Mountains make it the country's most beautiful site for racing. In the May 2001 issue of *House Beautiful*, David Hay likened it to "the fantasy creation of a motion picture art department." When a project was announced that would permanently alter the track's original architecture, conservationists considered it sacrilegious.

Racecourses

■ *Indianapolis Motor Speedway:* The bricks still exist at "The Brickyard," home of the Indy 500, even though most of them are buried under the Speedway's asphalt surface. Out of reverence to its colorful past, the famous "yard of bricks" is exposed at the start/finish line.

■ *Daytona International Speedway, Daytona Beach, Fla.:* At Daytona USA, the racing-themed tourist attraction located just outside the track, fans linger at NASCAR's newest shrine—a nine-foot bronze statue of Dale Earnhardt unveiled in February 2002. The statue includes the now-famous lucky penny that was Earnhardt's good luck charm in his 1998 Daytona 500 win. In homage to No. 3—or maybe just for good luck—fans leave pennies and other mementos at the statue.

Tennis Venue

■ *Arthur Ashe Stadium, Flushing, N.Y.:* The 23,000-seat home of the U.S. Open was named for the tennis icon and patron saint who died of AIDS in 1993. During the opening ceremonies in August 1997, former New York City mayor David Dinkins said, "Day after day, year after year, as people pass into that stadium, or pass by that stadium, they will see the name Arthur Ashe and those who do not know of him will be told by people like we who did what a wonderful, magnificent human being he was."

ship facing a mutinous crew, the first mate standing and staring him down face-to-face, and it looked as though he had lost control of the situation.

"But then damned if the master didn't triumph again. After just a moment's hesitation, he said, 'All right. Now that's the kind of attitude I want to see. Who else feels that way?'

"Well, at this very moment, Willie Davis was nervously rocking back and forth on his metal folding chair. **Willie was known as Dr. Feelgood, because every day at practice, with everyone limping around and tired and moaning and complaining, somebody looked over and asked, 'Willie, how you feel?' He always said the same thing. 'Feel good, man!'** So there was Dr. Feelgood rocking back and forth and you know how low those chairs are. He lost his balance and he fell forward! He fell forward right out into the middle of the room . . . onto his feet; it looked as though he had leapt from his chair just as Lombardi asked, 'Who else feels that way?' And Willie sort of grinned sheepishly and said, 'Yeah, me too, I feel that way, man!' Lombardi said, 'All right, Willie, that's great.' And it swept through the room; everybody said, 'Yeah, hell—me too!' and suddenly you had 40 guys that could lick the world. That's what Lombardi created out of that situation. He went around to each player in the room with the exception of the rookies—he skipped the four of us rookies—and as he looked in each man's face, he said, 'Do you want to win football games for me?' And the answer was, 'Yes, sir,' 40 times. He wended his way through that mass of people sitting around in that disarray of chairs and looked each guy nose-to-nose two inches from his face and he said that thing: 'Do you want to win football games?' and every man said, 'Yes, sir,' and we did not lose another game that year."

■ Well, I can see why he's on your list.

Curry told me that he often coached from a tower at midfield, so that his oft-repeated cries ("What the hell's going on out there?") seemed to come out of the sky. Very god-like. Actually, Lombardi, a very religious man, at least off the field, often quoted St. Paul . . . a high-church rhetoric that was an extenuation of his oft-quoted remark about "winning is the only thing." It was: "Know ye not that which run in a race run all, but one receiveth the prize. So run, that ye may obtain."

Bill told me that "winning is the only thing" is not what he remembered Lombardi saying; it was that the will to win is the only thing.

■ It's easy to think of coaches being god-like because of what they are asked to do—inspire, manipulate, control . . .

Max McGee, who was a tight end with the Green Bay Packers, once said of Lombardi, "When he says sit down, I don't even bother to look for a chair."

Not Named in Vain (continued)
GOD-GIVEN NAMES

God Shammgod: Former star point guard for Providence.

Deacon Jones: Five-time all-pro defensive end with the Rams (1965-69).

Priest Holmes: Current running back for the Chiefs.

Moses Malone: Led NBA in rebounding six times, was three-time MVP.

(Many of the names in this and previous sidebars were provided by Terry W. Pruyne, author of Sports Nicknames: 20,000 Professionals Worldwide.*)*

■ Whew! Well, who else?

Well, I certainly would put Bill Russell, the great Boston Celtics center, at the top of the list, both as a coach and a player. I spent some time with him when I was with the Celtics during their training season in 1968. Of course, he looked like a god—6-foot-10, loose-limbed (he was a track star at San Francisco and could high jump 6-9 and long jump 24). His team-mate John Havlicek says Russell could have been a decathlon champion. In his last years, he coached the Celtics as well as playing for them and won the 1969 championship against the Lakers. Coaching came easily to him. **"I don't worry," he said. "I'm not going to get ulcers coaching, I'm going to give them." A true leader.** He bore himself like one, his head imperious, eagle-like, chin invariably jutting out as he went down the court, set off with a small black goatee. He was a leader off the court as well, on one occasion organizing a boycott of a game in Lexington because of race discrimination in Kentucky's hotel coffee shops.

He was hugely competitive, very often throwing up before a game, which delighted his fellow players. It meant that he was keyed up for the game. They'd nod. "Man, we're going to be all right tonight."

Though thought cold by the press and fans (Russell wouldn't give autographs on the grounds that writing should be reserved for friends), he was a man of great humor, blessed with an enormous open-jawed, rackety laugh easily heard through a couple of walls.

I went with him once to a small gathering where another god, Willie

Believe it or not, Bill Russell grew up dreaming of being an architect. Working from prints, he tried to reproduce the paintings of Michelangelo and Leonardo da Vinci—a couple of gods in their own right. The results? "It always looked," said Russell, "as if Michelangelo had sent his work into the nursery for completion." On the other hand, Michelangelo would have been lucky to get a shot off against Russell in the paint.

Mays, was in attendance. It was a cold autumn day outside, and Willie was standing in front of the fireplace, bouncing up and down on his toes. Russell began jawing him about how hard a game baseball was to play. He went into a monologue: **"Baseball . . . really damn brutal. You get to the ballpark at 4 o'clock for a night game. You sit around and shoot some pool. Then you eat a sandwich maybe, and you drink some pop. Then you sit around and do a lot of cussing at each other. Then you pull yourselves together, and it's time for some more pool.** After a while you get dressed. On the field you lounge around the batting cage. Then you lie down and read the day's lineup. Finally, you go back out and the game begins. The only people who do anything are the pitchers and catchers. What does everyone else do? Well, they lean forward on their toes, and they pound their fists into their gloves. Sometimes they spit on the ground. Just for a change. When the pitcher gets three men out, everybody walks into the dugout, where they hold their chins in their hands. And what then? They stare out at the field until it's time to go out and start pounding that glove again. It's really brutal."

It was really a wonderful monologue. Mays was a little disturbed by the ribbing; I remember him bouncing on his toes and finally he said, "Aw, come on."

Russell once said something worth remembering about being the object of adulation: "I have never seen an athlete, including myself, who I think should be lionized. There are very few athletes I know whom I would want my kids to be like. The only kids I try to set an example for are mine."

So to be a sports god, one doesn't necessarily have to be adulated, worshipped, and so on?

Well, obviously it helps. One thinks of Arnold Palmer and his adoring "Army" crowding the fairways, very much the kind of crowds following Tiger Woods these days. One area of sport where there is that kind of fan reaction is automobile racing. One thinks of Dale Earnhardt. The effect of his death from the crash at Daytona in 2001 on the racing fraternity and its fans was devastating, the kind of mourning one associates with the highest level of popularity, even to mythic heights—Elvis Presley, James Dean.

I had a sense of this kind of crowd worship when I spent some time with Jackie Stewart, the Grand Prix Formula One race driver. I watched him race at Monza in Italy, a country not of his birth (he is a Scot), but he is treated there as if he were indeed a god. Though he had not finished the race, on his way to the van where I and others were waiting for him, he could barely get through the crush of adoring fans, shouting his name over and over.

In his memoir *Faster*, he gives a vivid description of what it is like to be a god in the Formula One world of racing, at least in Italy. Three years earlier, in August 1969, he had won the race. The crowd, as he was stand-

---

Not Named in Vain (continued)
GOD'S FAMILY

Doomsday Defense: The Cowboys' tenacious D of the mid-'60s to early '70s, included Bob Lilly, Randy White and Harvey Martin, among others.

Four Horsemen (aka *Four Horsemen of the Apocalypse*): Knute Rockne devised the lineup in 1922, and two years later Grantland Rice coined the name for the Fighting Irish backfield— quarterback Harry Stuhldreher, fullback Elmer Layden, and halfbacks Jim Crowley and Don Miller. They led Notre Dame to a 10-0 record and the national championship in 1924.

God Squad: In 1978, the moniker was given to the San Francisco Giants, a team that included several born-again Christians. The Squad was later criticized by a few teammates who thought their spirituality made the team less aggressive.

The Faithful: Fans who attend games or support their teams religiously.

ing on the winner's rostrum, began to surge forward, trying to get at him . . . as if they wanted to carry away the laurel wreath he was wearing. The police were helpless. The pressure from so many people was beyond controlling. All the police could do was to get Jackie and his wife, Helen, into the club office. When the crowd broke through the door, the two fled into a bathroom and locked themselves in with the trophy and the wreath around his neck. **The police were outside the window, and Jackie remembers climbing up on the toilet seat, trying to attract their attention for almost an hour before police reinforcements were called up and they were able to get out the rear door.** Helen was taken to the safety of another office and Jackie ran for the Dunlop van . . . but some of the crowd saw him and surged, and he dove beneath the lorry and came out the other side, where there were Dunlop mechanics with tire irons, and it was they who got him inside.

But the crowd hadn't diminished at all . . . Italians chanting "Jackie! Jackie!" Every now and then he'd go outside and wave, trying to make them happy, but it didn't work and they finally went wild. The van in which Jackie was hiding with about 40 people weighed five or six tons or so, filled with all kinds of heavy tire-balancing equipment . . . it was a 10-wheeler, really huge, and yet the crowd went to work on it, first rocking it back and forth in cadence to the chanting, and then they had it completely up and off its wheels on one side, leaning against another truck, heeled

A three-time world champion, Jackie Stewart discovered last year that he wasn't just getting older at 62, he was getting better. First, he was knighted by the Prince of Wales, making him Sir Jackie. Then he was named the inaugural Scotsman of the Year (and his wife Helen was named the first Scotswoman of the year, making them easily the first Scots Family of the Year).

Not Named in Vain (continued)
ACTS OF GOD

Miracle Braves (1914): Last on July 18, Boston roared back to win the NL pennant by taking 68 of 87 games, and then swept the heavily favored A's in four games to win the Series.

The Miracle at Coogan's Bluff (1951): Bobby Thomson's playoff-winning homer in the ninth against the Dodgers' Ralph Branca capped an improbable playoff push by the Giants, who were 13 games out in August.

The Immaculate Reception (1972): Down 7-6 . . . fourth-and-10 at their 40 . . . 22 seconds remaining . . . Terry Bradshaw's pass downfield to Frenchy Fuqua was popped backward and into the air, when he was hit by the Raiders' Jack Tatum. Franco Harris caught it at his shoe tops and ran 42 yards for the touchdown and the first Steelers playoff victory.

The Original Hail Mary (1975): Roger Staubach said a Hail Mary and threw a 50-yard bomb to Drew Pearson as the Cowboys upset the Vikings in a 1975 NFC playoff game.

The Holy Roller (1978): Oakland was trailing San Diego 20-14 in Week 2, when QB Kenny Stabler intentionally fumbled the ball forward, rather than be sacked on the game's final play. Pete Banaszak and Dave Casper, using hands and feet, advanced it into the end zone, where Casper fell on it. The league soon changed the rules to forbid this.

The Miracle on Ice (1980): The inexperienced U.S. hockey team reached the gold medal game by beating the Soviet Union, then defeated Finland in the final, 4-2.

The Hand of God Goal (1986): Argentina's Diego Maradona scored two goals, one with his hand that the referees somehow didn't see (it was confirmed by TV replay) in a World Cup quarterfinal victory over England.

40 Minutes of Hell (1994): That season, Nolan Richardson's hellish full-court defense helped Arkansas win the NCAA title.

The Music City Miracle (2000): The Titan's Kevin Dyson took a lateral on the kickoff and ran 75 yards for the winning TD with three seconds left in a 22-16 playoff victory over the Bills.

over at maybe 30 degrees. The barrier was in the way, so they couldn't turn it over completely, but everyone was still inside, bottles crashing and tires rolling about. Stewart describes how he made a break out the back door for the Mercedes of a friend who literally drove him out through the crowd. "How he didn't kill half a dozen," he remembered, "I'll never know. How he didn't kill me, for that matter, is as baffling." **All the way along the overcrowded spectator route heading for his hotel on Lake Como he kept thinking, "My God, I've won the championship, and now I'm going to be killed on the very night I've won it."**

I spent some time with Jackie at a very fancy spa and resort called La Costa near San Diego. They say Jimmy Hoffa is buried by the second hole, but I won't vouch for that. We were doing a documentary on Jackie's life. During the course of it, he said that the greatest regret of his life was missing a clay pigeon during the Olympic tryouts for the English skeet-shooting team. One bird, that was the difference. He said he'd trade one of his Grand Prix victories (there were 27 of them) to have hit that target.

La Costa is adjacent to the Camp Pendleton Marine Base, where, as luck would have it, there is a skeet-shooting range. The documentary's producers thought it would be a nice bit of footage to have the two of us compete on the U-shaped range, a contest that indeed was arranged through the help of a Marine colonel from Camp Pendleton public relations. Jackie did not miss a shot. My showing was abysmal by comparison. As we moved from one station to the next, I noticed down in the valley a number of tanks maneuvering about, and the sight inspired me to ask the colonel if he could arrange a tank race between the two of us—a means by which, since I had been a tank driver in the army, I could avenge my defeat in skeet-shooting.

Somewhat to my surprise, the colonel said he didn't see why that couldn't be arranged ("after all, the tanks need exercise" was his exact quote, almost as if he were talking about horses), and that afternoon, watched by a large detachment of marines ("Jackie Stewart?! You're kidding!"), we raced M-1 Abrams tanks over a 500-yard course. **The tank I climbed into had nothing to do with the tractor-like M-4 General Shermans with two long brake handles to make turns and five shifts of gear I knew something about, but instead was equipped with a small steering wheel, like a Kiddie Kart's, and a hydromatic shift. Stewart won by 100 yards.** It turned out he had test-driven Peugeot tanks for the French military. So I was down two contests to none. Later that afternoon, we played tennis—doubles—with Pancho Segura, the club professional, as Jackie's partner. Tennis is not a game Jackie knows much about, but he ran around, quick as a fox, blocking shots back, letting Segura take charge of points, and we lost. That was all right. I could blame my partner, the assistant pro. But that evening we played backgammon. Jackie won $50. So in one day I had lost at backgammon, tennis, skeet-shooting and tanks.

That is not the way to acquire a god-like stature.

I mention this to indicate what it is like to be humiliated by a contemporary god. The Greek gods, to go back to them, couldn't resist humiliating the odd mortal, if they felt it was warranted. Very often they used their power quite thoughtlessly, in particular, Dionysus, who was the god of wine, and perhaps imbibed too much of the stuff to do such things.

Once, when the three daughters of King Minyas would not go to a party with him, he turned one of them into an owl, the second into a screech owl—a smallish owl with a high, scratchy voice—and the third into a mouse . . . which was difficult for her, having two owls as sisters.

Hardly a happy household.

Speaking of that occasion with Jackie Stewart, I am reminded of a similar episode with Jim Brown. He would certainly be high on my list, of course, the great Cleveland running back. He ran through defensive lines, whatever they could throw up to stop him, for about nine miles, leading the NFL in that department for eight of the nine years he played. Sam Huff, the middle linebacker for the New York Giants, said that the only way to stop him was to "mug him on the way out of the locker room." He retired at the comparatively early age of 30, punctuating the end of his career in fine style by scoring three touchdowns in the Pro Bowl. In 1988, he creat-

One of the greatest all-around athletes ever, Jim Brown lettered in football, lacrosse, basketball and track—plus he qualified for the 1956 Olympics in the decathlon, though he opted to finish school instead. But the years and all those carries have taken their toll. In 1994, when she was 11, Brown's daughter Kimberly was asked if she knew her father was once a great athlete. "He walks slow," she said. "I beat him in races all the time. I really don't believe he ran that fast before."

ed Amer-I-Can, an organization founded to promote the welfare of disadvantaged kids. He's an activist. Terrific!

I remember playing tennis with him on one occasion on the court at Hugh Hefner's mansion in Holmby Hills. Roses had burst through the wire fences, very much in flower when we played, a backdrop of deep red, but also bristling with thorns so that going back for a deep lob or retrieving a ball from under the branches very often meant extricating oneself carefully from their grip—a painful business. So I remember the roses, and also that Jim Brown was dressed entirely in black. I have played tennis all my life, am at ease with it, while Jim Brown I don't think had played much at all . . . a great athlete obviously (at Syracuse one of the finest lacrosse players who ever lived), but on the tennis court quite awkward, running around his backhand and so forth, and my thought, seeing this, was that I'd play a "gentleman's game," keeping it close, giving him some setups and so forth. After a while, I realized I was in serious trouble; every ball came back, often accompanied by a gruff grunt of effort. Twice he sent me into the thorns. **I remember the last point, a winning smash of his, went into the roses and stuck there. I didn't bother retrieving the ball. I couldn't quite believe I had lost. I walked to the net, and he said, "Do you play chess?"**

I said I did, upon which I climbed on the back of his enormous motorcycle, holding onto his shoulders as we drove up into the hills to his home above Bel Air. Out on the patio, he set up the chessboard. He beat me in 12 moves or so. All of this was done in a somewhat joyous way, but he joked about it the next time I saw him.

■ Well, at least he didn't have a backgammon board!

Thank goodness.

■ You are a Red Sox fan. I would think Ted Williams would be on your list.

He is indeed. I sat next to Ted Williams once at a banquet in the Waldorf-Astoria. He is surely a god in my mind. When he was 20, he said in so many words that all he wanted out of life was that, when he walked down the street, folks would say, "There goes the greatest hitter who ever lived." And, of course, that happened. At dinner, he didn't really want to talk about baseball. Fishing. So we talked about that. I wanted to ask him about a story he told on himself . . . which was that before the war (the Korean War, in which he served as a fighter pilot, interrupting his baseball career for most of two seasons—he also missed three seasons during WWII), he'd try to foul a ball into the stands at anyone who was heckling him excessively and noticeably. No way he could do it, he admitted, but he'd try to pop them in there nonetheless until there were two strikes. Then he'd try to get a hit. He always said that was "silly," but that's what he did.

FLAWED GODS

When baseball scouts think of what-might-have-been and use words like potential and upside,
no doubt Steve Dalkowski springs to mind. A pitcher from New Britain, Conn., Dalkowski's high school games
were the stuff of legend. The typical box score would read 17 strikeouts . . . and 18 walks. Ah, scouts thoughts,
but with professional training, the kinks would iron themselves out, and Dalkowski would be able to find the plate.
He was drafted by Baltimore and it was estimated he could throw the ball 110 mph or more,
making him easily the hardest throwing pitcher of all time. But no matter what they tried to help Dalkowski,
his tragic flaw—control problems—stood squarely in the path of greatness. And he wasn't the only
flawed god to have angels herald his arrival . . . only to watch him fall down and never get up.

BASKETBALL

Flying High
Earl "The Goat" Manigault

■ Might be the best player to have never made it to the NBA. The 6-foot-1 Manigault battled against Lew Alcindor and Connie Hawkins on even terms in the asphalt playgrounds of New York City during the '60s, but his heroin addiction cost him a shot. Played collegiately at Johnson C. Smith University but fought with the coach and returned to the Harlem courts. He was jailed in 1969-70 for drug possession and again in 1977-79 for a failed robbery. He ultimately kicked his heroin habit, but never played professional basketball. He died in 1998 at the age of 53 of heart failure.

A Loss of Face
LaRue Martin

■ The first overall pick in the 1972 NBA draft by the Portland Trail Blazers was a solid collegiate performer, averaging more than 18 ppg. And Portland's talent evaluators had seen Martin, 6-11, hold his own against top collegiate centers during a pre-draft camp. But Portland coach Jack McCloskey asked Martin to face the basket in the pros, something he never did in college at Loyola-Chicago, and Martin never made the adjustment. He was out of the league four years later with a career average of 5.3 ppg.

FOOTBALL

Technical Difficulties
Tony Mandarich

■ Everybody agreed: There was no possible way this beast could miss when Green Bay used the second overall selection of the 1989 draft to grab the OT from Michigan State. None . . . at least not until he completely bombed. Mandarich was injury-plagued and lacked great technique—the perfect combination for failing to star in the NFL, which he disappeared from after three frustrating years with the Packers. (He would later play three years with the Colts.)

Running Into Trouble
Lawrence Phillips

■ The super-talented tailback from Nebraska couldn't stay out of trouble before—or after— being selected sixth by the Rams in 1996. He began to build an impressive yellow sheet in Lincoln—among other things, he was arrested for assaulting a girlfriend—and ultimately Phillips played only parts of three seasons with three different NFL teams, his dismissal from each related to his being arrested for various crimes. Most recently, in 2001, he was dismissed from the Arena League for leaving his team with no explanation.

HOCKEY

Slop Shot
Scott Scissons

■ The Islanders drafted Scissons in 1990 with the sixth overall pick, and he played a grand total of two NHL games. His problem? He had one of the worst shots in the history of the game, which made him more of a threat to fans cowering in the stands than opposing goaltenders. He never scored a point.

BOXING

Taking the Low Road
Andrew Golota

■ The Polish heavyweight was considered by boxing experts to have an excellent chance to become heavyweight champion, but his irrational behavior in the ring was his undoing. After dominating title holder Riddick Bowe for nine rounds, he needlessly hit Bowe with a series of low blows, which caused him to be disqualified and set off a riot at Madison Square Garden between fans. Later, he would lose a second fight to Bowe under the exact same circumstances, and he also quit in the second round in a non-title fight against Mike Tyson.

Weak Chin Music
Duane Bobick

■ A U.S. Olympian and heavyweight contender in the '70s, the next great white hope could have been a dominant champion . . . or, at least, that's what legendary trainer Eddie Futch thought. In 1977, Futch scheduled a match against a supposedly washed-up Ken Norton, what was supposed to be just a tune-up for a shot against Larry Holmes for the title. Bobick was knocked cold in just 58 seconds, thanks to a glass jaw that couldn't hold up against quality fighters (his career record of 49-4 was achieved mostly against stiffs).

TRACK AND FIELD

The Fast Life Kills
Houston McTear

■ As a high school junior from Milligan, Fla., McTear turned the track universe upside down when he set a world record in the 100-yard dash, covering the distance in 9.0. Obviously, McTear was a gifted athlete, but he liked to smoke cigarettes between races and skipped school regularly. His inability to read and write prevented him from accepting aid from the University of Florida, and McTear went on to develop drug problems. He did eventually kick his habit and move to Sweden to work as a personal trainer, but he still kicks himself for not training harder as a kid.

ICE SKATING

Pipe Dreams
Tonya Harding

■ An excellent figure skater and athlete who won the U.S. women's championship in 1991 and again in 1994—during rival Nancy Kerrigan's absence due to an "injury." The injury occurred when Harding's ex-husband Jeff Gillooly and an accomplice arranged to have Kerrigan hit in the knee with a pipe to prevent her from qualifying for the '94 Olympics. Harding pled guilty to conspiracy to hinder an investigation into the incident. Although Harding has repeatedly denied any involvement in planning the attack, Gillooly and three cohorts all said Harding had prior knowledge of the plan. As a result of the attack, Harding has been barred for life from sanctioned competitions.

Interestingly enough, the most unintentional incident this brings to mind is an occasion when Bob Feller threw a pitch that was fouled off and hit his mother, breaking her glasses. It happened in Comiskey Park, Chicago, and the date, May 14, 1939, is hard to believe: Mother's Day!

■ The gods intervened for some quixotic reason.

It would appear so. I would like to mention that surely on my list I would put Secretariat, whose owner, Penny Chenery, once said of him, "This red horse with blue-and-white blinkers seemed to epitomize an American hero." He raced for only 16 months, starting 21 times, winning 16, but his specialty was winning the big races; he was the first to win the Triple Crown (1973) in 25 years. He won the Belmont by 31 lengths, an all-time record, running the mile and a half in 2:24, knocking $2\frac{3}{5}$ths seconds off the track record. **He was so far ahead that it looked as though either he was the last horse in the preceding race or the starting gate in the next race had not opened for the others.**

Racing fans fell in love with him. Heywood Hale Broun, the famous sportscaster who wore a colorful sports jacket that looked like it was constructed from an Amish quilt, kept a photograph of Secretariat in his wallet, so creased and worn that when he took it out to show me, the prized document almost fell apart. Broun was hardly alone in his opinion that Secretariat was the Zeus of thoroughbreds.

At the millennium, when varied TV sports programs and writers list-

What becomes a god most? How about membership in two halls of fame? Yes, Ted Williams is generally considered the best pure hitter ever. But he is also the greatest all-around fisherman of all time, according to no less an authority than Curt Gowdy, long-time host of ABC's American Sportsman.

ed the great athletes of the preceding century, Secretariat inevitably made the lists, the only non-athlete to do so. He was No. 35 on ESPN's Classic SportsCentury list, and picked in the top 10 by *Time*.

Perhaps the most astonishing discovery was made after his death at the age of 19 at Claiborne Farms in Kentucky. An autopsy was performed by Dr. Thomas Swerczek, a professor of veterinary science at the University of Kentucky. All the vital organs were normal in size except for the heart.

"I was shocked," the doctor said, " . . . nothing I've ever seen compared to it. The heart of an average horse weighs about nine pounds. This was almost twice the average size, and a third larger than any equine heart I've ever seen. And it wasn't pathologically enlarged. All the chambers and the valves were normal. It was just larger. I think it was why he was able to do what he did."

I watched Secretariat race at Arlington, near Chicago, the first time the horse raced in the Midwest. It was a summer day. I left the press box and went down to the rail to watch him go by. It was during the Watergate mess, and **I remember thinking he was about the only honest institution, if one can call a horse such a thing, left in the country at the time.** The schools were out, a weekend possibly, and I found myself standing among a cluster of coeds leaning against the railing and chattering among themselves. Then Secretariat came by, an overwhelming sight from that close—enormous, flaming chestnut in color, the epitome of power, such a magnificent sight that some of the coeds leaning on the fence burst into tears. I noticed and wrote it into my copy for *Sports Illustrated*. I had a feeling the editor probably winced when he read that particular paragraph about the weeping. But he left it in.

The only thoroughbred ever to appear on the covers of Sports Illustrated, Time *and* Newsweek *simultaneously— even Bruce Springsteen never hit that trifecta —Secretariat was so popular that a crowd of 5,000 once showed up at Chicago's Arlington Park just to watch a morning workout.*

■ Do you have any surprising gods on your list?

I have always been fascinated by athletes blessed with god-like gifts who somehow, as if the pesky Greek gods had taken a hand, have had their skills tampered with, or even deprived of . . . minor examples like Mackey Sasser, a catcher with the New York Mets, who had trouble throwing the ball back to the pitcher, or the two second basemen, Steve Sax and Chuck Knoblauch, who had fits trying to get the ball to first base. And Steve Blass of the Pittsburgh Pirates who, after a wonderful season, couldn't get the ball over the plate to such a degree that a common expression in baseball today for a pitcher who's having control problems is: "Oh-oh, he's Steve Blassing it."

Tops on that melancholy list of mine is Steve Dalkowski, who may well have thrown a baseball faster than any known pitcher and yet never made it to the major leagues. I actually talked to someone who knew him, Pat Jordan, a fine writer who wrote a classic baseball memoir entitled *A False Spring*. The two attended Connecticut high schools and competed against each other. Dalkowski struck out as many 18, 19 batters a game. Jordan told me that he had a small, compact delivery. His arm flicked out from the side of his body. The Orioles, who had signed him, felt that the secret of his speed lay in a curiously thin and elongated wrist. Dalkowski himself had no idea. It was a gift.

■ So his problem?

Control. There were any number of legends—he had supposedly thrown a ball through a home-plate screen. Batters swung in self-defense to get back to the safety of the dugout. Orioles management tried all sorts of measures to straighten him out, the most extreme putting a batter on either side of the plate so he could learn how to groove it down the middle. Imagine how those unfortunates felt! Luckily, his control problems were vertical rather than horizontal. They say his pitches rose a foot as they came in. I remember Jordan saying that the ball left Dalkowski's hand the size of a white dot, the proverbial aspirin, then disappeared . . . and then all of a sudden it appeared at the plate the size of a moon! It exploded. Batters went white.

■ How fast was he?

No one knows for sure. The Orioles tried to measure him at the Aberdeen Proving Grounds with a radar device. The findings were not especially conclusive. He threw not from a mound but from the level ground, which meant a loss of perhaps 10 miles per hour. It took him over half an hour to get the ball into the parameters of the device. So that meant a few more lost miles per hour. He had pitched the night before and surely followed that with a binge in the bars. That would have slowed him down, as well. Still, as it was, the mechanism clocked him at 93.5. The consensus was that given all the right circumstances, his fastball would have clocked out

at well over 110 mph. Maybe more. The record at present is 100.9.

I collect stories about him. Ted Williams, after he'd retired and was working as a spring training instructor for the Red Sox, couldn't resist stepping up to the plate against Dalkowski. After one pitch, he called out, "I'm getting out," laid down his bat, confessed that he never saw the ball and added that he'd be damned if he'd ever step into the cage with Dalkowski on the mound again. Bob Lemon, the Hall of Fame pitcher, said that he saw a Dalkowski pitch that got away from him sail over the backstop into the stands and hit a guy who was buying a hot dog.

■ ### He's a strange choice for a sport's god.

Well, he had Zeus' thunderbolt and couldn't direct it. Mind you, I'm also fascinated by those who, quite unlike Dalkowski, have no gifts at all, and yet have the temerity to try to become gods. **They suffer from what the Greeks called *hubris*—overweening pride or self-confidence, stepping onto a platform reserved for the gods and thus incurring their displeasure and often retribution.** They are like the *espontaneo* in bullfighting, the lunatic onlooker who leaps over the *barrera* into the bullring and tries to play the bull, fresh out of the gate, with a homemade cape—trying to emulate the gods, if you will—and who pays for his attempt with a trip either to prison, because obviously, it's very much against the law, or to the hospital.

I remember at a Colts-Dolphins game a fan leapt out of the stands and made for the line of scrimmage just as the Dolphins were breaking from the huddle, his intent, apparently, to make off with the ball which was lying uncontested in front of the Colts defensive four. He might have

Steve Dalkowski was what one frightened hitter called "stupid wild. I didn't want to go to the plate, didn't want to get hurt." Supposedly, Dalkowski once tore a batter's ear off with an errant fastball, and broke an ump's mask, putting him in the hospital for three days with a concussion.

gotten away with it had it not been for Mike "Mad Dog" Curtis, the Baltimore middle linebacker whose function is geared to removing a football from whomever is carrying it. Curtis hit the man with a shoulder block from behind that launched him up as if from a trampoline, the ball fell away, and he was carted off by two policemen, hurrying him along with his toes barely touching the ground. Some time after the incident, I found out where the fan was. Telephoned him. He was a bartender working in Kansas. Originally from Rochester, N.Y. **The consequences of what he had done had been considerable. Jailed. He was black and blue from his knees to his shoulders. He turned out to have a pinched nerve at the base of his spine** that kept him out of his job at Kodak for such a long period of time that he was eventually let go. His picture had appeared in the local paper, the *Rochester Democrat and Chronicle*, which didn't help matters. His wife left him. Things hadn't been going too well anyway, and when she saw the pictures she said, "Well, that's the last straw." The worst of it were the phone calls. He'd become a celebrity. Most of them wanted to know why he had done it. He told me he didn't know himself. "I never could give them an answer . . . the game was sort of dull, so suddenly I turned to my friend next to me and handed him my binoculars and football program. 'Eddie,' I said. 'How about holding these for a minute? I'll be right back.' " He told me that he'd finally left Rochester. A friend called him in Kansas the following year to say that the headline that day in the *Democrat and Chronicle* read: NOT GOING TO THE GAME THIS YEAR, and everyone in town knew what it referred to.

So he didn't do it to get his name in the papers—like the guys who drop onto the baseball field and try to run the bases?

On impulse, apparently. No, there are those who do it simply to get attention, in a sense to be immortalized by being in the proximity of the gods. That was supposedly why the temple of Diana at Ephesus, one of the Seven Wonders of the ancient world, was burned down. The arsonist, a man named Herostratus, admitted under torture that he'd done so because he could think of no other way to be remembered by future generations. Of course, there are many ways of attracting attention.

Battling Siki, a light heavyweight from Senegal, comes to mind. He went to Paris when he was 15, where he was supposedly kept by a rich actress who nicknamed him "Phal"—which was the name he took because he didn't know his real one—after the most striking part of his anatomy. He fought in the First World War, winning the Croix de Guerre and the medaille militare for, among other things, clearing out a German machine gun nest single-handed. A brawler, he fought Georges Carpentier for the world title in 1922 and won by a knockout in the sixth round. It was the first million-franc fight in France, 40,000 in attendance in the Buffalo Velodrome. Carpentier was hugely favored, and indeed it was thought the

---

Not Named in Vain (continued)
BLESSED TEAMS (College)

Angels: Meredith College, Raleigh, North Carolina

Athenas: Joint team of Harvey Mudd College, Claremont, California; Claremont McKenna College, Claremont, California; and Scripps College, Claremont, California

Battling Bishops: North Carolina Wesleyan College, Rocky Mount, North Carolina; Ohio Wesleyan, Delaware, Ohio

Crusaders: Belmont Abbey College, Belmont, North Carolina; Capital University, Columbus, Ohio; College of the Holy Cross, Worcester, Massachusetts; Clarke College, Dubuque, Iowa; Eastern Nazarene College, Wollaston, Massachusetts; University of the Incarnate Word, San Antonio, Texas; Northwest Nazarene College, Nampa, Idaho; Maranatha Baptist Bible College, Watertown, Wisconsin; Point Loma Nazarene College, San Diego, California; Southeastern College, Lakeland, Florida; University of Dallas, Dallas, Texas; Valparaiso University, Valparaiso, Indiana; Villa Maria College, Buffalo, New York; William Carey College, Hattiesburg, Mississippi; Alvernia College, Reading, Pennsylvania; Cardinal-Stritch College, Milwaukee, Wisconsin; Circleville Bible College, Circleville, Ohio; Crown College, St. Bonifacius, Minnesota; Dallas Christian College, Dallas, Texas; Evangel College, Springfield, Missouri; Great Lakes Christian College, Lansing, Michigan; Madonna University, Livonia, Michigan; Manhattan Christian College, Manhattan, Kansas; Mount Mary College, Milwaukee, Wisconsin; Northwest Christian College, Eugene, Oregon; Susquehanna University, Selinsgrove, Pennsylvania; Tennessee Temple University, Chattanooga, Tennessee; University of Mary Hardin-Baylor, Belton, Texas

Deacons: Bloomfield College, Bloomfield, New Jersey; Eugene Bible College, Eugene, Oregon

Evangels: Johnson Bible College, Knoxville, Tennessee

Fighting Saints: Carroll College, Helena, Montana

Friars: Providence College, Providence, Rhode Island

fix was in, and it probably was. Carpentier went down for the count in the sixth round, but the referee ruled that Siki had tripped him and was thus disqualified. The crowd, though pro-Carpentier, took huge exception to this; the three judges, fearing a riot, overrode the referee's decision. Siki took to parading around Paris with two Great Danes on a leash, often a pet lion, and even a pistol, which he fired on occasion, scattering pedestrians and sending the patrons in the cafes scuttling under the tables. **He lost his title in Dublin, on St. Patrick's Day, 1923, beaten by Mike McTigue—a lousy choice of place, date and opponent.** He could not have been a man of much judgment. He was shot to death two years later in New York's Hell's Kitchen, supposedly (according to his wife, Madame Lillian Phal) by a man named "Jimmy" over a $20 debt. I liked reading about him because, in many ways, he was a precursor of the kind of showmanship developed by many fighters, in particular Archie Moore and, of course, Muhammad Ali. "Ah, Monsieur Georges," he taunted Carpentier, "I can't feel your punches."

■ **But these aren't the infiltrators you're talking about. Siki was a professional fighter.**

You're right. My list of people trying to emulate the gods are mostly amateurs. I have notes on one or two golfers. One of them, an English crane operator named Maurice Flitcroft, though he had never played a full 18

As befits a god, Battling Siki had a more interesting afterlife than his actual life. Fifty years after Siki was murdered in 1925 and laid to rest in an unmarked grave, a former boxer named Albert "Scoop" Gallello raised $500 for a headstone, which features a misspelling of his nickname ("Battleing Siki") and the slogan "Lest We Forget." Eventually, officials of Siki's homeland arranged to have his remains transported to his birthplace of St. Louis, Senegal, where they were buried in a proper shrine. Gallello's headstone, left behind (perhaps the Senegalese were put off by the large cross, since Siki was a Muslim), now belongs to the International Boxing Hall of Fame, which is still trying to figure out how to display it.

THE HOLY TRINITY

In sports, it has been said, "Winning is not the best thing, it's the only thing."
In religion, winning souls is the only thing. And in the motion picture biz, winning box-office
numbers is the only thing. If you still don't understand that this is a perfect recipe for a heavenly
ménage à trois, then consider the following sports movies with religious themes:

Here Comes Mr. Jordan
(1941): Joe Pendleton, an up-and-coming boxer, crashes while flying his single-engine plane. He is plucked up by a heavenly messenger who learns that Joe was to live another 50 years and become the heavy-weight champ. It's up to an archangel, Mr. Jordan, to help Joe find another body for the remainder of his life.

Angels in the Outfield
(1951): The prayers of an orphan girl prompt Angel Gabriel to help the cellar-dwelling Pirates. A reporter blames the temperamental manager, but he changes his ways and more angels— baseball legends from the past—appear. With their help, the Pirates climb to the top of the standings.

Chariots of Fire (1981):
An inspirational true story about the cost of victory. Eric Liddell, a Scot, runs for the glory of Jesus. Harold Abrahams, an English Jew, seeks acceptance. They compete at the 1924 Olympics in Paris. The real-life Liddell became a Christian missionary, went to China, and eventually died in a Japanese POW camp. Abrahams, who won the race, was later knighted.

Heaven Can Wait (1978):
In this remake of Mr. *Jordan*, Joe Pendleton is an L.A. Rams quarterback who is prematurely ushered to heaven by a bumbling celestial messenger. An archangel restores Joe to life in the body of a wealthy indus-trialist. Determined to play in the Super Bowl, Joe buys the Rams and hires his old coach to help him train.

Miracle on Ice (1981):
Driven mercilessly by coach Herb Brooks, the U.S. hockey team heads for the 1980 Winter Games after swallowing months of defeat. The team achieves stunning victories over the Soviet and Finnish teams to win the gold, which qualifies as a religious experience for a nation in the Cold War era.

The Natural (1984):
Compelling as a baseball film or morality play, the plot revolves around an odyssey to the big leagues by a farmboy who yearns for greatness. Fifteen years later, Roy Hobbs is a major league rookie—with a mystical homemade bat called "Wonderboy"—seeking redemption as a player and as a man.

Field of Dreams (1989):
Urged on by a mysterious voice, an Iowa farmer believes that if he builds a baseball stadium in his cornfield, his late father's hero, Shoeless Joe Jackson, will come to play. Soon, an amazing gathering of baseball ghosts appears. The farmer avoids bankruptcy when a prediction that the flock will visit his field comes true.

School Ties (1992):
A working-class Jewish quarterback is given a scholarship to a prestigious New England prep school in the 1950s. He is told to be discreet about his faith or he will not be accepted. But as his popularity grows, the player struggles with how to practice his faith.

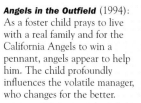

Angels in the Outfield (1994):
As a foster child prays to live with a real family and for the California Angels to win a pennant, angels appear to help him. The child profoundly influences the volatile manager, who changes for the better.

The Sixth Man (1997):
A heart attack takes the life of Antoine Tyler, a college basketball player. As the team begins to fall apart, he appears in ghostly form, ready to help. Eventually, his brother Kenny and his teammates ask their heavenly friend to leave them to win or lose on their own.

holes of golf, managed to get into the qualifying round of the 1976 British Open. He had taken up golf in 1974, hitting balls up and down a beach.

On the course at a place called Formby, his game collapsed and he scored an 11 at the short 10th hole. The local committee was so appalled he had slipped through the net that they refunded the entry fee of 30 pounds to the two unfortunates who were playing with him. Quite undaunted, Flitcroft tried again in 1983, this time masquerading as a Swiss professional named Gerald Hoppy. Playing his qualifying round at Pleasington, he got as far as the ninth hole, at which point the Royal and Ancient people caught up with him and suggested rather forcefully that he retire. **"Everything was going well and according to plan," mourned Hoppy, "until I five-putted the second."**

Another *espontaneo's* name I had in my notebooks was one Walter Danecki, a middle-aged postman from Milwaukee who with seven years of driving-range experience (he had never joined a club) managed to obtain an entry form for the 1965 British Open. In the space provided he wrote down "professional," posted a first-round 108 in qualifying on the par-70 course and a 113 at Ainsdale in the second round, missing the cut by 70 strokes. In an interview, he said he would have done better but for "a sore right hand."

Perhaps the best known of my *espontaneos*, although he was in fact a legitimate member of the 1988 British team at the Winter Games in Calgary, Alberta, is a ski jumper, Eddie Edwards, better known as "the

Eddie "the Eagle" Edwards is now as earthbound as you can get—he's a 38-year-old law student at De Montford University in Leicester, England. However, if Saville Productions of L.A. can find financial backing, the Eagle could fly again— in a movie of his life, scheduled to begin shooting next year.

Eagle." A 24-year-old plasterer from Cheltenham, one of his main problems was that he couldn't see; he was a wearer of bottle-bottom glasses that misted up on him halfway down the jump. His remark to the press, who often referred to him as Mr. Magoo on skis, was, "I just hope they clear by the time I reach the bottom."

He was the sole representative of British ski jumping and thus scheduled to compete in both the 70- and 90-meter events. After he finished a predictable last in the 70-meter jump, the authorities tried to ban him from going down the awesome 90-meter hill on the grounds that he might very well not survive. He wasn't so sure himself: **"When I looked from the top of the jump, my bum shriveled up like a prune."** As for the authorities, one said: "The Eagle doesn't fly—he drops like a stone." Somewhat surprising everyone, Edwards managed to jump without incident, finishing last (as expected), 47 meters behind the winner, Norway's Matti Nykaenen. The result of all this was that he came away from Calgary almost the most renowned figure of the Games, admittedly thought by some to be simply a self-serving clown, but most agreeing with *The Calgary Sun* that he was the biggest thing to come out of England since the Beatles.

Finally, I can't resist adding the Jamaican bobsled team, which became a darling of the 1988 Winter Olympics Games at Calgary, largely for the oddity of coming from an island that had never seen snow. They finished last (as everyone expected), but then came back six years later at Lillehammer, where their four-man sled finished in 14th place, ahead of, as it happened, both sleds entered by the United States. One reason for their success is that a good time is secured by an excellent push down the first 50 meters of the run before hopping aboard—a sprint, if you will, and the Jamaicans have always been very good at the short events in track. Their fame as bobsledders is such that there is a drink named a Jamaica Bobsled, which is half-vodka, half-banana liqueur.

■ ## Can we get back to the more traditional heroes?

By all means.

■ ## If you had to identify with one, which would it be?

Well, I've always wanted to be a major league pitcher. I actually tried it in real life, in a postseason All-Star game in Yankee Stadium in order to write about the experience for *Sports Illustrated*. It didn't work out as I had hoped. Among other things, control problems largely, Frank Thomas of the White Sox hit a home run into the third deck. Ernest Hemingway described the experience as the "dark side of the moon of Walter Mitty."

But the dream has never gone away. I often think of Walter "The Big Train" Johnson. I never saw him pitch, of course, but I read about him, the greenest rookie, by his own admission, that there ever was. The evening after the first game he ever pitched in Washington, he was standing on the sidewalk when a man walked up to him and said, "You're already famous.

Not Named in Vain
BLESSED TEAMS (College)
(continued)

Gaels: Saint Mary's College of California, Moraga, California; Iona College, New Rochelle, New York

Missionaries: Whitman College, Walla Walla, Washington

Monks: St. Joseph's College of Maine, Standish, Maine

Preachers: Johnson Bible College, Knoxville, Tennessee; Lincoln Christian College, Lincoln, Illinois

Prophets: Oklahoma Baptist College and Institute, Oklahoma City, Oklahoma

Quakers: Guilford College, Greensboro, North Carolina; University of Pennsylvania, Philadelphia, Pennsylvania; Wilmington College, Wilmington, Ohio

Saints: College of Saint Joseph, Rutland, Vermont; Emmanuel College, Boston, Massachusetts; Flagler College, St. Augustine, Florida; Hillsdale Free Will Baptist College, Moore, Oklahoma; Limestone College, Gaffney, South Carolina; Marymount University, Arlington, Virginia; Maryville University, Chesterfield, Missouri; North Georgia College and State University, Dahlonega, Georgia; Pennsylvania State University-McKeesport, McKeesport, Pennsylvania; Siena College, Loudonville, New York; Siena Heights College, Adrian, Michigan; St. Lawrence University, Canton, New York; Aquinas College, Grand Rapids, Michigan; College of Saint Francis, Joliet, Illinois; College of Saint Scholastica, Duluth, Minnesota; Manna Bible Institute, Philadelphia, Pennsylvania; Mission College, Santa Clara, California; Mount Senario, Ladysmith, Wisconsin; Notre Dame College, Manchester, New Hampshire; St. Martin's, Lacey, Washington

See? They named a hotel after you." He looked across the street and, sure enough, there was a big illuminated sign that read "Johnson Hotel." Johnson stood there gawking, actually believing what he had been told.

Both Ty Cobb and Johnson himself later described the game that afternoon, August 2, 1907. It was Johnson's big-league debut. Cobb's first impression was that they had picked a rube out of a cornfield to pitch—"a tall, shambling galoot of about 20, with arms so long they hung far out of his sleeves, and with a sidearm delivery that looked unimpressive at first glance." The Tigers began ragging the opposite bench: "Get the pitchfork ready, your hayseed's on his way back to the barn." Then Cobb went up to bat and, as he put it, "something went by me that made me flinch . . . every one of us knew we'd met the most powerful arm ever let loose in a ballpark." It was about Walter Johnson that a Chicago White Sox outfielder, Ping Bodie, after being struck out, remarked famously, "You can't hit what you can't see."

Incidentally, the Senators lost that game. The Detroit batters began laying down bunts. Johnson fell all over himself trying to field them. In his memoir, Johnson speaks of the people in the stands laughing themselves sick. "I was so confused I missed the bus back to the hotel . . . and was walking in my uniform when some fans gave me a lift."

■ When there's talk of green rookies, I always think of Joe DiMaggio being asked for a quote and not knowing what a quote was. He thought it was a soft drink.

Hey, you're breaking into my daydream. So that's it essentially. Walter Johnson is a little like Odysseus, whom I mentioned at the feast of King Alcinous, taunted, made fun of, and then able to still the voices with his god-like talent. It is the oldest boyhood dream—to walk on to the field, up to the pitcher's mound, get handed the ball, bases loaded, the best hitter at the plate, and then, in the midst of jeers, to strike him out. Walter Johnson, what an extraordinary record—113 shutouts! Any pitcher would be pleased to amass that number of wins, much less shutouts. All fastballs.

It was said that Clark Griffith, who owned the Senators, once threatened Johnson with a fine every time he threw a curveball, because that meant the hitter had a better chance to connect.

■ So Walter Johnson rounds out the list.

Well, wait a minute, there are others. You mentioned DiMaggio. He's on my list. Henry Aaron, Joe Torre, Arthur Ashe, Byron Nelson, Ken Dryden, Magic Johnson, Bear Bryant, George Foreman. There are some horses I have in mind . . .

■ Sorry. Time's up. Let's go out and have a couple of Jamaican Bobsleds.

Walter Johnson was a walking myth. "Everyone knew what was coming, but still couldn't hit him," said Chief Meyers, who caught for the New York Giants. "Walter's right arm was different than yours or mine. It was special, like Caruso's lungs or Einstein's brain."

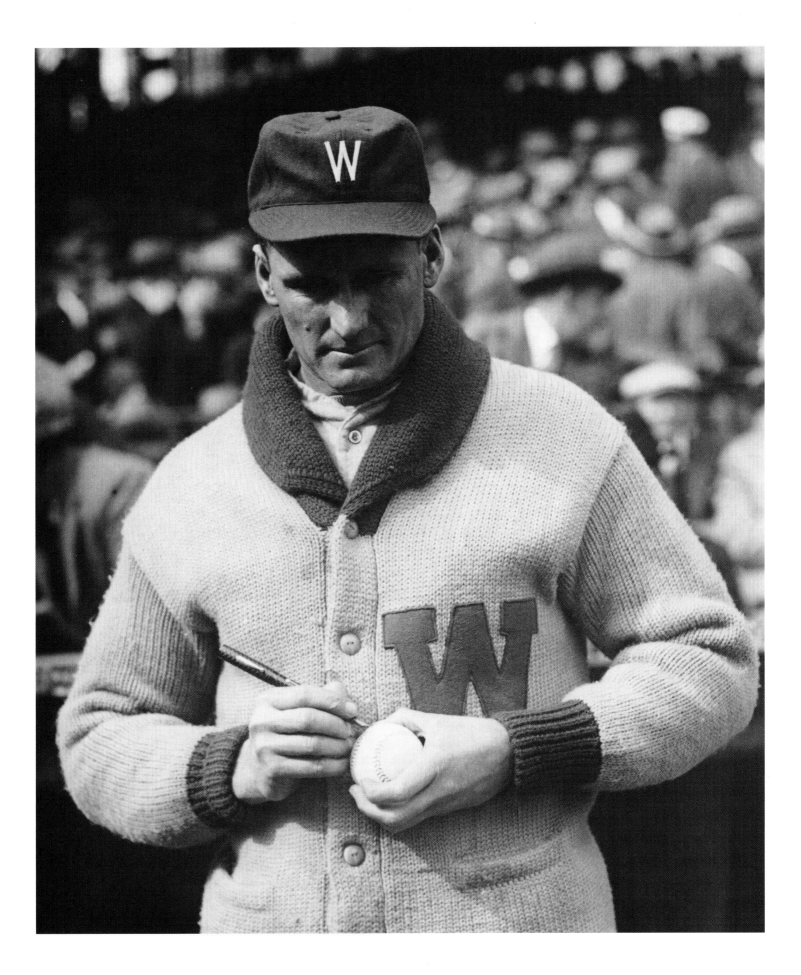

Picture Credits

Cover (from top):

Left Down: Hulton Archive Getty, Will Hart, Ken Regan/Camera 5, Kaplan/MLB.

Center Down: University of Iowa, Hulton Archive Getty, Blake Sell/Hulton Archive Getty, Duomo.

Right Down: Tom DiPace, Hulton Archive Getty, Vernon and John Biever/Allsport Getty, Rick Stewart/Hulton Archive Getty.

Ctsy. Neal Adams: 10, 40.

Allsport Getty: 48/Tony Duffy, 110 (right)/Andy Lyon, 181/Ken Regan, 184/Craig Jones, 193 (top) Al Bello, 198, 229/Mike Cooper.

The Advertising Archive: 10, 167 (top).

AP/Wideworld Photos: 7, 10 (center 2), 13 (bottom), 18, 21 (bottom), 23 (4), 25, 27, 28, 31, 34 (top), 35, 36 (left), 37, 39 (bottom), 43 (2), 46, 49, 52 (3), 53 (top 2), 56, 57 (leftmost 4 and centermost 3 on right), 58, 65, 74 (center 2), 78, 80, 81, 83, 85 (top and bottom), 87, 89, 91 (2), 93, 97, 99 (2), 103, 105 (left), 107 (2), 108, 109 (2), 110 (left), 111 (2), 112, 134, 136 (left), 142, 145, 148 (2), 150 (bottom), 152, 153 (right), 158, 164, 176 (right), 178 (bottom), 183, 187, 188, 192, 193 (bottom), 194, 197, 201 (2), 205, 207 (bottom right), 224 (center).

Ctsy. Arned Arter: pg. 30.

The Art Archive: Title page, 11.

Art Resource: Contents, Introduction, 61, 115, 117, 161, 211, 219, 220.

The Babe Ruth Museum: 162, 165.

The Baseball Hall of Fame: 62 (right), 68 (left), 159, 163, 165, 174 (7), 215 (left), 237.

The Billie Jean King Foundation: 44, 47.

Brown Brothers: 14, 150, (top 2), 166, 172.

Christies Images: 42.

Coca-Cola: 70 (right).

Michael Cole: 55.

The College Football Hall of Fame: 215 (center).

Corbis Images: 19, 39 (center), 45, 51, 57 (bottom center), 66, 71, 72, 73, 92 (bottom), 94, 95, 102, 137, 139, 195, 217, 224 (bottom), 225 (top and center 2), 231, 235, 239, 245.

Tom Corcoran: 3.

Dave Coverly: 86.

Culver Pictures: 62 (left), 216.

Tom DiPace: 182.

Ctsy. Chris Donofry: 149.

Duomo: 199, 203, 207 (bottom left), 208.

The Everett Collection: 60, 64, 105 (right), 169.

Carl Fischer: 29, 213.

Bill Gallo: 77, 92, 141, 177, 196.

Will Hart: 12 (center), 75 (2), 76 (right).

Ctsy Rudy Hoglund: 41.

Hulton Archive Getty: 10 (bottom), 12 (top), 13 (top), 17, 32 (bottom), 33, 39 (top), 53 (bottom), 54, 69, 79, 96, 98, 100, 101, 106 (left), 178 (top), 179, 190, 191, 205 (right), 207 (2), 221, 223, 224 (top), 225 (bottom), 227, 234.

Neil Leifer: 4, 155, 192.

Neil Leifer/ Sports Illustrated: 153 (left).

Tony Leonard: 146.

Library of Congress: 59, 68 (right).

Major League Baseball: 165 (right), 175 (left).

Joe McNally: 143.

Ctsy. MS. Magazine: 55 (bottom).

National Racing Museum/Reeves: 157.

Newsport: 180/Mitch Layton, 242/Popperphoto.

Gabe Perillo: 67.

Photo Assist: 160, 170, 175 (right).

Photofest: 36 (right), 57 (top right), 70 (left), 90, 104, 168 (2), 171 (2), 173, 176 (left), 185, 189, 240 (5), 241 (5).

Sipa Press: 39 (top left).

Lane Stewart/Sports Illustrated: 135.

The Tiger Woods Foundation: 200.

TimePix: 11/Mark Kaufman, 34/Bob Gomel, 38, 76 (left), 154/Jerry Cooke.

Topps Company: 74 (top left), 88, 116, 138.

Tribune Media Services: 26, 50, 186.

G.B. Trudeau/Universal Press: 84, 106 (right), 204.

University of Illinois: 12 (bottom), 16, 20, 21.

University of Iowa: 113, 118 through 131 (22), 133.

The World Golf Hall of Fame: 215 (right).

Special thanks to:

John Walsh and John Skipper of ESPN.

Natalie Kaire, Gretchen Young, Linda Prather and Bob Miller of Hyperion.

Scott Siebers, Jeff Ausiello and Kris Schwartz of ESPN Classic.

Billie Jean King for permission to use her personal photos, and Bill Schoen for his help with the King material.

Kathy Hodson of the U. of Iowa archives, and Robert Chapel of the U. of Illinois archives.

Ken Grayson for his Ruffian memorabilia.

Jim Anderson of the Detroit Tigers.

Robert Bradley of the Association for Pro Basketball Research.

Scott Chipman of the Big Ten.

Tom Gilcoyne of the National Museum of Racing and the Thoroughbred Hall of Fame, and Fran LaBelle of the New York Racing Association.

Phillip Haddy, U. of Iowa sports information.

Shirley Ito of the Amateur Athletic Foundation of LA.

Bob Kendrick of the Negro Leagues Baseball Museum.

Peter Siegel of Gotta Have It! Collectibles Inc.

Russell Wolinsky of the National Baseball Hall of Fame and Museum.